The End of Philosophy of Religion

The End of Philosophy of Religion

Nick Trakakis

continuum

Continuum International Publishing Group
The Tower Building
11 York Road
London SE1 7NX

80 Maiden Lane
Suite 704, New York
NY 10038

www.continuumbooks.com

British Library Cataloguing-in-Publication Data
A catalogue record for this book is available from the British Library

ISBN-13: PB: 978-4411-4970-1

Typeset by Newgen Imaging Systems Pvt Ltd, Chennai, India
Printed and bound in Great Britain by Biddles Ltd, King's Lynn, Norfolk

For Lydia
sic itur ad astra

In my end is my beginning.

— T. S. Eliot, "East Coker"

Philosophy, as I have understood it and lived it so far,
is a life lived freely in ice and high mountains – a seeking
after everything strange and questionable in existence,
everything banned by morality so far.

— Friedrich Nietzsche, *Ecce Homo*

The way I understand the philosopher, as a terrible
explosive that is a danger to everything, how remote my
idea of a philosopher is from anything that includes
even a Kant, let alone academic 'ruminants' and other
professors of philosophy.

— Friedrich Nietzsche, *Ecce Homo*

Art-in-art is art.
The end of art is art-as-art.
The end of art is not the end.

— Ad Reinhardt

CONTENTS

CHAPTER 1

INTRODUCTION: THE BEGINNING OF THE END

In a series of almost indistinguishable black paintings created in the 1960s, with one monochromatic colourless five-foot-square canvas after another, Ad Reinhardt sought to make the last paintings that anyone could make. In each black canvas and with a sense of impending finality, Reinhardt saw himself as working through to the end of painting. A parallel could be drawn here with contemporary philosophy. Just as Reinhardt's black paintings, in their austere purity and emptiness, symbolized "a kind of zero beyond which painting could not progress," as one critic put it,[1] so too much of the philosophy that is studied and practised in the academies today appears 'colourless' and monotonous, even mournful and melancholic in its endlessly futile attempts to render everything rationally comprehensible. In effect, philosophy has brought about its own demise.[2]

However, rumours of the death of philosophy, like proclamations of the death of painting and the infamous declaration of the death of God, are routinely dismissed as exaggerated and premature.[3] The practice of philosophy, like the worship of God, has not disappeared and even shows signs of resurgence and renewal in many quarters. But the case of God and religion should lead us to be more wary. Nietzsche's Zarathustra was to learn that the death of God must be followed by a long twilight of piety and nihilism,[4] and Nietzsche elsewhere pointed out that there may be caves for centuries to come where the gruesome shadow of God will continue to be displayed.[5] Similarly with philosophy, at least in the Anglo-American world where the so-called 'analytic tradition' holds sway (a tradition of philosophy that, as will be explained in Chapter 3, models itself on scientific inquiry and reasoning). This kind of philosophy may not, as a matter of historical fact, have come to an end, but a growing awareness of the unduly narrow ends that can be pursued under its banner, as well as the personal and political dangers involved in the pursuit of such ends, is leading to widespread calls for an end to be finally put to this approach to philosophy.

The present study claims to drive one further nail into the coffin of philosophy as it is usually practised in the analytic tradition, but with one peculiar twist: the focus will be on the philosophy of religion, the subdiscipline that is concerned with the meaning and truth of religious beliefs. Metaphilosophical debates are usually conducted in a very generalized way that does not take into account the specificities of the particular fields or discourses within philosophy. I attempt to correct this tendency by considering the presuppositions and consequences of some competing philosophical approaches to religious faith. My aim will be to show that the analytic tradition of philosophy, by virtue of its attachment to scientific norms of rationality and truth, cannot come to terms with the mysterious transcendent reality that is disclosed in religious practice.

But there is also a positive side to what follows. Just as the 'death of painting' signalled only the end of a particular way of thinking about painting and the emergence of new and exciting art forms that challenge conventional ideas, so too the end of analytic philosophy need not spell the end of philosophy *simpliciter*. I therefore aim to substantiate Levinas' comment that, "In the contemporary end of philosophy, philosophy has found a new lease of life."[6] Specifically, I attempt to show that alternatives to analytic philosophy of religion are available, not only within the various schools of so-called Continental philosophy, but also in explicitly narrative and literary approaches that achieve greater philosophical insight than what is usually offered in the purely academic and highly professionalized settings of contemporary philosophy.

Robert Nozick began his monumental *Philosophical Explanations* with the declaration: "I, too, seek an unreadable book: urgent thoughts to grapple with in agitation and excitement, revelations to be transformed by or to transform, a book incapable of being read straight through, a book, even, to bring reading to *stop*."[7] Nozick's book, of course, does not live up to this promise, or even tries to. After ploughing through the dense volumes and specialized journals of analytic philosophy, one soon discovers that they also are unreadable – not because they present "urgent thoughts" that force one to put the text down and think deeply for a change, if not to act and do something differently, but because they have the very opposite effect of putting serious contemplation and engagement to an end, perhaps even knocking one out cold, like an anaesthetic. This also is the effect, I contend, of much analytic philosophy of religion, even though philosophy of religion is the last place one would expect to find such a disconnection between life and thought, between the lived praxis of faith and the philosophical pursuit of wisdom (philo*sophia*). Clearly, new ways of reading and writing philosophy of religion are urgently required.

The investigation begins, in Chapter 2, in one of the heartlands of analytic philosophy of religion, the 'problem of evil', that is, the problem of reconciling the existence of a loving God with the innumerable instances of human and animal suffering we observe in the world. A traditional response to this problem has involved the construction of theodicies, or the search for greater goods that might plausibly justify God's permission of evil. This project is often criticized on the grounds that it has systematically failed to unearth any plausible reasons as to why God would permit suffering. But theodicists also face a deeper challenge, one that places under question the very attempt to look for any morally sufficient reasons God might have for creating a world littered with evil. This 'anti-theodical' view argues that theists (and non-theists) ought to reject, primarily for moral reasons, the project of 'justifying the ways of God to men'. Unfortunately, this view has not received the serious attention it deserves, particularly in analytic philosophy of religion. Taking my cues from such anti-theodicists as Kenneth Surin, D. Z. Phillips and Dostoyevsky's Ivan Karamazov, I defend several reasons for holding that the way of thinking about God and evil enshrined in theodical discourse can only add to the world's evils, not remove or illuminate them. Given this negative assessment of theodicy and the centrality of theodical discourse in analytic philosophy of religion, the question is initially raised as to whether the analytic approach is the most helpful one to take in philosophical studies of religion.

The discussion then proceeds, in Chapter 3, on a higher plane: rather than considering the merits of a particular response (theodicy) to a particular question in the philosophy of religion (the problem of evil), I examine the nature and function of philosophy of religion itself. The issue, in other words, is the metaphilosophical one of how the philosophy of religion is best pursued. To this end, I discuss the widely divergent approaches of the two currently dominant players in the field, the analytic and the Continental traditions. I begin with a comparison of the stylistic differences in the language of the two traditions, taking the work of Alvin Plantinga and John Caputo as exemplars of the analytic and Continental schools respectively. In order to account for these stylistic divergences, however, it is necessary to delve further into metaphilosophy. I go on to show how each philosophical school models itself on different theoretical practices, the analytic school mimicking the scientific style of inquiry, while in Continental philosophy it is the arts – especially literature and literary criticism – rather than the sciences that provide the model for philosophical discourse. By situating themselves in such different genres, analytic and Continental philosophers have inevitably developed contrasting, if not mutually exclusive, methods for pursuing the philosophy of religion.

The first half of Chapter 4 is taken up with an elaboration of what is perhaps the most important characteristic of contemporary Continental philosophy of religion: its rejection of 'scientism', the conviction that truth, rationality and progress can only be secured through the emulation of the methods of the natural sciences. The rejection of scientism by Continental philosophers is underwritten by, first, a commitment to the doctrine of perspectivism ("facts is precisely what there is not, only interpretations," as Nietzsche expressed the doctrine), and secondly, the adoption of a 'non-realist' perspective on religious language, according to which the reality of God cannot be understood in a purely factual or objective way. The second half of the chapter considers objections that analytic philosophers have raised against Continental philosophy of religion, beginning with objections to the language and style of Continental writing, and then proceeding to criticisms made of some doctrinal commitments of Continental religious thought, specifically, perspectivism and non-realism. I defend perspectivism against the charges of self-referential inconsistency and dialectical ineffectiveness, and I then defend a non-realist account of religious discourse, drawing upon the work of D. Z. Phillips and other Wittgensteinians in this area.

Things take a quite different turn in Chapter 5, where I delineate a further way in which the philosophy of religion may be pursued, but this time without confining myself to the standard literary and rhetorical devices that are deployed in academic philosophical writings in either the analytic or the Continental camp. I do this by drawing upon, and engaging with, Nikos Kazantzakis' brilliant novel on St Francis of Assisi, *The Poor Man of God* (written in 1953). The end result is a 'philosophy without philosophy', one that is inevitably experimental and unorthodox, and hence unlikely to appeal to the academic establishment. But it is precisely challenges of this sort that are required if the prevailing paradigms as to what counts as 'good' or 'proper' philosophical writing are to be overturned.

In the concluding chapter, I briefly contemplate the current dismal state of academic philosophy, analytic philosophy in particular. Philosophy departments in the English-speaking world, where analytic philosophy flourishes, have recently come under attack for encouraging a 'scientistic' and highly professionalized approach that limits itself to the search for *knowledge* without due regard for *wisdom*. The same holds *a fortiori* for analytic philosophy of religion, where the existential and lived dimension of religious faith continues to be disregarded. I call therefore for a completely fresh start where philosophy is re-envisioned as something greater than a narrow specialization beholden to scientific forms of thinking. To achieve this, however, requires more than a re-orientation in philosophical practice; it also demands fundamental change at the institutional level, replacing the managerialism and corporatization that currently dominate universities with a holistic approach that integrates life, learning and meaning.

For helpful comments on previous drafts, I would like to thank John Caputo, Lawrence Cunningham, Kevin Hart, Mark Manolopoulos, Darren Middleton, Marcel Sarot, Chris Tucker and participants in the weekly discussion group at the Centre for Philosophy of Religion at the

University of Notre Dame. Much of the present work was written during a postdoctoral fellowship at the Centre for Philosophy of Religion (to the regret, perhaps, of some of the members of this analytic stronghold), and I would like to thank the Centre and the Notre Dame community for their generous hospitality.

Finally, I am grateful to the original publishers (and, in one instance, to my co-author) for permission to re-use material from the following previously published papers:

"Nietzsche's Perspectivism and Problems of Self-Refutation," *International Philosophical Quarterly*, vol. 46, no. 1, March 2006, pp. 91–110.

"Meta-Philosophy of Religion: The Analytic-Continental Divide in Philosophy of Religion," *Ars Disputandi: The Online Journal for Philosophy of Religion* [http://www.ArsDisputandi.org], vol. 7, 2007.

"Religious Language Games" (co-written with Graham Oppy), in Andrew Moore and Michael Scott (eds), *Realism and Religion: Philosophical and Theological Perspectives* (Aldershot: Ashgate Publishing, 2007), pp. 103–30.

"Kazantzakis' Poor Man of God: Philosophy without Philosophy," *Colloquy: Text, Theory, Critique*, issue 15, June 2008.

"Theodicy: The Solution to the Problem of Evil, or Part of the Problem?," *Sophia: International Journal for Philosophy of Religion, Metaphysical Theology and Ethics*, vol. 47, no. 2, July 2008, pp. 161–91.

CHAPTER 2

THEODICY: THE SOLUTION TO THE PROBLEM OF EVIL, OR PART OF THE PROBLEM?

No statement, theological or otherwise, should be made that would not be credible in the presence of the burning children.

—*Rabbi Irving Greenberg*[1]

Apart from a few lonely voices in the wilderness – such as those of Kenneth Surin and D. Z. Phillips – there is little discussion today within analytic philosophy of religion of the meta-theodical question of whether it is legitimate (in some significant sense) to offer a theodicy in response to the problem of evil. The recent resurgence of 'sceptical theism' has, of course, emphasized that we should not expect to know, at least in many cases, what God's reasons are or might be for permitting evil, and so it is thought that it is somewhat presumptuous of us to construct theodicies. But the meta-theodical question I am asking is much more radical than that, for it questions the crucial presupposition lying behind all theodicies: the very idea that God has morally sufficient reasons for permitting evil, whether these be beyond our ken or not. In other words, does it make sense – specifically, *moral* sense – to speak of God as permitting his creatures to suffer some evil, or inflicting suffering on them, for the sake of some 'greater good', such as free will or soul-making? In my previous work on the problem of evil[2] I benightedly assumed that the answer was so obvious that the question did not even need to be asked. But now I think otherwise, and this chapter is my attempt to explain why.

1. What is a Theodicy?

To begin with, what exactly is a 'theodicy', what is its nature and what does it attempt to achieve?[3] Very briefly, a theodicy is the attempt to "justify the ways of God to men," as John Milton famously put it.[4] In other words, a theodicy aims to vindicate the justice or goodness of God in the face of the evil and suffering found in the world. This purported vindication is, in turn, thought to be contingent upon the degree to which a 'reasonable' or 'plausible' explanation has been provided as to why God allows evil to abound in his creation. And the God under discussion – or under trial – is invariably the God of philosophical theism, an omnipresent person-like being that is omnipotent, omniscient, perfectly good and the sole creator and sustainer of the universe.

Theodicies come in all shapes and sizes, some more comprehensive and ambitious than others, some more abstract and technical than others, and some more tied to a specific religious tradition than others. Theodicies, I suggest, can best be understood by looking at them from three distinct perspectives.

First, we can understand theodicies in terms of the range of evils they attempt to explain. Following the typology introduced by William Rowe,[5] at the least ambitious end of the scale we have theodicies that seek to explain why God permits *any* evil at all. Such a theodicy may seek to explain why there is some evil rather than none at all, or it may seek to account for at least one instance of evil. Next, there are theodicies that purport to explain why there are the various *kinds* of evil we find in our world, the two principal evil-kinds being 'moral evil' (evil brought about by the intentional misuse of human free will) and 'natural evil' (evil not resulting from the culpable misuse of human free will). Thirdly, there are theodicies that endeavour to explain why there is the *amount* of evil that we find in the world. Finally, and most ambitiously of all, there are theodicies that strive to account for every particular instance of evil, thus showing how it can be the case that, for every instance of evil, God is justified in allowing it.[6]

A second way in which the nature of theodicies can be clarified is in terms of the kinds of goods that are invoked. A theodicist, as indicated above, attempts to explain God's permission of various evils, and this is achieved by ascribing to God some reason for allowing the evils to take place. This exculpating reason is thought to be a 'morally sufficient reason', a greater good for the sake of which God permits some evil and is morally justified in doing so.

The first thing to note here is that the greater good identified by the theodicist need not constitute God's *actual* reason for permitting evil. It would suffice, for the purposes of theodicy, if it can be shown that, were the obtaining of the good in question God's aim in permitting some evil, then God would be justified in permitting the evil. Secondly, the goods identified by the theodicist must in some sense be *greater* than the evils they justify (this is usually understood in quantitative terms, so that the positive value of the good state of affairs must outweigh the disvalue of the evil state of affairs).[7] Thirdly, whatever goods are presumed to result from God's permission of evil, it is often thought that – in at least the most extreme cases, involving intense, involuntary and undeserved suffering (e.g., child sex abuse) – these goods must include 'patient-centred goods', that is to say, goods that directly benefit the sufferer. Fourthly, the relation-ship between the goods invoked by the theodicist and the evils (or, more precisely, God's permission of the evils) that these goods are intended to justify is one of *logical necessity*: when God's permission of evil is explained in terms of some greater good this means, in part, that God's permission of the evil is logically necessary (and not merely causally neces-sary) in order for the good to obtain.

A third way of interpreting the project of theodicy is in terms of the explanations that theodicists seek to offer. The theodicist's explanations are not intended to be merely logically possible, for then a theodicy would be indiscernible from a 'defence', as this term is standardly used in the context of the so-called 'logical problem of evil'. (Plantinga's free will defence, for example, only attempts to show that it is logically possible that God and evil co-exist.[8]) Rather, the kind of explanation sought by the theodicist is one that would illuminate and make sense of our experience of evil from a theistic perspective, and to this end the theodicist must provide not only an internally consistent story (as to why God permits evil), but also one that is, in some significant sense, *reasonable* or *plausible*. The precise sense in which the theodicist's story must be reasonable or plausible is much contested, with some requiring that theodical stories need only be true 'for all we know' (i.e., not explicitly ruled out by such things as commonsensical views about the world and widely accepted scientific beliefs),[9] and others demanding that a theodicy be not merely epistemically possible, but more likely to be true than not true.[10]

2. Sketch of a Theodicy

The next step I want to take is to put some flesh onto this meta-theodical structure, in order to give some idea as to how theodicies are put into action. This is well-trodden terrain, familiar to most readers, and so I can afford to be somewhat brief.[11]

Two of the most common theodicies are the *soul-making theodicy* and the *free will theodicy*, which are intimately connected and perhaps better seen as a single theodicy comprised of two separate elements.

Soul-making. Inspired by the thought of the early Church Father, Irenaeus of Lyon (c.130–c. 202 CE), John Hick has put forward in a number of writings, but above all in his 1966 classic *Evil and the God of Love*, a theodicy that appeals to the good of soul-making.[12] According to Hick, the divine intention in relation to humankind is to bring forth perfect finite personal beings by means of a 'vale of soul-making' in which humans may transcend their natural self-centredness by freely developing the most desirable qualities of moral character and entering into a personal relationship with their Maker. Any world, however, that makes possible such personal growth cannot be a hedonistic paradise whose inhabitants experience a maximum of pleasure and a minimum of pain. Rather, an environment that is able to produce the finest characteristics of human personality – particularly the capacity to love – must be one in which "there are obstacles to be overcome, tasks to be performed, goals to be achieved, setbacks to be endured, problems to be solved, dangers to be met."[13] A soul-making environment must, in other words, share a good deal in common with our world, for only a world containing great dangers and risks, as well as the genuine possibility of failure and tragedy, can provide opportunities for the development of virtue and character. A necessary condition, however, for this developmental process to take place is that humanity be situated at an 'epistemic distance' from God. On this view, if we were initially created in the direct presence of God we could not *freely* come to love and worship God. So as to preserve our freedom in relation to God, the world must be created religiously ambiguous or must appear, to some extent at least, as if there were no God.[14] And evil, of course, plays an important role in creating the desired epistemic distance.

Free will. The appeal to human freedom, in one guise or another, constitutes an enduring theme in the history of theodicy. Typically, the kind of freedom that is invoked by the theodicist is the *libertarian* sort, according to which I am free with respect to a particular action at time t only if the action is not determined by all that happened or obtained before t and all the causal laws there are in such a way that the conjunction of the two (the past and the laws) logically entails that I perform the action in question. My mowing the lawn, for instance, constitutes a freely performed action only if, the state of the universe (including my beliefs and desires) and laws of nature being just as they were immediately preceding my decision to mow the lawn, I could have chosen or acted otherwise than I in fact did. In this sense, the acts I perform freely are genuinely 'up to me' – they are not determined by anything external to my will, whether these be causal laws or even God. And so it is not open to God to cause or determine just what actions I will perform, for if he does so those actions could not be free. Freedom and determinism are incompatible.[15]

The theodicist, however, is not so much interested in libertarian freedom as in libertarian freedom of the *morally relevant* kind, where this consists of the freedom to choose between good and evil courses of action. The theodicist's freedom, moreover, is intended to be *morally significant*, not only providing agents with the capacity to bring about good and evil, but also making possible a range of actions that vary enormously in moral worth, from great and noble deeds to horrific evils.

Armed therefore with such a conception of freedom, the free will theodicist proceeds to explain the existence of moral evil as a consequence of the misuse of our freedom (though some, most prominently Richard Swinburne, have attempted to extend the free will theodicy to natural evil[16]). This, however, means that responsibility for the existence of moral evil lies with us, not with God. Of course, God is responsible for creating the conditions under which moral evil could come into existence. But it was not inevitable that human beings, if placed in those conditions, would go wrong. It was not necessary, in other words, that humans would misuse their free will, although this always was a possibility and hence a risk inherent in God's creation of free creatures.

The free will theodicist adds, however, that the value of free will is so great as to outweigh the risk that it may be misused in various ways. It may be held, for example, that free will of the morally significant kind provides us with the opportunity to engage in soul-making, thus providing us with deep responsibilities (e.g., the responsibility for the sort of person we become and the choices we make) and giving us the ability to enter into relationships of love with others, including God. Given that freedom has such great value, it is better that God create a world with agents who possess free will, even though they may misuse it, than to create a world of mere automata.

Although not a theodicy in itself, the idea of a *heavenly afterlife* is usually appended to free will and soul-making theodicies, providing an eschatological perspective without which (it is often thought) these theodicies would simply collapse. This is particularly evident in Hick's soul-making theory, which includes a universalist eschatology that extends the soul-making process beyond the grave. The motivation behind this extension arises from the following sort of objection: Although there are some people whose character is strengthened and transformed through the challenges and dangers they encounter, there clearly are many others who either make little progress due to dying young, or regress after finding themselves in terribly adverse circumstances. It seems, then, that the soul-making process, if it exists at all, is quite ineffective. As a way out, Hick speculates that this process does not terminate at death, so that anyone unfit for communion with God by the end of their earthly life continues on the course of moral and spiritual growth until they too attain the ultimate heavenly state of an eternal life of love and fellowship with God. This final state is described by Hick as an "infinite because eternal future good that justifies and redeems all the pain and suffering, sin and sorrow, which has occurred on the way to it."[17]

Theodicy 11

3. The Anti-Theodical Critique

Now, what is wrong with all this? Isn't it merely a reasonable and valiant, even if ultimately unsuccessful, attempt to make sense of the human predicament, plagued as it is by all manner of strife and disaster. The overwhelming consensus within Anglo-American (or analytic) philosophy of religion is that there is nothing, in principle, wrong or mistaken in the idea that God has morally sufficient reasons for permitting evil, and that we can at least try to discern what these reasons might be. I, for one, subscribed to this view, and in a number of previous publications I attempted to show that the kind of theodicy sketched out above provides us with some clues as to why God permits many sorts of moral evil, although such a theodicy (I argued) does not throw any light on God's permission of natural evil.[18] These arguments, I have now come to see, were not considered carefully and thoroughly enough, and so the conclusions were arrived at in a somewhat rash manner. In fact, I would venture to say, along with critics such as Kenneth Surin and D. Z. Phillips, that the theodicist's way of proceeding evinces a failure to take suffering seriously. If the matter were pursued on an even deeper level, something that will be reserved for the following chapters, it may well be discovered that the heart of the problem lies with the kind of God, or the specific conception of God, that forms the basis of discussion in analytic philosophy. However, this is not to endorse a reductive or projectionist account of God-talk, or religious discourse more generally, as is often feared, nor is it to fall back on some kind of invidious fideism or anti-intellectualism. Rather, it is to call attention to the nature of the divine reality that is taken to be experienced in the world's religious traditions, a reality that cannot properly be understood with the tools of formal logic and empirical science, if it can be understood at all. But this, as I mentioned, will be the subject of the chapters that follow.[19] For now, I wish to delineate some of the problems faced by those who offer theodicies in response to the problem of evil, showing in the process that these problems are in essence *moral* problems.

It is surprising to see that the recent revival of interest in both the phenomenon of evil and the theological problem of evil has given rise to very few anti-theodical critiques of the kind I am advancing here. In theological circles and in the so-called Continental stream of philosophy, such critiques of theodicy are also rarely offered, but this is usually because the morally problematic nature of theodicies is taken to be too obvious or too widely accepted to require explicit argument and defence.[20] But while many on the theological and Continental sides are already convinced, the majority in the Anglo-American camp are far less sanguine, or even interested, about the prospects of the case against theodicy. There are therefore very few systematic defences of the anti-theodical view, particularly ones that engage with the concerns of analytic philosophers of religion. The most notable such defences that have made it to print are Kenneth Surin's *Theology and the Problem of Evil* (1986), Terrence Tilley's *The Evils of Theodicy* (1991) and most recently D. Z. Phillips's *The Problem of Evil and the Problem of God* (2004).[21] As is well-known, Phillips consistently waged war for many decades against (what he called) 'the friends of Cleanthes', those who attempt to shore up religious beliefs with empirical evidence and philosophical demonstrations, thereby doing greater damage to religion than those who proclaim themselves to be atheists and agnostics. Although his recent book on the problem of evil was not his first foray into this subject, the book offers his most comprehensive critique of the theodical project. In the two sub-sections that follow, I will concentrate on two lines of thought that Phillips advances, as I think these expose the moral dangers of theodicy in a particularly lucid way.

Those familiar with Phillip's book will notice that Phillips brings an entire barrage of criticisms against the various theodicies that are currently on offer.[22] Many of Phillips's criticisms, however, are not directed against the very idea of God having morally sufficient reasons for permitting evil, but are rather offered as 'immanent critiques', that is to say, criticisms that operate within the terms of reference of the theodicy under discussion. For example, in reply to the theodical view that the evils suffered either by ourselves or by others provide us with the opportunity to be shown at our best in the ways we respond to such evils, Phillips counters that this view suffers from a fatal generality: it suppresses or ignores obvious examples of the disastrous effects suffering has had on human beings.[23] These sorts of criticisms can be important in loosening the stranglehold theodicies have on our thinking. More, however, is clearly required if we are to finally stop playing the game of constructing divine reasons for evil, only to have them shot down in the next issue of our favourite learned journal, this in turn prompting us to reconfigure the original divine reasons or to offer new ones, only to have these debunked, and so on. Phillips is not unaware of this, and in at least two places he goes beyond an immanent critique and offers what might be termed a 'global offensive' that is intended to undermine the very foundations of the theodicist's project.

3.1 Suffering the consequences

Phillips's first offensive takes the form of an insightful argument that sets out to show that if, as theodicists suppose, God had to permit (or inflict) evil in order to bring about some ultimate good which somehow redeems that evil, it would be impossible to attribute anything resembling perfect goodness to God.[24]

Phillips begins by noting that he will be granting, for the purposes of argument, the theodicist's assumption that God is a moral agent who shares a moral community with us and is therefore subject to the same moral standards as we are. If this assumption be granted, then we are bound to draw our moral judgements regarding God from what we already know and believe about moral matters. (The importance of the assumption that God shares a moral community with us will become evident soon, but it is not one that Phillips accepts.)[25]

The theodicist, then, tells us that God had to allow evil to exist in order to fulfill some overall good purpose of his. So, the evils that exist are the unavoidable consequences of God's purposes. As Phillips points out, the predicament of having to allow something unfortunate or bad to occur in order to achieve some goal is not something we cannot understand or appreciate, for it is a situation "with which we are *already morally familiar.*"[26] We know perfectly well what is involved in such situations, what is said about people who find themselves in these predicaments and, indeed, what such people say or feel about themselves. This is not strange or alien territory, but ground with which we are all familiar and may have even traversed ourselves. But if this is so, then – recalling the assumption made at the outset, that God is a member of our moral community – what should we say about a God who must permit (or inflict) evil that good may come, and what would we expect this God to say of himself?

To answer this question, Phillips raises a further question, this time one which is structured as a dilemma: Does God do what he has to *with or without a second thought?*

To carry out or permit an evil *without even so much as a second thought* is to have no hesitation whatsoever, no scruples, no doubts and no remorse about one's behaviour. It is clear what is said about people who act in this way: they are called callous and insensitive, and this even if they had no choice but to permit the evil for the sake of some worthwhile goal. If we defer, then, to the standards of our moral community, which we have agreed to do for the sake of argument, then to think of God as permitting an evil such as the Holocaust without a second thought is, in effect, to condemn God as callous and insensitive. God, on this view, would not be at all bothered or troubled by the predicament he is in, and he would be indifferent to the fate of those who will suffer as a result of the implementation of his 'master plan'. In that case, it would make no sense to speak of the perfect goodness of God.

Perhaps, then, we should think of God as allowing evil only *after a second thought.* But this does not make things any better. For to say that

God permitted some evil after a second thought is to say that "he did what he had to do, but gave full weight to the evil it involved."[27] Giving full weight to the evil involved, however, implies acting reluctantly and 'with a heavy heart', not excusing or absolving oneself for having taken this road, but rather seeing oneself as sullied with 'dirty hands' and hence in need of penance and forgiveness. But if God stands in need of penance and forgiveness, again it would make no sense to attribute perfect goodness to him.

Phillips therefore concludes that whether evil is allowed with or without a second thought, God has to "suffer the consequences," the consequences being either moral insensitiveness or dirty hands. This is an ingenious and provocative argument, and one that is reminiscent of Camus' statement in *The Rebel* that, "When man submits God to moral judgement, he kills Him in his own heart."[28]

To illustrate the force of the argument, Phillips examines how characters in literature and film are depicted when they find themselves compelled to do something evil: What is said of them, and what do they say of themselves? One of the characters he discusses is Sophie Zawistowska from William Styron's novel, *Sophie's Choice*. Upon arriving at Auschwitz, Sophie was forced by an SS officer to make the terrible choice of whether to send her son or her daughter to the gas chambers. If she refused to make a choice, both children would be killed. As it happens she chooses to save her son, and so her daughter is taken away to be murdered. But consider the torment and anguish this choice caused her:

> Her thought processes dwindled, ceased. Then she felt her legs crumple. 'I can't choose! I can't choose!' She began to scream. Oh, how she recalled her own screams! Tormented angels never screeched so loudly above hell's pandemonium. '*Ich kann nicht wählen!*' she screamed.[29]

The torment and anguish bore so heavily on Sophie that, two years after being liberated from the death camps, she gave up her own life. The moral of the story is not that Sophie should be condemned for letting one of her children be taken to the gas chambers. Rather, the point, as Phillips explains, is that she never thinks of her act of giving up her daughter as something to be excused in the light of the total situation. But if Sophie "suffers the consequences," it would be unimaginable to think that God doesn't, as Phillips points out:

> If God shares a common moral community with Sophie and ourselves, what should we say of his allowing the Holocaust to happen? Is God to be the object of pity? Is creation a moral tragedy in which God is necessarily involved in evil? And what of God's view of what he has done? Does the

Holocaust stay with him? Does he think that it can be excused in the light of the greater good that made it necessary, or does he recognize he has something to answer for? It will be obvious that within these moral parameters, there is no logical space for talk of God's perfect goodness.[30]

3.2 The teleology of suffering

A second problem with the theodical project lies with its *teleology of suffering*. To say that suffering has a teleology is to say that suffering has some (God-given) point or purpose, and for theodicists the ultimate purpose of suffering must be moral in nature (though some theodicists countenance non-moral – e.g., aesthetic – ends) and must be worth the devastation it leaves in its wake.

Phillips discusses some problems attaching to the idea of a teleology of suffering with reference to two specific theodicies,[31] though I think his criticisms have more general appeal. The first theodicy he discusses is Hick's soul-making theory, which considers evil as an opportunity for character development, while the second theodicy examined by Phillips holds that the existence of evil makes it possible for one to be morally responsible by coming to the aid of those who are victims of evil. This latter view, usually formulated in the context of the soul-making theory, is championed most prominently by Richard Swinburne, who writes that evil is the price that must be paid if we are to have "great responsibilities for each other" and that "the sufferer is of use to us in helping us to grow."[32]

The morally problematic nature of the appeal to soul-making is nicely summarized by Phillips:

> We are told that in allowing evils to exist, God is providing the conditions needed to give us the choice of moulding our characters in one direction or another. This offer of God's morally sufficient reason suffers from a fatal objection. *To make the development of one's character an aim is to ensure that the development will not take place.* This is because the endeavour so conceived is self-defeating: *it lacks character.*[33]

Phillips goes on to explain that if we understood the evils that exist as opportunities for character development, then we would be motivated to respond to evil at least in part in order to build our characters. But, notes Phillips, "it seems to be both a logical and moral truth that to seek one's character development is to lose it."[34] For example, if someone acts bravely in difficult circumstances – say, they save a child from a building that has caught fire – but does so (partly or purely) out of self-regarding reasons (e.g., so as to build up their character, or make a name for themselves, etc.), then that would detract, or even annul, the moral worth of the action. In short, the soul-making theodicy promotes an indulgent concern with one's self rather than the development of one's character.

The underlying problem, observes Phillips, is a self-centred instrumentalism that is antithetical to the genuine spirit of morality. This is evident once more in those theodicies, such as Swinburne's, that view evil as an opportunity for developing and displaying moral responsibility. As before, Phillips criticizes this theodicy as morally incoherent: to say that another person can be regarded as an *opportunity* for us to grow morally or to develop moral responsibility does not make sense, since morality cannot be furthered by this sort of instrumentalism. As Phillips states, Swinburne's morality "would make it possible for the Good Samaritan to say, on coming across the victim of the robbers, 'Thank you, God, for another opportunity to be responsible'."[35] Similarly, as Phillips again points out, it would make it possible for God to multiply our pains in order to multiply compassion, a crazy view but one to which the theodicist (of the sort under consideration here) is committed.[36]

These, I submit, are perceptive observations, ones that would repay greater consideration by mainstream analytic philosophers. Unfortunately, as Phillips states later in his book, "philosophers of religion, for the most part, do not pause to consider whether *the logic* of economic management, the calculus of gain and loss, should be introduced into discussions of human suffering."[37] As a result, philosophical discussions on the problem of evil invariably presuppose a 'teleology of suffering', a framework which only compounds (albeit inadvertently) the evils we are subjected to, rather than illuminating or ameliorating them. I will return to this theme in Section 5, but in the interim I wish to stress that we must be careful about how we write and how we think about human (and animal) suffering, for it is the carelessness displayed in this area by so many that has raised the ire of critics such as Phillips.[38]

One can appreciate, then, why Phillips consistently and stridently opposed Swinburne's philosophical theology, particularly as it impacts on the problem of evil. Phillips's critique, in fact, remained largely unchanged from the time it first appeared in the published proceedings of a conference held in 1975, where Phillips responded to a paper presented by Swinburne on the topic of theodicy.[39] In an unfortunate but not atypical section of his paper, Swinburne wrote:

> . . . Hence it follows that one who knows much more about the probable consequences of a quarrel may have no duty to interfere where another with

less knowledge does have such a duty – and conversely. Hence a God who sees far more clearly than we do the consequences of quarrels may have duties very different from ours with respect to particular such quarrels. He may know that the suffering that A will cause B is not nearly as great as B's screams might suggest to us and will provide (unknown to us) an opportunity to C to help B recover and will thus give C a deep responsibility which he would not otherwise have.[40]

Something has clearly gone wrong here, and on Phillips's diagnosis the problem runs deep indeed:

> It is true that sometimes considering a matter further is a sign of reasonableness and maturity. But this cannot be stated absolutely, since at other times readiness to be open-minded about matters is a sign of a corrupt mind. There are screams and screams, and to ask of what use are the screams of the innocent, as Swinburne's defense would have us do, is to embark on a speculation we should not even contemplate. We have our reasons, final human reasons, for putting a moral full stop at many places.[41]

In his reply, Swinburne defends his methodology as one that is entirely in keeping with, if not mandated by, his theoretical enquiries:

> When we are doing philosophy and are justified in doing so (as I hope that we are now), it is *never* a "sign of a corrupt mind" to be open-minded about things. In all areas of life what seems most obviously true sometimes turns out to be false, and it is not the sign of a corrupt mind but the sign of a seeker after truth to examine carefully views which initially seem obviously true. It seemed to many men obvious that the Earth was flat; we may, however, be grateful that despite this, they were prepared to listen to arguments to the contrary. Sometimes, too, moral judgments which seem obviously true turn out on investigation not to be so at all – and this for both moral and factual reasons.[42]

It is fair to say that this response, or something close to it, would be endorsed by most of Swinburne's peers who toil in the fields of analytical philosophy of religion. But Swinburne's response reinforces, rather than discredits, the initial charge of moral insensitivity. To see this, consider the following comments Kenneth Surin makes in the light of the above quote from Swinburne:

> It *is* precisely the sign of a corrupt mind to speak easily of two different realities, say, the world of the Flat Earth Society on the one hand and the world of Auschwitz on the other, as if they are interchangeable. To be 'open-minded' about certain realities, and 'more tellingly' to *insist* on retaining such a contemplative disposition, is to show oneself incapable of making

certain exigent moral discriminations. In the worst of cases, this incapacity to acknowledge that a particular reality is mind-stopping betokens an irremissable moral blindness, in less serious occurrences it testifies to a real lack of moral imagination, to an unshakeable moral coarseness. But in *all* cases the failure to lend a voice to the cries of the innocent (and there can be few more glaring instances of this failure than the willingness to construct a divine teleology out of innocent suffering) is to have lost the capacity to tell the truth.[43]

Surin glosses these "rather aggressive remarks" (as he admits they are) with a quote from Theodor Adorno:

> The need to lend a voice to suffering is a condition of all truth. For suffering is objectivity that weighs upon the subject; its most subjective experience, its expression, is objectively conveyed.[44]

Surin, like Phillips, accepts that open-mindedness is quite often a virtue that we should aspire to embody, but warns that open-mindedness is not always a virtue, and that the kind advocated by Swinburne and other theodicists – an open-mindedness that does not hesitate to ask what use or purpose someone's sufferings could serve – betrays a fundamental misunderstanding of morality. To quote Surin again,

> To think that morality is something that can be intellectually constructed in this way, that it can be slotted into a matrix of purposes (whether divine or otherwise), is to negate the concept of morality. In the domain where human beings have to think and act, there are irreducible realities – realities 'extra-territorial to reason' (to borrow a phrase of George Steiner's) – which halt the tongue, afflict the mind with blankness. To be resolutely 'open-minded' when confronted with these morally surd realities is to have lost any possible accordance with the truth (Adorno). It is to have lost one's own humanity (Cavell).[45]

Here we have the convergence of three distinct, but inter-related, themes: the teleology of suffering exemplified in theodicies displays a deep moral incoherence (morality just doesn't work that way), an inexcusable moral insensitivity (treating people as mere means) and an equally culpable moral blindness (which refuses to countenance the possibility of unjustified and inexplicable evil).[46]

4. The Challenge of Ivan Karamazov

In developing the charges of moral insensitivity and moral blindness further, one can do no better than turn to Dostoyesvsky's masterpiece, *The*

Brothers Karamazov. Indeed, the failure of analytic philosophers of religion to appreciate the import of these charges stems in large part from their refusal to engage with literary works when philosophizing. But as Stewart Sutherland notes, "the separation of philosophical from literary inquiry is detrimental to both."[47] Philosophers, however, have not always been oblivious to the insights that works of literature can afford. A prime example is Alexander Boyce Gibson, a former Professor of Philosophy at the University of Melbourne, who noted the impact Dostoyevsky's novel had on subsequent thinking on the problem of evil:

> By sheer force and sincerity he [Dostoyevsky] changed the face of theology. Since he wrote, it has become unfashionable, not to say impious, to contend that all is for the best in God's world. Henceforward, no justification of evil, by its outcome or its context, has been possible; Ivan Karamazov has seen to that.[48]

Gibson, in fact, goes on to say, a few pages later, that he first read the infamous exchange between Ivan and his brother Alyosha "fifty years ago, and my theology has never been the same since."[49]

Let's turn, then, to this part of Dostoyevksy's novel, where we find the well-educated and atheistic Ivan Karamazov meeting with Alyosha in an inn. Ivan has returned from his journalistic career in Moscow to stay at the family home in the provinces, while his younger brother has taken up the monastic life under the discipleship of the religious elder, Father Zosima. During their conversation, Ivan recounts a series of harrowing stories taken from a "fine collection"[50] of such stories he has been collecting from newspapers and other sources. The most poignant of the atrocities recounted by Ivan involve the abuse and torture of children. There is the case of a soldier shooting a baby boy in the head even while the infant was in the hands of his mother; a five-year-old girl being constantly subjected to beatings and floggings by her parents, who went so far as to lock up their daughter during one freezing night in the outside latrine after having smeared her eyes, cheeks and mouth with faeces; and a general ordering an eight-year-old boy to be hunted down by a pack of borzoi hounds simply because the boy accidentally bruised the leg of the general's favourite beagle.[51] Having described these horrors in some detail, Ivan challenges Alyosha to square these facts with the traditional theodicies offered by theists in defence of their belief in a providential God.

Ivan begins with the idea, central to 'contrast theodicies', that evil provides a necessary contrast to the good. One way of spelling this out is in epistemic terms: just as we could not learn what the colour red is without experiencing the contrast between it and other colours, so too if we had no experience of evil we would have no knowledge, understanding, or appreciation of the good. To this, Ivan offers the following response:

> Without it [i.e., evil and suffering], they say, man would not be able to survive upon earth, for he would not know good from evil. Why recognize that devilish good-and-evil, when it costs so much? I mean, the entire universe of knowledge is not worth the tears of that little child addressed to "dear Father God". I say nothing of the sufferings of grown-ups – they have eaten the apple, and the devil with them, and the devil take them all, but the children, the children![52]

Ivan's view is that no good is great enough to morally justify the sufferings of innocent children ("the entire universe of knowledge is not worth the tears of that little child"), in which case the very project of constructing a theodicy, at least for the evils suffered by children, becomes impossible to carry out.

There is a strong contrast in Ivan's thinking between *deserved* and *undeserved* suffering: children do not usually deserve the suffering they experience, whereas adults who "have eaten the apple" may well deserve to suffer. But it would be a mistake to think that Ivan is merely trying to say that children are innocent, or their sufferings are undeserved, and therefore no moral justification for such suffering can be provided. Although Ivan would accept this, the main point he is trying to express is that there is something gravely wrong in the idea that the suffering of children can be used, or made to serve, some higher purpose. It is an anti-instrumentalist argument of the sort we encountered in Phillips. What Ivan is therefore gesturing towards is the existence of evil that is in principle unredeemable and incomprehensible. Theodicists, however, habitually turn a blind eye to the possibility that no moral justification for (God's permission of) many evils may be available. As Surin points out,

> Theodicy, by its very nature, involves the application of the principles of *reason* to a cluster of problems which are essentially such that they cannot be resolved by the mere application of rational principles. Evil and suffering in their innermost depths are fundamentally mysterious; they confound the human mind. And yet the goal of theodicy is, somehow, to render them comprehensible, explicable.[53]

Surin is not merely making the epistemic point that our rational faculties are unfortunately not well suited to the task of uncovering the underlying meaning behind suffering. Rather, his point is the far stronger one that at least some evils have no point – they are inherently inexplicable. It is this that gives life its tragic dimension, a dimension not easily recognized by philosophers in the grip of theory (such as the Principle of Sufficient Reason, which posits a reason for everything that happens) or by lay people intent on playing the victim and finding a scapegoat for their misfortunes ("Someone is going to pay for this!", and if no person or corporation can be sued for damages, then God can always be made to pay). But what gets lost in all this is the tragic sense of life, where notions of 'blame', 'responsibility' and 'explanation' are entirely out of place.[54]

The immorality of thinking otherwise, of indulging in rationalizations and assuming that just any evil can be justified, is again contested later on in the dialogue by Ivan:

> If everyone must suffer in order with their suffering to purchase eternal harmony, what do young children have to do with it, tell me, please? It is quite impossible to understand why they should have to suffer, and why should they have to purchase harmony with their sufferings? Why have they also ended up as raw material, to be the manure for someone else's future harmony?[55]

Some philosophers have interpreted Ivan here not as challenging the entire practice of developing theodicies, but as laying down a principle we met earlier in Section 1, a principle that is thought to function as a criterion that any satisfactory theodicy must meet. The adequacy condition in question is usually understood along the following lines: God could permit a person to suffer intensely, involuntarily and undeservedly only if, by their sufferings, a greater good will result *in which they themselves can participate*. A growing number of contemporary philosophers of religion, theists and non-theists alike, have come to accept this view. Eleonore Stump, for example, argues that "there is something morally repulsive about supposing that the point of allowing a child to suffer is some abstract benefit for the race as a whole and, therefore, that the good which justifies a child's pain must be a benefit *for that child*."[56] To speak as Ivan would, a person should not be reduced to "manure for someone else's future harmony."[57]

But there is much more to the immediately preceding quote from Ivan than simply an endorsement of an adequacy condition for theodicies. For Ivan's message is that, even if the adequacy condition were rejected and so we accepted that "everyone must suffer in order with their suffering to purchase eternal harmony," it is terribly wrong to subject children to this scheme: there is no reason why they should have to "purchase harmony with their sufferings." This is not so much an attack on some extravagant form of utilitarianism, but a criticism levelled against those who cannot see the inviolable sanctity of childhood.[58]

The idea of 'purchasing eternal harmony by means of one's suffering' comes under further question by Ivan, who criticizes the very coherence of this notion:

> I decline the offer of eternal harmony altogether. It is not worth one single small tear of even one tortured little child that beat its breast with its little fist and prayed in its foul-smelling dog-hole with its unredeemed tears addressed to "dear Father God"! It is not worth it because its tears have remained unredeemed. They must be redeemed, or there can be no harmony. But by what means, by what means will you redeem them? Is it even possible? Will you really do it by avenging them? But what use is vengeance to me, what use to me is hell for torturers, what can hell put right again, when those children have been tortured to death?[59]

The typical theodical tactic of appealing to a heavenly afterlife for the victim and a hellish post-mortem existence for the perpetrator, the former as a compensatory award and the latter as a just punishment, is shown by Ivan to be totally irrelevant, for it does nothing to *redeem* (or make up for) the underserved sufferings of a child. Such sufferings, Ivan suggests, cannot be redeemed in any way, and without such redemption there can be no prospect of achieving an 'eternal harmony by means of one's suffering'. Phillips makes a similar point when arguing against the idea that, in the afterlife, God will either compensate us for, or in some way redeem, all the evils we have suffered in this life (an idea which, as indicated earlier, is not a theodicy as such, but is often appended to theodicies as a further defence of God's benevolence):

> Given the nature of many of the evils human beings undergo, it would make little sense to speak of compensations for them after death. It does not even make sense to speak of compensation, in this life, with respect to many of our losses – the loss of a child, the end of a friendship, various forms of injustice which create harm, a harm done to someone who dies before any restitution can be made and so on. In some of these circumstances, the law decrees financial compensation, but one almost always hears those who receive it say, 'Nothing, of course, can compensate for . . .' Faced with this undeniable fact, the picture cannot change by changing the landscape from an earthly to a heavenly one.[60]

In the remainder of the chapter, Ivan continues his anti-theodical critique in some of the most moving and memorable words to be found in any literature:

> I do not want the mother to embrace the torturer who tore her son to pieces with his dogs! Let her not dare to forgive him! If she wants, she may forgive

him on her own account. She may forgive the torturer her limitless maternal suffering; but as for the sufferings of her dismembered child, those she has no right to forgive, she dare not forgive his torturer, even if her child himself forgave him! And if that is the case, if they dare not forgive, where is the harmony? Is there in all the world a being that could forgive and have the right to forgive? I do not want harmony, out of a love for mankind I do not want it. I want rather to be left with sufferings that are unavenged. Let me rather remain with my unavenged and unassuaged indignation, *even though I am not right.*[61]

If to forgive the torturer is tantamount to imposing a meaning or justification to the child's suffering ('I forgive him because he knew not what he was doing/because such-and-such a good would not have been possible if the suffering did not take place', etc.), then in forgiving we are not taking suffering seriously, we are not showing proper respect to the sufferer, but are diminishing them by trying to diminish their sufferings. If we have "a love for mankind," therefore, we must refuse the temptation to 'forgive', to construct theodicies, and must remain instead with our "unavenged and unassuaged indignation." And all this "even if we are not right": even if as a matter of 'objective fact' the theodicists have it right and all our sufferings are necessary to purchase some greater good, we should protest on moral grounds against such a scheme of things (that is to say, this scheme, even if true on some level, can never be morally acceptable).

> . . . And so I hasten to return my entry ticket. And if I am at all an honest man, I am obliged to return it as soon as possible. That is what I am doing. It isn't God I don't accept, Alyosha, it's just his ticket that I most respectfully return to him.[62]

The 'entry ticket' to the heavenly afterlife where an eternal harmony will reign is too expensive; it is not worth the sufferings – particularly the sufferings of children – that it demands. But, as the above quote indicates, this does not lead Ivan to some form of conventional or speculative atheism, whereby one merely adopts a particular attitude (viz., cognitive dissent) towards a particular proposition (viz., 'God exists'). Rather, Ivan is, as some have labelled him, a 'moral atheist' or a 'protest atheist', someone who passionately rebels against God. As Kenneth Surin explains,

> Ivan already believes that the world is a providential place, he accepts, albeit most unwillingly, that history will probably take a course according with Christian eschatology (though he finds it quite wrong that one should acquiesce in the outcome promised by this scheme of things). What he cannot accept, therefore, is the price, in terms of innocent human suffering, that is exacted so that men and women may come to enjoy eternal harmony.

God has a providential relationship with his creation, yes, but this divine providence is just too costly. Ivan, it seems, has steeled himself (in the end his spiritual turmoil drives him insane) to the point where he decides that he must decline to be the masochistic accomplice of this God – we ought not to allow ourselves to be loved by such a God.[63]

Alyosha responds, "This is mutiny," but Ivan raises the tempo of his challenge even further:

"Imagine that you yourself are erecting the edifice of human fortune with the goal of, at the finale, making people happy, of at last giving them peace and quiet, but that in order to do it it would be necessary and unavoidable to torture to death only one tiny little creature, that same little child that beat its breast with its little fist, and on its unavenged tears to found that edifice, would you agree to be the architect on those conditions, tell me and tell me truly?"

"No, I would not agree," Alyosha said quietly.[64]

Ivan here succinctly reinforces points made earlier: anti-instrumentalism with respect to human suffering (which can be seen as an instance of the Kantian categorical imperative to always treat another human being as an end in himself or herself and never simply as a means[65]), a defence of the sanctity of childhood, and the impossibility of redeeming the tears of a child – in short, the rejection of theodicy as traditionally practised.[66]

5. Theoretical and Practical Problems of Evil

Another factor contributing to the morally suspect nature of theodicy is the almost exclusively *theoretical* character of the enterprise: the machinery of deductive and probabilistic logic plays an important role in the formulation of arguments, the debates are often couched in a highly abstract, technical and ahistorical language, and little attention is given to the concrete, emotional and practical problems that the occurrence of evil brings in its wake. As a result of this 'professionalization' of the problem of evil, a spirit of cool and detached reflection pervades the increasing number, and often quite repetitive and barren, journal papers and monographs dealing with the subject of theodicy. Detached reflection of this sort is, of course, to be found in all areas of academic scholarship and is not in itself something to be lamented. However, when our gaze turns to the evil and horrible suffering we inflict upon each other on a daily basis, dispassionate and abstract theorizing (at least of the kind recommended by theodicists) seems wholly inappropriate.

In attempting to make sense of the realities of evil and suffering, theodicists inculcate a sense of detachment both in themselves and in their readers. They never stop to ask, however, whether we should, or even could, be detached from the stark realities of evil in the ways they propose. No question is ever raised as to whether there might be some moral danger involved in promoting a strategy of detachment. But as Kenneth Surin and Terrence Tilley have emphasized, a number of dangers follow unavoidably from a purely theoretical and disinterested study of the problem of evil. Tilley, for example, calls attention to the harms that might accrue to readers who follow the theodicist's counsel that, "it is in regard to the issues that raise the greatest passion that we must try to be the most dispassionate" (the words, in fact, of the process theodicist, David Ray Griffin[67]):

> The theodicist encourages readers to "distance" themselves from the evils of the world to "understand" them. Yet should readers distance themselves from their own sins, and refuse to own them?... It is just those who can't or don't own their lives – including their sins – who are fated to continue the process of dehumanizing victimization without reconciliation.[68]

Thus, the distancing strategies promoted by those who approach theodicy as a purely theoretical undertaking only add to the evils of the world, rather than illuminating or counteracting them. For as Tilley explains, "accepting the recommendation of detachment when considering evils may render one oblivious to the commitment, practical wisdom and constancy needed to counteract some evils," predisposing one instead to a quietistic fatalism or a kind of masochism or escapism.[69]

Kenneth Surin, similarly, argues that the theoretical pursuit of theodicy can have disastrous moral consequences, not only for writers and readers of theodicies, but for society at large. To view theodicy as an exclusively academic undertaking, notes Surin,

> ... is already to possess the perspective on good and evil which Max Weber found to be characteristic of modern times; namely, an essentially bureaucratic view of the nature of good and evil. [Surin explains by way of a footnote that, "It is typical of the bureaucratic view of good and evil that it regards them in an abstract way, as something involving roles of office, administrative procedures, protocols, etc., but rarely personal guilt and responsibility. The evil bureaucrat *par excellence*, who rendered evil 'banal', was of course Adolf Eichmann."] If this is in fact the case, then to regard theodicy as a purely intellectual exercise is to provide – albeit unwittingly – a tacit sanction for the evil that exists on our appalling planet.[70]

The key premise in Surin's argument is that every theoretical discourse has a social dimension, or as he puts it, "all philosophical and theological reflection, no matter how abstract such reflection may be, inevitably mediates a certain social and political praxis."[71] The crucial question therefore is whether the praxis mediated by the work of theodicists serves to transform life and reality, or whether instead it legitimizes and mystifies the status quo. Surin's damning judgement is that theodicists have become complicit in the very evils they seek to explain:

> A theodicist who, intentionally or inadvertently, formulates doctrines which occlude the radical and ruthless particularity of human evil is, by implication, mediating a social and political practice which averts its gaze from the cruelties that exist in the world.[72]

The theodicist, then, tacitly sanctions evil when putting forward a doctrine or theoretical perspective which endorses the treatment of people as mere means towards some higher end; which is abstracted from the plight of those who are suffering, thus turning a deaf ear to their screams and reinforcing their powerlessness; which encourages (to borrow Surin's words) "serenity in a heartless world"[73] and which is blind to the harsh and gratuitous nature of much evil.[74]

The typical response made by theodicists is to draw a distinction between *the theoretical problem of evil* and *the practical problem of evil*. The theoretical problem of evil is the purely intellectual matter of determining what impact, if any, the existence of evil has on the truth-value or the epistemic status of theistic belief. It is customary to divide the theoretical problem into the 'logical problem of evil', which concerns the logical compatibility of theistic belief with the existence of evil, and the 'evidential problem of evil', which concerns the likelihood that theistic belief is true given the existence of evil. These issues are contrasted with the difficulties arising from the practical (or experiential) problem of evil, where the problem is how to adopt or maintain an attitude of love and trust towards God when confronted by evil that is deeply perplexing and disturbing. Although it is sometimes recognized that the theoretical and practical problems are interconnected – theoretical considerations, for example, may colour one's actual experience of evil, making it harder or easier to bear – it is usually thought that the two problems are distinct and therefore call for different approaches and answers. Alvin Plantinga, for example, writes:

> Confronted with evil in his own life or suddenly coming to realize more clearly than before the *extent* and *magnitude* of evil, a believer in God may undergo a crisis of faith. He may be tempted to follow the advice of Job's

"friends"; he may be tempted to "curse God and die". Neither a Free Will Defense nor a Free Will Theodicy is designed to be of much help or comfort to one suffering from such a storm in the soul (although in a specific case, of course, one or the other could prove useful). Neither is to be thought of first of all as a means of pastoral counseling. Probably neither will enable someone to find peace with himself and with God in the face of the evil the world contains. But then, of course, neither is intended for that purpose.[75]

The theist may find a *religious* problem in evil; in the presence of his own suffering or that of someone near to him he may find it difficult to maintain what he takes to be the proper attitude towards God. Faced with great personal suffering or misfortune, he may be tempted to rebel against God, to shake his fist in God's face, or even to give up belief in God altogether . . . Such a problem calls, not for philosophical enlightenment, but for pastoral care.[76]

Having distinguished in this way between theoretical and practical responses to the problem of evil, the theodicist may then proceed to argue that the criticisms made earlier – in particular, the criticism that the abstract and detached approach of theodicists promotes a callous and indifferent attitude towards the sufferings of others – have force only if the scope and aims of the theoretical and practical projects are conflated. David O'Connor expresses this view well in his reply to Kenneth Surin:

Theoretical theodicy is indeed a response to the actuality of evil in the world . . . Through and through it is an intellectual response. But it is not, and to my knowledge has never been offered as, a response in the quite different sense of being an address to the victims, of being an attempt to minister to the afflicted, or as a substitute for such a response. Surin, however, operating without an express distinction between the conceptual and existential dimensions of the problem of evil, supposes otherwise, and so gets to the view that theoretical theodicy is heartless, indifferent, and acquiescent in the face of real suffering. But, with the distinction made . . . between a conceptual and a ministerial response to evil in the world, and with the recognition that, to my knowledge, no philosophical theologian has ever supposed the former fit for the work of the latter, the alleged culpability, together with the grounds on which it is alleged, disappears.[77]

Michael Scott helpfully clarifies O'Connor's position as follows: Two distinctions may be drawn, the first of which focuses on the kind of problems evil creates for a religious believer:

(1) the theoretical problem of determining the logical consistency and probability-value of the theistic worldview, and
(2) the practical or existential difficulties in coping with evil.

The second distinction, however, is based on the different methods open to
the believer in responding to the above problems:

   (3) the application of the theoretical techniques used by philosophers and
        theologians, and
   (4) various practical strategies for helping one to combat or come to terms
        with evil.

Scott then restates O'Connor's argument in terms of the above distinctions: O'Connor is arguing that Surin's moral objections would be valid
only if the theodicist were conjoining (2) with (3), that is to say, were
employing the theoretical techniques of professional philosophers and
theologians to resolve people's practical or 'real-life' problems. But no
theodicist, at least as far as O'Connor is aware, is guilty of such an inhu-
mane response to the plight of victims of evil.[78]

   Surin, however, is not suggesting that the (theoretical) theodicist intentionally sets out to alleviate our personal struggles with hardship and
suffering. The theodicist is clearly not addressing his journal papers and
monographs to the poor and the afflicted, to the hungry and the homeless
(in any case, people who don't have a morsel to eat, or are not sure if they
can make it to the next day, are not likely to worry about whether the latest atheological argument from evil is logically valid). But on Surin's view,
the practice of theodicy has great practical implications that bear on the
religious life of believers. As Michael Scott shows, O'Connor admits as
much when he argues that theodicies provide believers with a necessary
bulwark against rival (i.e., naturalistic) interpretations of the world.[79]
Without a successful theodicy, O'Connor agues, the cognitive aspect of
religious belief – enshrined by the theory called 'theism' – would be under-
mined, and with it would collapse the 'life-guiding' dimension of religious
belief, that is, the religious practices that are a source of inspiration, comfort and hope to the religious community. In O'Connor's words:

> If religion is to be able to sustain its integral claim to a transcendent dimen-
> sion in human life, a claim crucial to its distinctive life-guiding power, it will
> need to be able to sustain an appropriate ontology and epistemology. That is,
> it must continue to earn a place in the debate over ultimate things to which
> technical philosophy, natural science, and increasingly the human sciences
> too, are evident contributors.[80]

And in its struggle to 'earn its place', religion cannot afford to do without
theoretical theodicy.

   The problem with this view is not merely that it assimilates religious
belief to the language of scientific explanation (an assumption criticized by
Scott[81]), but more importantly it completely misses Surin's point: *theodicies*

mediate a praxis that sanctions evil. No-one would deny O'Connor's claim that theoretical theodicists do not seek to redress the painful realities of everyday life. But Surin's claim is that in the very act of not seeking to redress these realities, theodicists impinge upon them in certain detrimental ways. The underlying assumption here, as noted earlier, is that all theorizing has a social dimension, which Surin expresses as "the principle that the text participates in society, that consciousness is not divorced from historical and social forces," from which it follows that "the philosopher and the theologian do not reflect and discourse *in vacuo*: it is their responsibility, therefore, to ask themselves, continually, what particular praxis their work mediates."[82] Abstract and disinterested approaches to the problem of evil, however, only legitimize – rather than 'interrupt' – the reality in which horrendous evil and its victims languish.[83]

By way of conclusion, I would like to return to Irving Greenberg's view, quoted at the outset of the chapter, that "No statement, theological or otherwise, should be made that would not be credible in the presence of the burning children." In light of the criticisms made above, the project of theodicy, of offering moral justifications for God's permission of evil, clearly fails Greenberg's litmus test. In the presence of the burning children, the declarations of theodicists are shown to be not merely morally confused, but morally scandalous.[84] But this raises the following curious question: If the theodicist's picture of the world can readily be unmasked as a falsifying one that does not answer to the grim moral realities we know and experience, then why do theodicists bother offering us such a picture at all? Who are they trying to convince? (Or, less charitably, who are they trying to fool?) Those presently undergoing suffering, in their time of despair and desperation, are hardly going to be persuaded, let alone comforted, by the reassurances of the theodicist. They are more likely to ask, just as the terrified Candide did, while trembling with fear and confusion, "If this is the best of all possible worlds, what can the rest be like?"[85]

This suggests that theodicies are addressed to those who have achieved a certain degree of detachment from either their own or other people's sufferings. The moral dangers of a detached posture have been spelt out before. But here I wish to emphasize a danger of a different kind. In seeking an 'objective' perspective from which we can reflect on the sufferings of others with the aim of determining whether any sense or meaning can be given to their predicament, the theodicist privileges the observer's point of view at the expense of the outlook of the one who is in the throes of pain and despair.[86]

But as Levinas points out, rather than imposing a meaning on the sufferings of others, we must view their sufferings as "useless" or "for nothing." For suffering in itself has no intrinsic value, and whatever value it has can only be conferred by the assent of the sufferer. Therefore, even if the individual victim may assign some meaning to their suffering, this is not the prerogative of the observer or bystander. Indeed, "the justification of the neighbour's pain," writes Levinas, "is certainly the source of all immorality."[87] But the theodicist's disregard for the testimony of the sufferer when seeking to impose an objective meaning to suffering leads us once more to the question of the theodicist's audience. Here the insights of Rowan Williams are pertinent:

> "Who is it for?" is a question very close to "In whose presence is it done?" If the answer to that is, "In the absence of the perspective of the sufferer as subject or narrator", how can it [i.e., theodicy] fail to evade – to evade not only humanity, but divinity as well?[88]

Theodicy, then, may set out with the noble aim of vindicating the justice of God, but only ends up effacing our humanity and God's divinity. With friends such as Cleanthes, as Phillips would say, who needs enemies? We may need to choose our friends more carefully, or to quote Williams again:

> Perhaps it is time for philosophers of religion to look away from theodicy – not to appeal blandly to the mysterious purposes of God, not to appeal to any putative justification at all, but to put the question of how we remain faithful to *human* ways of seeing suffering, even and especially when we are thinking from a religious perspective.[89]

META-PHILOSOPHY OF RELIGION: THE ANALYTIC-CONTINENTAL DIVIDE IN PHILOSOPHY OF RELIGION

If, as was argued in the preceding chapter, the approach customarily taken by analytic philosophers to the problem of evil is seriously flawed, the suspicion raised is that there may well be something fundamentally amiss in the analytic approach to philosophy of religion, if not in the analytic philosophical project as a whole. I want to see whether there is any substance to this suspicion, and to this end I will re-position the discussion on a higher plane: the focus will now turn from a specific issue within the philosophy of religion (viz., the problem of evil), to the nature and function of philosophy of religion itself. This will take the discussion to the metaphilosophical level of comparing the different ways in which philosophy of religion has been practised in the analytic and Continental traditions, examining the assumptions and commitments of each and how these have brought about two seemingly irreconcilable ways of philosophizing about religion.

1. The Great Divide

It so happened that I met A.J. Ayer last night, and our reciprocal interest kept us talking until about three in the morning. Merleau-Ponty and Ambrosino also took part . . . We finally fell to discussing the following very strange question. Ayer had uttered the very simple proposition: there was a sun before men existed. And he saw no reason to doubt it. Merleau-Ponty, Ambrosino, and I disagreed with this proposition, and Ambrosino said that the sun had certainly not existed before the world. I, for my part, do not see how one can say so. This proposition is such as to indicate the total meaninglessness that can be taken on by a rational statement . . . I should say that yesterday's conversation produced an effect of shock. There exists between French and English philosophers a sort of abyss which we do not find between French and German philosophers.[1]

This is how Georges Bataille described his encounter with A. J. Ayer that took place in January 1951.[2] There is indeed a long history of such sporadic encounters, either in person or in print, between analytic and Continental philosophers, usually resulting in mutual incomprehension and dismissive rejection of each other's views. We could point, for example, to Carnap's criticism that Heidegger's *das Nichts* counts as a prime piece of meaningless metaphysics;[3] the hostile exchange between Derrida and Searle on J. L. Austin's speech act theory;[4] and the infamous 1992 letter to the London *Times*, signed by a number of 'luminaries' of the analytic tradition and protesting against the granting of an honorary degree to Derrida by Cambridge University on the grounds that Derrida's work "does not meet accepted standards of clarity and rigour."[5]

A great gulf therefore separates the way in which Anglo-American analytic philosophers approach their subject from the approach (or approaches) taken by their Continental counterparts. One can appreciate, then, R. M. Hare's comments that there are "two different ways" in which philosophy is now studied, ways concerning which "one might be forgiven for thinking . . . are really two quite different subjects."[6] Hare was writing in 1960, but his remarks still ring true. William Charlton, for example, observed more recently that "at the moment English-speaking and Continental philosophers neither read each other's journals nor attend each other's conferences."[7] And Michael Dummett has been led to state that "we have reached a point at which it is as if we're working in different subjects."[8] This begs the question: How did we get to here?

One can look at this question from a historical perspective, tracing the different routes philosophy has taken over the centuries, and perhaps showing how the unity of philosophical endeavour that characterized the Latin Middle Ages and the Renaissance, and extended well into the Enlightenment, has effectively disappeared, leaving philosophy today in a deeply fragmented state. My approach, however, will be the more philosophical, or metaphilosophical, one of uncovering the divergent philosophical presuppositions at work within the analytic and Continental traditions.

Unfortunately, philosophers from both the analytic and Continental camps tend to be averse to the kind of introspective reflection demanded by metaphilosophical questions. Analytic philosophers have been particularly disinclined to examine the nature and history of their own tradition, let alone the traditions of alternative philosophical methodologies. But it is not only analytic philosophy that has been, and largely remains, unselfconscious in this way. Continental philosophers have also displayed little interest in metaphilosophy. Gilles Deleuze and Félix Guattari acknowledge this in the first few sentences of their book, *What Is Philosophy?*:

> The question *what is philosophy?* can perhaps be posed only late in life, with the arrival of old age and the time for speaking concretely. In fact, the bibliography on the nature of philosophy is very limited. It is a question posed in a moment of quiet restlessness, at midnight, when there is no longer anything to ask. It was asked before; it was always being asked, but too indirectly or obliquely; the question was too artificial, too abstract . . . There was too much desire to *do* philosophy to wonder what it was, except as a

stylistic exercise. That point of nonstyle where one can finally say, "What is it I have been doing all my life?" had not been reached.[9]

The situation, however, is beginning to change, and there is now an increasing willingness on the part of members of both philosophical traditions to take a step back from their daily philosophical routine and turn their attention to the nature, methods and objectives of the work they engage in. Somewhat surprisingly, philosophers of religion have been slower than most other philosophers in taking up these metaphilosophical problems, and in the ensuing pages I hope to begin correcting this deficiency.

In the present chapter, however, my primary aim will not be to adjudicate the analytic-Continental split as this has manifested itself in the philosophy of religion, or to provide reasons for preferring one side over the other – this, instead, will be the concern of the following chapter. My goal here will be the more limited one of attempting to achieve some understanding as to what, fundamentally, differentiates the two camps. My interest will therefore be in such questions as: How do analytic and Continental philosophers, particularly those who take an active interest in religious topics, practise their craft? And what does their practice reveal about the nature, methodology and aims of their work? Only if we can get some hold on these questions can we then set out to bridge or in some other way overcome the analytic-Continental divide (or even, if we are so inclined, to keep the divide open and perhaps widen it).

2. Preliminary Matters

To begin with, however, a number of preliminary matters need to be attended to. There is, first, the problem of defining analytic and Continental philosophy. I will work with a very rough and schematic definition along the following lines: *Analytic philosophy* refers to the kind of philosophy that takes Gottlob Frege, G. E. Moore and Bertrand Russell as its founding fathers, and is usually practised today in English-speaking philosophy departments. *Continental philosophy* describes the kind of philosophy that is derived from the European continent, especially Germany and France, and is heavily indebted to the writings of the 'three H's', Hegel, Husserl and Heidegger, as well as the 'masters of suspicion', Marx, Nietzsche and Freud.[10]

In offering these definitions, I am not assuming that a clear and precise line of demarcation can be drawn between analytic philosophy and Continental philosophy, or that each of these philosophical traditions can be represented as a unified whole. Various proposals have been made as to how best to characterize each tradition and how to explain the stark and obvious differences between them: Is it merely a matter of style? or methodology? or doctrine? or the sorts of questions being asked? or bibliographies and canons? or a combination of these? At times these proposals are offered in a polemical spirit, with the intention of demonstrating the superiority of one way of doing philosophy over the other, but occasionally (and more frequently of late) the goal is the more irenic and ecumenical one of building bridges between the traditions and offering a way of overcoming the differences. Despite the difficulties in providing a satisfactory account of the metaphilosophies that underwrite each tradition, I will proceed with the assumption that at least many of the *characteristic* features of these philosophical practices can be identified and discussed, even though they may not be essential or universally shared features within the practices in question.[11]

A second preliminary point relates to the category of 'Continental philosophy of religion', which is to an extent misleading, especially when it is set against the discipline of analytic philosophy of religion. Analytic philosophy, perhaps now more than ever, is a highly specialized field, divided into various sub-fields, such as the philosophy of mind, the philosophy of language and the philosophy of religion. These sub-fields are in turn divided into further sub-fields which become the preserve of a select group of practitioners working on a standard set of research problems, with each problem carefully dissected into its parts so as to be amenable to eventual resolution.

Continental philosophy, by contrast, is not characterized by any such 'division of labour', but is more integrative or synthetic in approach. Individual problems are usually dealt with in a systematic way, in the context of a larger and often interdisciplinary framework. It is typical, therefore, of Continental philosophers to not restrict themselves to strictly philosophical concerns, let alone to a particular sub-discipline within philosophy, but to disregard any such classificatory regimes and to investigate a broad array of problems – from meaning and metaphysics to ethics and politics – as these surface in the writings of their predecessors and contemporaries. So, strictly speaking, there is no 'Continental philosophy of religion', though there obviously are plenty of Continental philosophers who have various things to say about religion and theology.

As a final preliminary point, my method in this chapter is to look at a range of writers in the analytic tradition of philosophy of religion, but to concentrate predominantly on the work of John Caputo as an exponent of Continental philosophy of religion. The justification for the focus on

Caputo is threefold. First, in the English-speaking world, Caputo has done more than anyone else to promulgate and defend the Continental approach to philosophy of religion. As John Manoussakis states, "Caputo should be credited with the revival of continental philosophy of religion in North America".[12] Caputo's large body of publications and the series of conferences he has led at Villanova and now Syracuse have played a pivotal role in relating postmodern thought to religious faith.

Secondly, Caputo's writings can be used to highlight at least some of the reasons why the analytic and Continental schools are (and remain) divided with regard to the philosophical study of religion. To be sure, Caputo cannot be taken as representative of contemporary Continental philosophy of religion, if only because the field is too diverse for any single thinker to be held up as its 'representative'. Caputo's distinctive style of writing and his Derridean outlook (in particular his post-metaphysical conception of religion) have provoked much discussion, if not appreciation, from fellow colleagues within the Continental camp, but other styles and outlooks also flourish. Nevertheless, there is arguably enough similarity between Caputo's approach to religious questions and other Continental approaches to make it worthwhile to place the spotlight on Caputo.

Thirdly, the diversity within Continental philosophy of religion simply makes it more manageable and practical to concentrate on one of its better known exponents. Indeed, the writings of Caputo himself display a rich variety, reflecting an intellectual adventure that has taken Caputo from the French neo-Thomism of Maritain, Gilson and (especially) Rousselot to the enchanted world of medieval mystics and saints, Thomas Aquinas and Meister Eckhart in particular, while also negotiating powerful currents of thought encountered in modern Freiburg (Heidegger) and postmodern Paris (Derrida, Levinas).[13] Caputo not only engages with a diverse group of philosophers and theologians, but has also allowed his thinking to develop and change in significant ways, the most important of these being the move away from a broadly Heideggerian to a pronounced Derridean outlook as signalled most definitively in his 1993 publications, *Demythologizing Heidegger* and *Against Ethics*.[14] I should add, however, that I will be looking at a wide range of philosophers when discussing the general contours of Continental philosophy, though I will be focusing on Caputo when turning to Continental philosophy of religion (and then only on the more recent, Derrida-inspired Caputo).

To avoid a possible misunderstanding, I am not suggesting that Caputo has an explicitly and elaborately developed metaphilosophy. This does not mean, however, that there is no metaphilosophy lurking within his philosophical writings. Indeed, any philosopher, especially any philosopher who has published as extensively as Caputo, will at least have an *implicit* metaphilosophy, that is, a position as to how philosophy ought to be approached which can be distilled from what they have to say on purely (non-metaphilosophical) philosophical issues.

3. A Question of Style

Anyone who is brought up on a steady diet of analytic philosophy of religion and then turns to philosophical writings on religion and theology from the Continental tradition is immediately struck by the differences in the writing styles of the two groups. I will attempt to highlight this by comparing extracts from the writings of two prominent members of each group, Alvin Plantinga on the analytic side and John Caputo on the Continental side.

Some words of caution, however, might be in order. Faced with the quotations that follow, especially those taken from the analytic camp, some may feel that the passages in question have been so removed from their original context that their meaning has been distorted to some degree. There is an element of truth in this, for as will be seen shortly, I make little or no attempt to precisely explain the technical terms employed by the authors, and I only provide minimal clarification on the general setting of the quoted extracts. My aim, however, is not so much to clarify what the authors are attempting to say or establish in these passages, but to draw attention to the way in which they say what they have to say. It is style, not content, that concerns me here. (I will pay greater attention to issues of content later in the chapter.)

Also, it might be felt that the passages that follow are not typical or are not truly representative of the writings of the authors in question. I don't think this is the case, as anyone familiar with the writings of these authors will recognize. Nevertheless, there is an element of truth in this reaction as well. Each of the philosophers I have chosen, like any accomplished philosopher, does not write in one style only, but usually deploys a variety of linguistic registers in their philosophical corpus. However, the style of the passages below is not, I believe, atypical or unusual either within the whole corpus of the philosopher in question or the wider philosophical tradition within which they work.

With these caveats out of the way, let us begin with three quotations from the work of a quintessential analytical philosopher of religion, Alvin Plantinga.

Exhibit A1: Plantinga on the ontological argument
In *The Nature of Necessity*, Plantinga attempts to revive the famous ontological argument in support of the existence of God that originated with
Anselm in the eleventh century. Although Plantinga thinks that the argument as formulated by Anselm is open to objection, he contends that it can
be recast in a more rigorous form that succeeds in establishing the rationality of belief in God. But before presenting his reconstructed version of the
ontological argument, Plantinga briefly introduces Anselm's argument, first
by quoting at length chapter 2 of Anselm's *Proslogion*, and then by providing the following interpretation of Anselm's text:

> I think we may best understand him [Anselm] as giving a *reductio ad absur-
> dum* argument; postulate the non-existence of God and show that this sup-
> position leads to absurdity or contradiction. Let us use the term 'God' as an
> abbreviation for the phrase 'the being than which nothing greater can be
> conceived'. Then, sticking as closely as possible to Anselm's wording, we may
> put his argument more explicitly as follows: suppose

> (1) God exists in the understanding but not in reality.
> (2) Existence in reality is greater than existence in the understanding alone.
> (3) God's existence in reality is conceivable.
> (4) If God did exist in reality, then he would be greater than he is (from (1)
> and (2)).
> (5) It is conceivable that there be a being greater than God is ((3)
> and (4)).
> (6) It is conceivable that there be a being greater than the being than which
> nothing greater can be conceived ((5), by the definition of 'God').

> But surely

> (7) It is false that it is conceivable that there be a being greater than the being
> than which none greater can be conceived.

> Since (6) and (7) contradict each other, we may conclude that

> (8) It is false that God exists in the understanding but not in reality.

> So if God exists in the understanding, he also exists in reality; but clearly
> enough he does exist in the understanding, as even the fool will testify; there-
> fore he exists in reality as well.[15]

This way of presenting one's own or one's interlocutor's argument, with
individual propositions and their inferential relationships carefully set out,
is a regular feature of analytic philosophy of religion. In fact, this kind of

schematization is sometimes merely the first stage in the process of 'translating' an argument into the language of formal logic, so that the original argument is recast entirely in terms of logical symbols and rules of inference.[16]

Exhibit A2: Plantinga on warranted Christian belief

A second example of the kind of style that is commonly found in the analytic tradition is taken from Plantinga's *Warranted Christian Belief*, his most comprehensive study to date of the epistemology of religious belief, or the conditions under which religious belief can be held to be (in some significant sense) rationally acceptable. As Plantinga explains in the opening chapter of this book, his primary interest is in the question of whether it is rational, reasonable, justifiable or warranted to accept Christian belief, or whether there is something epistemically unacceptable or deplorable in so doing. Part of Plantinga's answer to this question involves showing when, if at all, belief in God would be warranted (in Plantinga's technical sense of 'warrant'[17]), and in the passage that follows he makes an opening move in this direction:

> On the other hand, if theistic belief is *true*, then it seems likely that it *does* have warrant. If it is true, then there is, indeed, such a person as God, a person who has created us in his image (so that we resemble him, among other things, in having the capacity for knowledge), who loves us, who desires that we know and love him, and who is such that it is our end and good to know and love him. But if these things are so, then he would of course intend that we be able to be aware of his presence and to know something about him. And if that is so, the natural thing to think is that he created us in such a way that we would come to hold such true beliefs as that there is such a person as God, that he is our creator, that we owe him obedience and worship, that he is worthy of worship, that he loves us, and so on. And if *that* is so, then the natural thing to think is that the cognitive processes that *do* produce belief in God are aimed by their designer at producing that belief. But then the belief in question will be produced by cognitive faculties functioning properly according to a design plan successfully aimed at truth: it will therefore have warrant. Again, this isn't certain: the argument is not deductively valid. It is abstractly possible, I suppose, that God has created us with a certain faculty *f* for knowing him; for one reason or another, *f* always malfunctions, and some other faculty *f'* created to produce some *other* beliefs, often malfunctions in such a way that *it* produces belief in God. Then our belief in God wouldn't have warrant, despite the fact that it is true. (This would be something like a sort of complex and peculiar theological Gettier problem.) And the abstract character of this possibility is perhaps strengthened when we think of the fact that human beings, according to Christian belief, have fallen into sin, which has noetic effects as well as effects of other

sorts. Nevertheless, the more probable thing, at least as far as I can see, is that if in fact theism is true, then theistic belief has warrant.[18]

Exhibit A3: Plantinga on the free will defence

In contrast to the plain and readable style of the above extract, the next quotation, again from Plantinga, is much more demanding. The passage is taken from chapter 9 of *The Nature of Necessity*, where Plantinga offers his well-known refutation of the logical argument from evil, an argument that attempts to show that the existence of evil is logically incompatible with the existence of God. In this passage, Plantinga develops his refutation by focusing on moral evil, and in particular by defending a version of the 'free will defence', the central thesis of which is that it is possible that it was not within God's power to create a world containing moral good but no moral evil. It is a lengthy extract, but it is worth reproducing in full to highlight the style that has characterized much analytic philosophy of religion. We pick up the action with Plantinga's statement of what it is that he seeks to achieve:

> To show this latter [that it is possible that 'God is omnipotent and it was not within his power to create a world containing moral good but no moral evil'], we must demonstrate the possibility that among the worlds God could not have actualized are all the worlds containing moral good but no moral evil. How can we approach this question?
>
> Let us return to Curley and his venality [Curley Smith, a purely fictional creature, is described as an unscrupulous mayor who accepts a bribe of $35,000 to drop his opposition to the building of a freeway]. The latter is unbounded; Curley's bribality is utter and absolute. We could put this more exactly as follows. Take any positive integer n. If (1) at t Curely had been offered n dollars by way of a bribe, and (2) he had been free with respect to the action of taking the bribe, and (3) conditions had otherwise been as much as possible like those that did in fact obtain, Curley would have accepted the bribe. But there is worse to come. Significant freedom, obviously, does not *entail* wrongdoing; so there are possible worlds in which God and Curley both exist and in which the latter is significantly free but never goes wrong. But consider W, any one of these worlds. There is a state of affairs T such that God strongly actualizes T in W and T includes every state of affairs God strongly actualizes in W. Furthermore, since Curley is significantly free in W, there are some actions that are morally significantly free in W and with respect to which he is free in W. The sad truth, however, may be this: among these actions there is one – call it A – such that if God had actualized T, Curley would have gone wrong with respect to A. But then it follows [by the argument outlined in the preceding section of Plantinga's book] that God could not have actualized W. Now W was just any of the worlds in which Curley is significantly free but always does only what is

right. It therefore follows that it was not within God's power to actualize a
world in which Curley produces moral good but no moral evil. Every world
God could have actualized is such that if Curley is significantly free in it, he
takes at least one wrong action.[19]

Plantinga here introduces his thesis of 'transworld depravity', which states
that any significantly free person created by God will commit at least one
wrong action. If this thesis is even possibly true, then it is possible that it
was not within God's power to create a world in which every person always
does that which is right, and so *contra* Mackie and McCloskey, the logical
argument from evil fails. No doubt there is much technical jargon in the
above quote (e.g., the ideas of 'actualization', 'strong actualization', 'significant freedom') that Plantinga does clarify and that would need to be
understood in order to properly appreciate the force of Plantinga's argument. But here the aim is not so much to understand and evaluate Plantinga's free will defence, but to appreciate the kind of language and style
within which he couches his defence.

I ask the reader to keep these passages in mind as I turn to some extracts
from Caputo's recent work in the philosophy of religion.

Exhibit B1: Caputo on the love of God
In the opening pages of his book, *On Religion*, Caputo is seeking to
describe the nature of religion, and he begins by identifying religion with
"the love of God." This, in turn, gives rise to the question Augustine posed
in the *Confessions*: "What do I love when I love God?" Here are some of
Caputo's thoughts on this question:

> I love this question in no small part because it assumes that anybody worth
> their salt loves God. If you do not love God, what good are you? You are too
> caught up in the meanness of self-love and self-gratification to be worth a
> tinker's damn. Your soul soars only with a spike in the Dow-Jones Industrial
> average; your heart leaps only at the prospect of a new tax break. The devil
> take you. He already has. Religion is for lovers, for men and women of pas-
> sion, for real people with a passion for something other than taking profits,
> people who believe in something, who hope like mad in something, who love
> something with a love that surpasses understanding. Faith, hope, and love,
> and of these three the best is love, according to a famous apostle (1 Cor.
> 13:13). But what do they love? What do I love when I love my God? That is
> their question. That is my question.[20]

Exhibit B2: Caputo on the love of God, again
In the concluding pages of *On Religion* Caputo again takes up this question, this time employing it to construct what he calls "three gradually

higher or more radical axioms of a religion without religion."[21] The first such axiom he summarizes as: 'I do not know who I am or whether I believe in God'. The second axiom states that, 'I do not know whether what I believe in is God or not'. The third and highest axiom, 'I do not know what I love when I love my God', is taken up at length in an earlier work, *The Prayers and Tears of Jacques Derrida*, where it is described in the following terms:

> That is to reach full stride, to open the throttle, to engage the *oui, oui*, to let life dance, to let the forces play, to be impassioned by the secret, impassioned by the passion for the impossible. That is the formula over which I pray and fast, around which I dance, the motto that I meditate upon night and day, that I have inscribed on the plaque that hangs over my desk, around which I have organized my life's task. When I awake in the middle of the night and jot down my dreams, I always write the same thing. I take my stand with love, and with God, and I am driven by a passion for God.[22]

Exhibit B3: The prayers of Caputo
Caputo ends his recent book, *The Weakness of God*, with a concluding prayer "for theology, for the truth, for the event." Here are several excerpts of what he says (and prays) over the course of his last chapter:[23]

> I am praying not to be lost, praying because I am already lost, praying not to get any more lost than I already am, praying that my prayer does not make things worse. I am trying to think while praying, to pray while thinking, praying like mad – for theology, for theology's truth, for the event. The event for me is not an object but a matter for prayer. (p. 283)
>
> . . . I am praying to God, preyed upon by God, turned to God – by God (*à Dieu*). Each night upon retiring I pray for the truth, for the truth of the event, for the courage of the truth, for the courage to welcome the event. I am praying for a thought, for a thought that is engendered in prayer, praying for theology, for theology's truth, praying for the courage of the truth of theology. (p. 284)
>
> . . . I am praying with both hands. On the one hand – what is the sound of one hand praying? – to confess the name of God is to profess it and affirm it, endorse it and countersign it, pray and weep it, again and again, yes, yes, for I am turned by God to God (*à Dieu*).
>
> But on the other hand – the sound of the other hand praying – if the truth be told, to be turned in prayer to the event is to risk being overturned and turned out in the cold . . . (p. 286)
>
> . . . Indulge for a moment my authorial conceit that the present study is to be viewed as my *Confessions*. If the honest truth be told, I have never done anything memorable enough to be worthy of confession, never even dared to steal pears (I don't even like pears) or to wear my trousers rolled. But I will nonetheless dare here to speak in these concluding pages of my confessions, which are a way of praying and writing with both hands,

praying for the truth, praying not to die from the truth, praying that the truth will set me free.

. . . I am praying for theology to come true. In my anarchical way of looking at things, which is not without precedent, prayer brings not peace but the sword (Matt. 10:34). To call upon the name of God is to call for trouble, for it is to call for loosening up the grip of the world, which threatens to be all in all. To turn to God in prayer one must be willing in return to be overturned by God, to be submitted to an infinitely subversive turn in things, which destabilizes the present order. To pray for theology to come true – where theology is taken to be prayer's own thought – is to want to break up the presence of the world, to prevent the world at present from closing over and sealing off an event that the world cannot contain. (p. 287)

. . . I am praying because I am lost, praying not to get any more lost than I already am, fully conscious that every prayer worthy of the name suffers through a dark night of the soul, suffers a loss of faith and its own kind of prayerful atheism. Not knowing whether anyone hears our prayer, we pray in the dark to cold and indifferent heavens that seem unmindful that we here below beseech them. We pray *sans voir, sans avoir, sans savoir*, every prayer worthy of the name being to an unknown God. (p. 292)

. . . Every prayer worthy of the name is a prayer to an unknown god. If I knew and had assurances about the addressee of my prayer, I would be too self-assured to need to pray. To pray to an unknown God is not only possible but it may be, in the end, the only possible prayer. Derrida's "*s'il y en a*" or "*peut-être*" may be the very form of prayer. Oh, God, my God (if you are there). Oh, God, my God, you are all in all (perhaps). (p. 295)

As is evident from the two above groups of quotations, the styles of each group are remarkably different. Rephrasing a comment made by David Cooper, we instantly recognize to which tradition Plantinga or Caputo belongs, before grasping what he is saying, merely from the way he says it.[24] Indeed, it is possible to distill from these quotations a set of implicit prescriptions as to how philosophy ought to be written. In Exhibits A1–A3 the overriding virtues of good philosophical writing are those that have become commonplace in the analytic tradition: *clarity* and *rigour*. Clarity, of course, is almost an obsession among analytic philosophers. The general rule is to write in such a way that a reader with even moderate understanding of the topic under investigation can follow, with not too much difficulty, the line of argument that is being proposed. Analytical philosophers therefore tend to adopt a certain simplicity of style, expressing themselves in short, crisp and concise sentences, avoiding as much as possible any rhetorical embellishments, and drawing as much as they can from the vocabulary of 'ordinary language' (this perhaps being an expression of analytic philosophy's unwillingness to steer too far away from the dictates of common sense). As many have noted, this style of writing, in the hands of its best practitioners (Russell and Quine come to mind), achieves a degree of beauty and elegance that is often found only in more literary circles.

However, there is also a strong pull in the direction of rigour, which often obstructs rather than furthers the goal of clarity. The virtue of rigour can be subdivided into two component virtues: cogent reasoning and precision. What qualifies as a cogent form of reasoning in the context of a philosophical discussion is usually left unclear, but the general idea is that arguments (whether they be one's own or one's opponent's) should be set out in a logically rigorous way, where this may involve clearly identifying the premises, the conclusion and the inferences employed, and perhaps also formalizing the argument with the help of the tools of a logical calculus. Once it is clear what exactly the argument is, it can then be assessed for validity and soundness according to commonly accepted criteria. The second component in the drive towards rigour is precision. Here we meet the customary practice in analytic philosophy of scrupulously defining key terms, making relevant distinctions, providing finely grained analyses and introducing technical vocabulary where necessary to avoid the ambiguities of ordinary language.

Exhibits A1–A3 exhibit many of these characteristics. With the possible exception of A3, where argumentative rigour may, for some readers, be an obstacle to comprehension, these extracts have both a broadly scientific or technical style, while also retaining a firm footing in ordinary language. Further, the mood created is one of disinterested and detached investigation in pursuit of objectivity: personal interests, feelings and commitments give way to unbiased judgement, so that the reader is led to believe that the author is merely following the argument or evidence wherever it leads. One could even say, at least analytic philosophers would be inclined to say, that the passages in A1–A3, as well as the entire books from which they were taken could, in principle, be 'translated' into a formal language, such as that represented by the predicate calculus, almost without remainder, without loss of meaning. Of course, the texts would thereby become impenetrable to all but an elite few who have the requisite training, but this does not detract from the significance of the fact that (it is believed that) such a thing could be pulled off.

In contrast to the style prevalent in analytic philosophy, philosophical works from the Continental tradition are more literary than scientific in character. There is, of course, a long history within Continental philosophy of engagement with literature and the arts, whether it be by crossing genres

(Sartre and Camus, for example, wrote philosophical works as well as highly acclaimed novels and plays) or by writing sensitively about painting and literary texts (e.g., Deleuze and Guatarri write on Kafka, while Derrida publishes *The Truth in Painting*).[25] It is no surprise, therefore, that in the Continental tradition clarity and precision – at least as these are usually understood within analytic philosophy – are not viewed as overwhelmingly important (though this is not to say that they are altogether eschewed). The works of Heidegger, Levinas and Derrida are notoriously difficult to read, as they are saturated with dense sentence constructions, highly idiosyncratic (even experimental) forms of language, all manner of literary devices or tropes and technical jargon that is rarely precisely defined. Like the writings of his mentor, Jacques Derrida, Caputo's texts, as evidenced by Exhibits B1–B3, are also replete with rhetorical flourishes – including prayers, parables, pseudonymous discourses, witty jokes, wordplays, paradoxical turns of speech, irony and metaphor – that would only cause consternation, if not exasperation, in comparatively 'sober' analytic circles.[26] And when one ventures into the writings of those who are not philosophers in any straightforward sense but who have significantly influenced Continental philosophy – and here I have figures such as Jacques Lacan, Georges Bataille and Maurice Blanchot in mind – the level of obscurity only seems to be compounded. Whether this constitutes a criticism of Continental philosophy is not obvious, and will be examined in the following chapter.

In line with their rejection of an 'objective' or scientific style, Continental philosophers frequently adopt a very personal and intimate tone. This is especially evident in Exhibit B3, where Caputo, in the manner of Augustine, tells us that he will "dare here to speak in these concluding pages of my confessions," writing repeatedly in the first-person of his experience of prayer, of truth, of God and of his very self. No attempt is made to downplay the emotions or to remove them from view: indeed, Caputo's language is charged with passion and enthusiasm. One is reminded of another Continental philosopher, Slavoj Žižek, though the name of Nietzsche also comes to mind. In a recent review of Žižek's book, *The Puppet and the Dwarf: The Perverse Core of Christianity*, the reviewer (Jeremy Biles) did a fine job, I thought, of characterizing the kind of style that is typical not only of Žižek, but also of many other writers in this tradition (Caputo included): Žižek's language is described as "consistently emphatic: there is an implied exclamation point at the end of nearly every sentence."[27] The reviewer goes on to note that, in the book under review, "the Slovenian bulldozer does what he does best: with engine roaring, he ploughs through history and philosophy, overturning conventional understandings and turning up potentially new ground for thought."[28] Further on still, the reviewer states that,

> With Zizek, there is a great deal of sound and fury, signifying – what, exactly? Yet the cumulative effect of reading Zizek is indeed compelling, partly because the prose is cloaked in an aura of importance . . . I have never read a book in which my marginalia has so frequently consisted of asterisks paired with question marks. For this reader, at least, everything in this book seems very important, but nothing is entirely clear. Nearly every point I found important I also found either dubious or incomprehensible.[29]

The criticisms of lack of clarity (or even intentional obfuscation) and lack of plausibility are often voiced by analytic philosophers against their Continental brethren. Rather than entering into these disputes here, I simply wish to underscore the stylistic qualities displayed by both Žižek and Caputo. Clearly, neither writer is in the business of advancing formalized arguments, where precisely crafted propositions are translated into logical symbolism so that the validity or invalidity of the argument can be made transparent. Instead, we are presented with a range of rhetorical strategies that make for a flamboyant, even hyperbolic and polemical, style of writing that regularly draws upon various fields across the humanities (including literary and cultural theory, history, politics and psychoanalysis, thus giving Continental philosophy a distinct interdisciplinary focus[30]). The overall effect, as Žižek's reviewer discovered, is inevitably perplexity and incomprehension, though this may also be accompanied by a sense that there is something *compelling* here.

But differences in style, all on their own, cannot tell the whole story. This is not to say that stylistic differences are superficial, something that can be overcome relatively easily while keeping the analytic-Continental divide fundamentally intact. Rather, stylistic differences point to disagreements on a much deeper level. As A. W. Moore has stated about his style of 'conceptual philosophy', in comparison with Derrida's deconstructive style, "the sense in which these are styles of philosophy is a deep sense. It is not a matter of icing on the cake; not a matter of how you dress something that could be presented with some completely different kind of dressing."[31] In order, therefore, to account for the stylistic divergences between the analytic and Continental schools, we need to turn to the domain of metaphilosophy. At this level, where one's underlying assumptions as to how philosophy ought to be pursued are made explicit, we will see what exactly it is that separates Caputo from his analytic counterparts.

4. Entering Deeper into Meta-philosophy: Analytical and Continental Approaches

The style employed in Exhibits A1–A3 indicates that analytic philosophers of religion like to think of their inquiries as somewhat analogous to those pursued in a scientific discipline. This, of course, is a trait of analytic philosophy in general. As Pascal Engel has stated, analytic philosophy "mimics the scientific style of inquiry, which proposes hypotheses and theories, tests them in the light of data, and aims at widespread discussion and control by peers."[32] In Continental philosophy, by contrast, it is the arts or humanities – especially literature and literary criticism – rather than the sciences that provide the model for philosophical discourse. This, as we shall see, has wide ramifications in the philosophy of religion. For in situating themselves in such different genres, the two schools of thought take on widely divergent perspectives on the philosophy of religion: there is little agreement as to what philosophy of religion is for (its aims and purpose) and how it ought to be pursued (its methodology), and these differences both inform and are informed by disparate philosophical positions on a range of issues.

4.1 Analytic philosophy

Analytic philosophy cannot be circumscribed within the narrow confines of a particular school of thought, or a set of doctrines, or a specific methodology. Since its origins in the early twentieth century as a movement against British idealism, analytic philosophy has undergone extensive change and development, encompassing a diverse range of doctrines and methods. Peter Hacker, for example, has documented four distinct phases in the history of analytic philosophy: (i) logical and conceptual analysis as practised by Moore and Russell in the early years of the twentieth century (e.g., Russell's theory of descriptions, celebrated by Ramsey as a "paradigm of philosophy"[33]); (ii) a linguistic turn initiated by Wittgenstein's *Tractatus*, where the analysis of language, its forms and structure, take centre-stage in philosophical investigation; (iii) the Cambridge school of analysis active in the 1930s (responsible for founding the journal *Analysis*), and the logical positivism of the Vienna Circle; and finally (iv) the post-WWII period of linguistic analysis (or 'ordinary language philosophy'), its chief representatives being Gilbert Ryle and J. L. Austin.[34] Although Hacker's historical outline is by no means uncontroversial (e.g., as he acknowledges, some take the linguistic turn to have originated with Frege, not Wittgenstein), his overview succeeds in demonstrating the multi-faceted nature of what has come to be known as 'analytic philosophy'. Indeed, in its contemporary manifestations, analytic philosophy is distinguished by the variety of ways in which its very *modus operandi* – analysis – is understood and put into action. As Michael Beaney has stated,

> Analytic philosophy . . . is a broad and still ramifying movement in which various conceptions of analysis compete and pull in different directions. Reductive and connective, revisionary and descriptive, linguistic and psychological, formal and empirical elements all coexist in creative tension; and it is this creative tension that is the great strength of the analytic tradition.[35]

Similarly, A. P. Martinich and David Sosa note in their 2001 anthology on analytic philosophy that, "No one, two, or three ways of doing philosophy and no small class of problems dominated the last quarter century. A thousand philosophical flowers have bloomed."[36]

Despite this variety within the analytic tradition, there remains – at least in many quarters of the tradition today – a common way of pursuing philosophy, a methodology that is not beholden to any one conception of analysis but nevertheless has a distinct orientation and character. (There is, then, no presumption made here that this methodology is universally accepted within the analytic tradition, but only that it has become a distinguishing feature of this tradition.[37]) The method in question is broadly scientific in spirit and is underwritten by the assumption that philosophy is or should be in some sense continuous with (or an extension of) the sciences. On this view, philosophers should not only take the results and discoveries of science seriously, but should also model their enquiries on the language, methods and techniques of science (including the formal sciences of logic and mathematics). This is evident, for example, in the tendency towards specialization that has come to play an increasingly important role in analytic philosophy. A philosophical career in the analytic tradition is typically built almost exclusively around a few distinct sub-fields (such as the philosophy of mind and metaphysics), and even then only around certain issues or problems within these sub-fields (such as the mind-body problem, or the compatibility of free will and determinism).[38] This growth in specialization reinforces, and is reinforced by, a piecemeal or semi-independent approach to philosophical problems, with only a narrow set of questions open at any one time for intensive scrutiny – hence the great popularity of short journal papers in the analytic tradition. But the piecemeal approach of the analytic philosopher also tends to be ahistorical in nature, again suggesting parallels with the (formal and natural) sciences.

It is not unusual, for example, to see propositions and forms of argumentation culled from the texts of the great philosophers of the past, with scant attention paid to the wider cultural milieu within which those texts were originally produced. As in mathematics and physics, what matters in analytic philosophy is not so much who formulated a particular doctrine and what motivated them to do so, but whether the doctrine itself can be demonstrated to be true. Generally speaking, then, the methodology of the analytic philosopher is the broadly scientific one of advancing a hypothesis or theory in response to a narrowly circumscribed problem, all of which is done without great concern for the historical and cultural context of the problem.

The next stage in this method involves subjecting the relevant hypothesis to various 'tests'. These tests do not, of course, require any laboratory experimentation (though a distant analogue might be the 'thought-experiments' and 'counterexamples' that have become a staple of analytic philosophy). What is involved, rather, is usually a test for *conceptual adequacy*, where some central philosophical concept (such as 'knowledge', 'cause' or 'free will') is examined so as to determine whether it can be given a coherent or adequate analysis. This is sometimes supplemented by a test for *evidential adequacy*, where evidence and arguments both in support of and against a hypothesis are carefully evaluated. Here, as in the scientific arena, criteria such as explanatory power, simplicity and fit with background knowledge may be used to assess evidence, while arguments are routinely formalized in the language of a logical calculus so that their deductive validity or inductive strength can be measured. In the end, a solution to the problem is proposed, and this may lead to the construction of a theory that, ideally, pushes in new directions a broadly defined research programme, such as physicalism or evolutionary naturalism. There is a sense, then, that some progress, however minimal, is being made, even if universal consent within the philosophical community (or even within those parts of the philosophical community that take an active interest in the problem at hand) is not forthcoming.

An approach of this sort also characterizes analytic philosophy of religion. The hypothesis that is usually under investigation is that the world is created and governed by God, where 'God' is standardly defined as a maximally great or absolutely perfect being, that is, a being perfect in power (omnipotent), perfect in knowledge (omniscient) and perfect in goodness, but also possessing a suite of other essential properties, including omnipresence, incoporeality, eternity, worship-worthiness, and (on some accounts) simplicity, immutability, impassibility and necessary existence. The overall aim is to determine whether 'the theistic hypothesis', as it

is called, is w   ypically, this project begins with a test
for conceptu   cept of God presupposed in the theistic
hypothesis c   s, an adequate definition or analysis of
each divine attribute is sought, with a view to determining whether any
inconsistency or incoherence in the divine attributes (either individually or
in combination) can be detected.[39] The analyses of the divine attributes
often face formidable challenges (such as 'the paradox of the stone' with
regard to omnipotence), and so the analyses quickly become convoluted
and technical.[40] But assuming these difficulties can be overcome and
satisfactory analyses are available, the project then proceeds to the crucial
second stage: Are there any good reasons for accepting the existence (or
non-existence) of God? The issue is now one of justification, rather than
conceptual clarification, and so a barrage of arguments for and against the
existence of God are offered and minutely scrutinized.[41]

Two points may be noted in regards to the foregoing account of analytic
philosophy of religion. First, the search for proofs and disproofs of the
existence of God has come under much fire of late, even within the analytic
camp. Natural theology, in particular, has been criticized for, among other
things, its dialectical ineffectiveness; an inability to produce or sustain
religious faith and commitment; a tendency to overlook the non-rational
factors that play an important role in the assessment of evidence and arguments; presupposing an evidentialist model of religious belief that can no
longer be accepted in our post-foundationalist era; and insensitivity to the
historical context in which theistic arguments were originally developed
(a glaring example of this being the treatment of Anselm's ontological
argument at the hands of analytical philosophers).[42] Natural theology,
however, continues to be practised by analytic philosophers, even if theistic
arguments are no longer thought to be necessary for the rationality of
religious belief, and even if the standards as to what counts as a successful
argument have generally been relaxed so that a 'knock-down' or universally convincing argument is rarely thought to be possible. Also, natural
atheology remains as popular as ever, with a large contingent of non-
theistic analytic philosophers of religion – including William Rowe, Quen-
tin Smith, Michael Martin and Jordan Howard Sobel – developing a variety
of arguments against the existence of God.

Secondly, analytic philosophy of religion, particularly as it has developed over the last few decades, is much broader in scope than the picture
painted earlier might suggest. Analytic philosophers are now increasingly
engaging in a much wider range of activities than merely the clarification
of the divine attributes and the projects of natural theology and atheology.
Analytic theists, in particular, are more likely to see their work in the

tradition of *fides quaerens intellectum*, attempting to understand what they already believe, as opposed to trying to convince non-theists of the meaningfulness and truth of what they (as theists) believe. There is, therefore, much work being done in such areas as the epistemology of religious belief (as evidenced by Exhibit A2), the nature of religious faith and practice (e.g., discussions on faith and reason, prayer and worship), the problem of religious pluralism, the relationship between religion and morality and the elucidation of distinctively Christian doctrines such as the Trinity and the Incarnation. Be that as it may, these investigations continue to be conducted in a scientific spirit. A specific problem, for example, is first identified, such as the 'Euthyphro problem' (Does God approve of what is good because it is good, or is it good because God approves of it?), or the conflicting truth-claims made by the various religions of the world. In an attempt to resolve such problems, hypotheses or theories are tentatively proposed. Norman Kretzmann, for example, answers the Euthyphro question by deferring to the idea of divine simplicity: on this view, there is an objective standard of goodness, but that standard is God himself.[43] And John Hick responds to religious diversity by putting forward his pluralistic hypothesis that the world's great religious traditions embody different but equally valid conceptions of a transcendent divine reality.[44] These hypotheses are, in turn, assessed in the light of commonly accepted criteria (and possibly more controversial ones, such as consistency with the teachings of a particular set of sacred scriptures or religious tradition) in the hope that progress can be made in resolving the issue in question.[45]

4.2 Continental philosophy

Continental philosophy proceeds along very different lines. It is difficult to characterize this kind of philosophy, at least in an accurate way that avoids caricaturing it, partly because it is made up of a plethora of schools and methodologies: existentialism, phenomenology, hermeneutics, structuralism, Frankfurt School Critical Theory, postmodernism, philosophies based on or influenced by psychoanalytic theory and so on. But as the two sets of quotes provided earlier in Section 3 indicate, there is a distinct flavour to this kind of philosophy. Perhaps one promising way of capturing this 'flavour' is to follow Neil Levy's suggestion that modernist art, and not modern science, provides the model for Continental philosophers.[46] So, in what way does the artist act as an exemplar for philosophers of the Continental variety? The idea, as Levy elaborates it, is that modernist art – typified by the work of the abstract expressionists in the United States in the 1940s and 50s (the so-called 'Irascibles', including the likes of Jackson Pollock, Willem de Koonig and Mark Rothko) – is geared towards novelty and revolution. Art of this sort cultivates the myth of the isolated and tormented genius who suffers for his art, is misunderstood by his peers and wider society, but nevertheless manages to break through existing styles and conventions, thus gaining access to new and deeper truths or realities. The aim here is not *continuous progress*, the gradual but steady accumulation of knowledge or accepted facts, as in modern science, but *continuous revolution*: rejecting received methods and styles with ones that are unforeseen or overlooked, so as to see the word anew.[47] Hermeneutics, the interpretation or re-interpretation of the world, therefore takes precedence over formalization or the mere advancement of knowledge. This, I think, is evident in the Caputo extracts above, B1–B3, where the aim is not to render something more precise or better established, but to destabilize common patterns of thought, to cast doubt on settled ways of thinking, and in the end to open up avenues of thinking about the divine and religion that have been dismissed by the confessional faiths and professional philosophers.[48]

Thus, the Continental philosopher *qua* avant-garde artist aims to provide a fresh and imaginative view of the world, with invention rather than analysis taking precedence (as Deleuze and Guattari's conception of philosophy as conceptual creation makes clear[49]). Cultural critique, furthermore, plays an important part in this quest. As David Cooper observes, "there is hardly a continental thinker of note, from Bergson and Unamuno to Derrida and Habermas, who has failed to include in his brief a critical assessment of the contemporary human condition, and to regard this as seamlessly connected with his wider philosophical enterprise."[50] Analytical philosophers, Cooper acknowledges, also engage in critical reflection on 'the human condition' (Bertrand Russell being a case in point), but when they do so one gets the impression, as Cooper puts it, that they are 'off duty', not working as professional philosophers but in some broader capacity as 'public intellectuals' who are concerned to discuss political or moral issues that may have little connection to their academic projects.[51] Continental philosophers, by contrast, typically see it as part of their job (or vocation) to overturn theories and structures that they perceive to be socially, if not spiritually, regressive and dangerous, a task which is integrally related to their philosophical work, rather than being extraneous to it. The concerns, then, of the Continental philosopher are not concentrated on a set of well-delineated and sometimes quite technical problems that may have few implications for life outside the academy. Rather, their goal is to provide a new vocabulary and a new vision that will inspire people of all walks of life to take up the struggle for 'liberation', however this is conceived. This explains, as Levy points out, the Continental philosopher's "constant urge to begin again, to question the foundations of philosophical systems, particularly of those systems that, she believes, shape the common-sense and everyday perception of her entire culture. Thus the problem of social transformation is the constant horizon of her work."[52]

Closely tied to this social vision is a certain kind of attitude to the hegemony of science in Western society, an attitude which may be labelled 'anti-scientism'. David Cooper provides a clear and succinct description of scientism:

> 'Scientism' denotes the conviction, explicit in thinkers like Comte, that it is in and through the practices epitomized by the natural sciences that the goals of European Enlightenment are to be attained. These goals would include progress towards better conditions of life, 'the dissolution of myths and the substitution of knowledge for fancy' (Adorno and Horkheimer's phrase), and, in Kant's famous words, 'man's emergence from his self-incurred immaturity . . . the courage to use your *own* understanding'.[53]

Continental philosophers uniformly and vehemently reject the elevation of science that is encapsulated in scientism. On their view, whatever the value and legitimacy of science itself, scientism is nothing less than theoretically and existentially bankrupt. On the theoretical side, first of all, scientism overlooks the thoroughly conditioned nature of all human knowledge in its pretensions to have privileged access to objective facts or truths. The adoption of a perspectival, or even relativistic, view of knowledge and truth helps to explain the emphasis Continental writers place on history and interpretive practices, and on situating philosophical texts in their social, cultural and historical milieu in order to properly understand them.[54]

Secondly, and on the existential plane, it is argued that the elevation of science as the model for all discourse and understanding has not produced a better world, but has rather ushered an "age of distress" (to borrow Heidegger's phrase) marked by all manner of ills: nuclear warfare, genocide on a scale previously unimaginable, totalitarianisms of the left and the right, the technological exploitation of natural resources, a 'calculating' mentality that feeds the excesses of capitalism while the third world languishes in abject poverty, a culture marked by a deep sense of disenchantment and disillusionment, where only Disneyland or drugs can offer stimulation or a way out and so on. The Enlightenment equation of reason, emancipation and progress is thereby undone. (However contentious such criticisms might be, it should be borne in mind that the connection being drawn is not between the practice of science and the evils of the twentieth century, but between these evils and a distorted and overblown conception of science or reason.) In direct contrast, then, to analytic philosophy's emulation of science, Continental philosophy is much more wary, viewing this kind of attachment to scientific thinking as having disastrous consequences. The blend of philosophical theory and cultural critique is here apparent.

I have yet to say anything in much detail about Continental philosophy of religion, as opposed to Continental philosophy in general. My next task, therefore, will be to discuss some features of the Continental approach to the philosophy of religion, focusing in particular on the recent writings of John Caputo. This, in turn, will pave the way for a discussion and assessment of some objections that analytic philosophers of religion typically raise against their Continental brethren.

CHAPTER 4

CONTINENTAL PHILOSOPHY OF RELIGION AND OBJECTIONS FROM THE ANALYTIC CAMP

In the previous chapter I explored the suggestion that Continental philosophy models itself in many ways after modernist art, as opposed to the broadly scientific approach of analytic philosophy. Another fruitful analogy, and one that is perhaps more apposite in discussions of religion, is that between Continental philosophy (of religion) and the tradition of prophetic speech in the Old Testament. This analogy is worked out in a remarkable but unjustly neglected essay published in 1973 by Merold Westphal, entitled appropriately enough, "Prolegomena To Any Future Philosophy of Religion Which Will Be Able To Come Forth As Prophecy."[1] Westphal's paper is a kind of 'Advice to Christian Philosophers', prefiguring Plantinga's influential address of that name by over a decade, and aiming, like Plantinga, to steer the philosophical study of religion in radically new directions. The picture that Westphal paints of what philosophy of religion could (and should) become has, in fact, largely materialized in the recent development of a 'post-metaphysical theology' among Continental philosophers of religion, including John Caputo, Mark C. Taylor, Jean-Luc Marion, Gianni Vattimo and many others. My aim in the first half of this chapter is to describe the programme put forward by Westphal, indicating along the way how this has been put into practice by Caputo, and thus offering at least one plausible image of what contemporary Continental philosophy of religion looks like. I will then proceed in the second half of the chapter to a discussion of various criticisms that the Continental way of philosophizing about religion is likely to provoke from members of the analytic camp.

1. Continental Philosophy of Religion

Westphal argues that philosophy of religion, properly pursued, will take on the following marks that distinguished the speech of the biblical prophets:

(1) *personal:* Unlike scientific discourse, prophetic speech is delivered in a very personal manner, in the mode of direct address. This is because, as

Westphal explains, prophetic speech "is the echo of God's address to man," as in the following excerpt from Exodus:

> I am the Lord your God, who brought you out of the land of Egypt, out of the house of bondage.
> You shall have no other gods before me. (Ex. 20:2–3)[2]

Acting as receptacles of the word of the Lord, the prophets are too intimately and personally involved to present their message in a neutral or objective way. Kierkegaard, as Westphal notes, also took such a personal approach: even if he does not preface his remarks, as did the prophets, with 'Thus saith the Lord', he "has sought to hear God's truth in a personal way and then to pass it on, albeit without authority, in an equally personal way."[3] This personal form of address, in Kierkegaard as in the prophets, takes as its target audience only a particular group of people (perhaps even only the troubled heart of a single individual) at a particular time, and this is why it often has an *ad hominen* character rather than the form of a universally binding imperative (a Kantian categorical imperative, for example) or a formal proof built from universally self-evident premises.[4]

(2) *untimely:* A further property of prophetic speech is its untimeliness. In Westphal's words, "Prophetic speech is conspicuously out of step with the spirit of its times. It is always minority speech, even when addressed to sectarian minorities. Hence it is lonely speech from the viewpoint of the speaker, while from the perspective of the hearer it is simply untimely and unwelcome."[5] By revealing truths that people prefer to keep concealed, prophets are seen as threatening and are therefore dismissed as mad, bad or worse – much like Nietzsche's 'untimely meditations' are customarily dismissed by analytic philosophers as the product of a madman.

(3) *political:* Westphal notes that the Hebrew prophets do not deify their monarchs, as did the surrounding nations, but rather view the monarch as subordinate and responsible to God himself. The prophets are therefore not afraid to enter the political fray, to question and confront not only their priests on religious issues (such as idolatry) but also their kings on matters of social justice. Indeed, as Westphal states, "the prophetic opposition to priest and king is an opposition to the whole dualism of sacred and secular which they represent. It is the call to a religion which functions seven days a week and to a politics whose piety is more visible in its policy than in its church attendance."[6]

(4) *eschatological:* The words of the prophets are geared towards the future, towards preparing the way of the Lord. The prophets, explains

Westphal, "see the history of salvation as continuing (since God is not dead), and thus they look forward to a whole new era of saving acts."[7] This re-orientation towards the future, however, is not escapist, but serves to represent the present in a new light. Seen from the eschatological vantage point, change on a socio-political level becomes less "an aberration in a fixed order due to bad luck or poor strategy," but "the harbinger of new saving acts which God is about to perform."[8]

Westphal thus encourages the development of a prophetic philosophy of religion that addresses its audience in a personal, untimely, political and eschatological manner. At the time of publication (in 1973), Westphal was forced to concede that, "It is hard to tell what the result [of such a philosophy of religion] would look like, and even harder to tell whether there would be any healing in it."[9] But over three decades later, the results are in. A distinct prophetic discourse of the kind advocated by Westphal has emerged, exemplified best in the writings of Caputo. There we find a discourse consciously molded in a prophetic, rather than in a Greek-philosophical, idiom: "The poetics of the Kingdom," Caputo writes, "is prophetic – a diction of contradiction and interdiction – that 'calls for' (*prophetein*) the rule of God, calls for things to happen in God's way, not the world's."[10] Such a poetics is marked by the four above qualities identified by Westphal. As mentioned in the previous chapter, Caputo brings to his texts an intensely personal and passionate style, a prophetic "passion for the impossible" as he likes to say, that many have found engaging and compelling. Caputo's work is also untimely in its advocacy of a 'religion without religion', that is, a religion without pretensions of being 'the one true religion' and a religion without the hierarchical and authoritarian structures of the institutionalized faiths[11] – views clearly out of step with the rising tide of religious conservatism and fundamentalism. But Caputo raises the ire not only of the religious authorities, but also the secularized academic establishment that is intent on keeping religion out of academia.[12] Further, the political and eschatological dimensions are evident in Caputo's appropriation of the Derridean themes of 'deconstruction as a radical call to justice' and 'messianicity without messianism'.[13] Like Derrida, Caputo eschews the violence and exclusivity created by the concrete messianisms of the religions of the Book, placing in their stead a formal messianicity described by Derrida as "the opening to the future or to the coming of the other as the advent of justice, but without horizon of expectation and without prophetic prefiguration."[14] Deconstruction, on this conception, "turns out to be a religion of the *tout autre*, a religious affirmation of what is to come, hoping and sighing, dreaming and praying for the coming of the wholly other."[15] "The first, last and constant prayer of deconstruction," Caputo continues, "is to shout, to pray, '*viens, oui, oui*'."[16]

But underlying these points of convergence between the Continental approach to philosophy of religion and the speech of the Old Testament prophets is an overall approach and attitude towards religion that is perhaps best viewed negatively as *non-scientific*. Indeed, Westphal's aim in drawing attention to prophetic discourse is "to explore the possibility that the model for the philosopher of religion can be someone other than the scientist."[17] Philosophy of religion, Westphal points out, often strives to be scientific, whether it be in the form of natural theology or atheology (as the attempt to establish the truth or falsity of religious beliefs) or in the guise of a phenomenology of religion that purports to merely describe the form and content of various religious beliefs and practices. These approaches strive to be scientific in that they actively pursue the scientific ideal of *objectivity*. Westphal nicely summarizes this ideal:

> The scientist is the one who brackets all personal interests, values, and commitments which would have any bearing on his investigations. By an heroic act of self-renunciation he becomes the transcendental ego, a nonparticipating spectator . . . He presents his results to other scientists who are able to verify what is really there for the common transcendental ego and eliminate what is due to the residual idiosyncrasies of the original investigation. The result is acclaimed as universal truth. In this sense of inter-subjective agreement one can speak of the public verification which renders scientific objectivity.[18]

The arguments of natural theology have traditionally been delivered in this detached and neutral (non-committal) way, so as to avoid (for example) any appeal to emotions and to ensure that the premises employed are not question-begging (i.e., do not presuppose what they set out to prove) and are acceptable to any 'rational' person. Similarly, phenomenology of religion aspires to be an objective science, but it does so by demanding an *epochē* of all questions of religious truth, as well as all personal and practical interests, thus paving the way for an objective characterization of religious phenomena.

Westphal, however, criticizes philosophy of religion for taking such a 'scientific turn'. He notes that

> . . . the notion of scientific objectivity, even without the ideals of mathematical precision and general laws, when torn from its natural habitat and transferred to the religious realm reveals the fundamental incongruity between itself and its newly assigned subject matter.[19]

Part of the reason why the scientific ideal is not appropriate in a religious context concerns the perspectival nature of religious knowledge:

> It seems as if Kant's discovery of the a priori as the unconditioned condition of all possible experience touched off a whole series of discoveries showing that there are some areas of thought where the a priori itself is radically conditioned by historical, sociological, and psychological factors. To say this is to say that the categories in which questions are framed and the principles by which answers are evaluated vary with the observer. Knowledge becomes radically perspectival and interest-bound. Who can doubt that religion is one such area of thought? When the question is about God and immortality, Where did I come from? Where am I going? What's it all about, Alfie, is it just for the moment we live? – is it not comical to speak of "pure *theoria*", the knower as "non-participating spectator" whose "fully disinterested seeing of the world" stems from "the *epoche* of all practical interests"?[20]

In contrast with the spirit of detached objectivity that is common to both science and the philosophy of science, religion as well as the philosophy of religion demand a far more conditioned and interest-relative conception of knowledge. Westphal further highlights this by means of some illuminating comparisons: Kant's proposal that objects must conform to our knowledge is contrasted with Barth's view that in coming to know God we become the mastered, not the masters, knowledge becomes acknowledgement, and our expression of this knowledge becomes confession; Aristotle's attempt to construct a science of the divine (a metaphysics) founded in sheer intellectual curiosity is contrasted with Socrates' experience of the darkness of the cave and his consequent desperate search for light and freedom.[21] Sin opens up another point of contrast between the scientific and religious points of view. "To talk about sin," Westphal observes, "is to talk about what concerns the individual in all his subjectivity . . . This is why, from the religious point of view, truth is not be found in objectivity."[22] Westphal therefore concludes that philosophy of religion, pursued under the banner of science, may serve as a pastime for the leisurely classes, but not as spiritual medicine in the crises of our time.

As Westphal indicates, the move away from a scientific mode of discourse in Continental philosophy of religion is regularly fuelled by a commitment to the doctrine of perspectivism.[23] This doctrine, made famous by Nietzsche's statement that "facts is precisely what there is not, only interpretations,"[24] is often presented as a challenge to a particular kind of metaphysics and epistemology. The metaphysics that perspectivism seeks to overturn is a realist one according to which, to quote E. E. Sleinis' succinct description, "the world has a fully articulated, fully determinate nature and structure independently of any awareness of it," that is to say, "mind-independently, there is a way the world is down to the finest detail."[25] Perspectivism, particularly in its Nietzschean guise, adopts instead an anti-realist metaphysics which rejects any conception of an objectively existing reality, a real world-structure of which there are interpretations, a way the world really is in contrast with our modes of interpreting it.[26] Perspectivism, moreover, rules out epistemological theories which hold that we can come to possess objective – that is, impartial and unconditioned – knowledge of the world. Knowledge-claims, for the perspectivist, are never impartial or unconditioned, but are always geared towards serving our interests, needs and desires, and are always influenced by (among other things) the nature of the knower, the placement of the knower, the conditions of knowing and the process of coming to know.[27]

Perspectivism enters Caputo's corpus by way of his 'radical hermeneutics', a hermeneutics radicalized by deconstruction so as to produce a structural 'blindness' or non-knowing described by Caputo in terms of the thesis that

> ...we are not (as far as we know) born into this world hard-wired to Being Itself, or Truth Itself, or the Good Itself, that we are not vessels of a Divine or World-Historical super-force that has chosen us as its earthly instruments, and that, when we open our mouths, it is we who speak, not something Bigger and Better than we. We have not been given privileged access to The Secret, to some big capitalized know-it-all Secret, not as far as we know. (If we have, it has been kept secret from me.) The secret is, there is no Secret ...[28]

Unlike analytic philosophers, who fear that such views are a threat to truth and rationality, for Caputo and other like-minded Continental philosophers the acceptance of perspectivism makes possible a new way of seeing and understanding, one in fact that opens the door to religion after it had been slammed shut by the modernist Enlightenment critique. As Caputo explains,

> The result of a more sober reading of Nietzsche is not relativism and irrationalism but a heightened sense of the contingency and revisability of our constructions, not the jettisoning of reason but a redescription of reason, one that is a lot more reasonable than the bill of goods about an overarching, transhistorical Rationality that the Enlightenment tried to sell us ... No one foresaw that Nietzsche's theory of fictions would converge with the biblical critique of idols, of mistaking our own graven images for the divinity. In this way of looking at things, the Enlightenment and its idea of Pure Reason are on the side of Aaron and the golden calf, while Nietzsche, God forbid, he who philosophizes with a hammer, stands on the side of Moses as a smasher of idols, and stands right beside Paul giving the Corinthians holy hell about the idols of the philosophers.[29]

No perspective, on this view, can provide the final answer on God and religion, and this applies not only to the creedal formulations of the mainstream Christian churches but also to the "unvarnished reductionism" of the Enlightenment, where religion is held up to be (e.g.) *nothing but* the expression of perverse psychological desires (Freud) or *nothing but* a way of keeping the ruling authorities in power (Marx). These, according to Caputo, are "just so many contingent ways of construing the world under contingent circumstances that eventually outlive their usefulness when circumstances change."[30] If this is so, however, the voice of religion can once again be heard, not this time as a totalizing and dogmatic pronouncement that purports to offer the absolute truth, but as a 'weak theology' that has the more modest aim of providing a non-confessional, pluralistic and tolerant outlook on religious matters.[31]

But perspectivism is only one plank in the Continental case against the scientific ideal of objectivity in the philosophy of religion. This ideal is also rejected on the grounds of what might be called 'non-realism', to which I now turn.[32]

2. The God of the Philosophers and the God of Abraham, Isaac and Jacob

After Pascal's death a note was found sown into the lining of a coat he was wearing, the note recording the so-called 'second conversion' he underwent in November of 1654 and containing the following famous words: "The God of Abraham, the God of Isaac, the God of Jacob, not of the philosophers and scholars." This dichotomy between the abstract God of speculative philosophy and the living God of the concrete religions is one that runs parallel to, and indeed informs and sustains, the analytic-Continental divide in philosophy of religion. To get somewhat clearer on these polarities, I will begin by outlining the conception of God accepted by most analytic philosophers and then comparing this with views about God prevalent in the Continental tradition. These differences, as will be seen, are largely underwritten by competing positions on the problem of realism and non-realism, where this is not to be confused with the issue of metaphysical anti-realism outlined earlier in my description of perspectivism, but is rather the question of whether the reality of God can be understood and expressed in a purely factual or objective way.

What exactly, then, is the 'God of the philosophers'? A helpful account is provided by Richard Messer, who in *Does God's Existence Need Proof?* argues that philosophers who think that belief in God is something that can be justified or falsified by means of evidence or proofs tend to presuppose a particular conception of God, a conception which is wildly at variance with the kind of God presupposed by Wittgensteinian philosophers of religion (such as Rush Rhees, Peter Winch and D. Z. Phillips) who reject theistic proofs and disproofs as alien to the practice of religious 'language games'.[33] Messer delineates a number of features of what he calls 'the traditional philosophical conception of God', this being the dominant conception of God within the analytic tradition and one which coheres well with the scientific ethos of this tradition (as described in Section 4.1 of Chapter 3). According to this understanding of God,

(1) *God is definable.* Swinburne, for example, has no difficulty in providing a definition of God, which he does in classical theistic terms (God is defined as "a person without a body (i.e. a spirit) who is eternal, is perfectly free, omnipotent, omniscient, perfectly good, and the creator of all things"[34]). Messer notes that underlying this procedure is an 'expressibility principle' to the effect that "God's attributes are largely expressible and that we can formulate a full enough definition of God to know almost exactly what we believe in or reject."[35]

(2) *God either exists or does not exist.* Having overcome verificationist qualms about the meaningfulness of either disjunct, analytic philosophers of religion today uniformly think that one or the other of these disjuncts must be true.

(3) *'God exists' is a factual claim.* Religious language has a fact-stating character, so that, as Messer puts it, "we can discover whether or not there is a God as we can discover whether or not any particular fact is correct: by weighing and assessing evidence."[36] The projects of natural theology and natural atheology therefore play an important role in the analytic tradition. Richard Swinburne and Michael Martin, for example, have devoted lengthy studies to the question of the existence of God, and the approach of each philosopher has involved the accumulation and evaluation of various pieces of evidence both for and against theistic belief.[37]

(4) *God is an explanatory hypothesis.* The case in support of the theistic hypothesis is largely built upon the presumed ability of this hypothesis to explain a wide variety of phenomena (including the existence of the world, its conformity to order, the evidence of miracles and religious experience). Theism is viewed as a theory which, like those advanced by scientists, can be judged according to its explanatory power.

(5) *God is an inference.* For many analytic theists, the existence of God is something that can appropriately be inferred from various empirical data.

(6) *God's existence is probable or improbable.* Analytic philosophers nowadays tend to defer to inductive arguments and (as in Swinburne's case) to the probability calculus, rather than to deductive considerations, when arguing in support of or against theism. Belief in God, then, is belief in what is merely probable.

(7) *God is an object.* Like other objects we are familiar with, God is – according to Swinburne – "something of which properties are true, which causally interacts with other recognisable observable objects, which can be distinguished from others as the subject of certain predicates which he has and they don't."[38]

(8) *God is comprehensible.* Through reason alone, we can understand who or what God is, and we can go at least some way towards settling the question of whether there is such a being.

This conception of God is rejected outright by Caputo. In the concluding pages of *The Prayers and Tears of Jacques Derrida*, Caputo mounts a scathing attack on the God of the Greek philosophers:

> That very finite Hellenistic creature called "God" is a being cut to fit the narrow needs of Greek ontology, of Parmenides and Plato, who were scandalized by time and motion and change, and of Aristotle, who did the best he could to make the name of matter and motion respectable among the Greeks. But from a biblical point of view, this highly Hellenic *theos* was an imperfect – may I say a pathetic, or better an *a*pathetic? – way to think of God. It had nothing to do with Yahweh who was easily moved to anger and jealousy, who was a God of tears and compassion, who suffered with his suffering people, who was moved by their sighs and lamentations, who was angered by their meanness of mind and had a well-known and much respected temper, who had, in short, a short fuse. Being "wholly other" was something other than being wholly unmoved by human suffering, for God or his prophets.
>
> The God of Hellenistic philosophers had as little to do with the God of the prophets as urbane, aristocratic Greek philosophers had to do with wild-eyed, half-naked (and sometimes not half) Jewish prophets. The prophets were outrageous and bombastic people, passionate and compassionate, fiery, fulminating, disturbing messengers who usually ended up getting killed because of their message which they delivered with sharp tongues and explosive tempers. Accordingly, the God of whom the prophets spoke, whose fire they delivered, had nothing to do with the *actus purus* of Athenian metaphysics.[39]

Drawing upon the prophetic tradition in precisely the way encouraged many years previously by Westphal, Caputo presents an image of God that sharply contrasts with the metaphysical God bequeathed to us by the

Greeks. It will be useful once again to defer to Richard Messer, who sets the eight above qualities of the traditional philosophical conception of God against the way in which God is conceived by the Wittgensteinian school and, we may add, by Caputo and many of his Continental brethren:[40]

(1) *God is wholly other.* Augustine is noted for saying, "Si comprehendis, non est Deus." God is holy other, the *mysterium tremendum et fascinans*, and is therefore also wholly other, *tout autre*. The incomprehensibility and radical alterity of God is, of course, an important theme in the writings of negative theologians and mystics, such as Pseudo-Dionysius and Meister Eckhart, who are regularly studied and discussed in Continental philosophy but are generally neglected in the analytic tradition. However, the conception of God as wholly other implies not merely that the standard philosophical definition of God (as given by Swinburne, for example) is inadequate, but that the very attempt to delimit God by means of definition fails to take due notice of the profound mystery that is God. Caputo expresses this point well:

> To say "God is good", "God is just", "God is wise", and the like is in each case a measured expenditure, reasoned and rationed, when what is called for is an expenditure without reserve in which one tears up the balance sheet of divine names and says, with a certain excess, "God is wholly other".[41]

The otherness of God, for Caputo, also manifests itself in our ignorance as to who or what God is. The question, 'What do I love when I love my God?', is left forever open, or undecidable. We are told "God is love" (1 John 4:8, 4:16), but Caputo asks: "Which one is the example of which? Is love a way of exemplifying *God*? Or is God a name we have for exemplifying *love*?"[42] On this view, in contrast to the expressibility principle as formulated by Messer, we cannot know what we believe in or reject when we say that we believe in or reject God: the believer/non-believer distinction begins to dissolve.[43]

(2) *God is not an existent or a being.* To treat God as an object, a thing or a being existing among other beings is to reduce God to creaturely proportions, to merely being "the biggest thing around" as David Burrell characterizes the God of 'perfect-being theology' (which conceives of God as a maximally perfect being).[44] Like the Wittgensteinians, Continental writers refuse to place God in the same ontological order as ordinary beings and objects. In the Continental tradition, this is customarily expressed as a refusal to conceive of God in metaphysical or onto-theological categories (e.g., "the *actus purus* of Athenian metaphysics," as Caputo states in the quote above). Jean-Luc Marion, therefore, challenges the primacy given to

being (*esse*) as a name for God, preferring instead to speak of God as 'without being', 'beyond being' and ultimately as the gift of love.[45] Richard Kearney interprets God not in terms of pure being (as in scholastic theology), nor in terms of pure non-being (as in apophatic theology), but in eschatological terms as a God who *may be*.[46] And Caputo develops 'a theology of the event', where "the name of God is the name of an event rather than of an entity, of a call rather than of a cause, of a provocation or a promise rather than of a presence."[47] But as Caputo goes on to emphasize, this is not to deny the reality of God or to adopt an anti-realist account of religious discourse where God is reduced to a metaphor or a projection of human wishes or some sort of fiction, but to refuse to delimit the reality of God within the horizon of being, presence, power and causality.[48]

(3) *God-talk is not fact-stating.* Although this view is common to both Wittgensteinians and Continental philosophers, the latter usually draw upon the doctrine of perspectivism in rejecting the idea of religious language as fact-stating. From the point of view of perspectivism, our language about God, like our language about anything else, cannot be 'factual' or 'objective', that is, something that corresponds with a mind-independent reality and can be known to so correspond by means of an impartial and disinterested investigation. As Caputo explains, this is not to deny the possibility of religious truth, but to reconfigure religious truth in practical or existential, as opposed to purely theoretical, terms:

> Religious truth is not the truth of propositions, the sort of truth that comes from getting our cognitive ducks in order, from getting our cognitive contents squared up with what is out there in the world, so that if we say "*S* is *p*" that means that we have picked out an *Sp* out there that looks just like our proposition. Religious truth belongs to a different order or sphere of what Augustine called "*facere veritatem*", "making" or "doing" the truth.[49]

Religious truth, on this view, is not to be assigned to the category of facts or propositions that get things right in an empirically verifiable way. Rather, religious truth belongs to the order of faith, not knowledge, so that it is a matter of "testifying (which is what the Greek *martyreo* means) to the love of God, doing something, a deed, making justice flow like water over the land."[50]

(4) *Belief in God is not scientific belief.* To construe religious beliefs as hypotheses, inferences or probability judgements is to model religious belief on the practice of science, a kind of scientism which, as mentioned earlier, the Continental tradition strongly disavows. Religious beliefs, unlike scientific theories, demand infinite commitment and passion, which

is why one cannot imagine Caputo's depiction of the Jewish prophets – "fiery, fulminating, disturbing messengers who usually ended up getting killed because of their message which they delivered with sharp tongues and explosive tempers" – applying in any way to the scientist (*qua* scientist). By contrast, one who treats theistic belief as a hypothesis may furnish evidence in its favour, and may even come to accept that belief as being more probable than not in the light of the available evidence, *all the while remaining personally indifferent to God.*

(5) *God is a concrete, not abstract, reality.* Philosophical conceptions of divinity tend to be abstractions such as the Unmoved Mover, the One, the Supreme Being, the Absolute Spirit, or the First Cause. Such a God, as Heidegger recognized, is religiously useless: "Man can neither pray nor sacrifice to this god. Before the *causa sui* man can neither fall to his knees in awe nor can he play music and dance before this god."[51] This also is Caputo's objection to the distant God of the Greek philosophers in the quoted passage reproduced earlier, where he contrasts the God of the philosophers with Yahweh, the 'living' God of the prophets who is roused to anger, tears and compassion, and whom Jesus addressed as *abba*, 'father'.

As the foregoing discussion suggests, different conceptions of God will have different and significant metaphilosophical implications, for how one conceives of God and language about God will greatly influence how one approaches the philosophy of religion. If one adopts the realist view, for example, where religious language is fact-stating and the reality of God is analogous to the reality of physical objects, then one naturally takes a scientific approach to the philosophical study of religion. The God of the philosophers is just the kind of God that can be precisely analysed and treated as a hypothesis to be rigorously tested and confirmed or disconfirmed. And this, as we have seen, is exactly the approach that has become standard in analytic philosophy of religion. On the other hand, if one takes the non-realist view, where the reality of God is wholly other, that is, infinitely removed from the order of contingent or creaturely reality, then clearly God will not be something that can be approached with neutral objectivity, rigorous proofs and clear and precise concepts – such tools are simply too blunt for the unfathomable divine reality. As theologian Hans Küng has stated:

> If the word 'God' is to mean anything at all, then it cannot mean an object like other objects, a being among other beings, a person like other persons. If the word is to retain a meaning today, it must denote the invisible and inaccessible, first and last reality which determines and permeates everything. And this reality would then be, not just another level, but a completely other

dimension, which cannot be discovered by the use of some sort of super X-rays. No, God would not be God if he could be empirically detected, worked out or deduced by mathematics or logic.[52]

This is a common theme in Continental religious thought, but as will be seen shortly, it represents a particularly sore point in analytic-Continental relations.

3. Objections from the Analytic Camp

How is Continental philosophy of religion, at least as it has been portrayed above, likely to be viewed by those working in the analytic tradition? There are, to be sure, a plethora of criticisms that analytic philosophers would want to raise, but here I will concentrate on some of the most important and recurrent objections that find their way in the literature and in discussion. I will divide the objections into those dealing primarily with matters of *form*, that is, the way in which Continental philosophy of religion tends to be written (its language and style), and those that are concerned with matters of *content*, that is, the key assumptions and doctrines that motivate much of contemporary Continental philosophy of religion.

3.1 Poor form: the language and style of Continental philosophy

The writings of Continental philosophers often lack the virtues of clarity and rigour. Indeed, in many cases one wonders whether the writing is not willfully obscure and imprecise. But how can the goals of truth and rationality, goals to which we all should aspire, be furthered by means of poor standards of reasoning and language that is vague and unclear, if not utterly incomprehensible?

This is a commonplace reaction among philosophers whose training lies exclusively within the analytic tradition, though even some Continental philosophers would admit to finding the language and style of certain figures or schools within their own and allied traditions to be woefully inadequate. The language of Continental philosophers often gives the impression that this group of philosophers has renounced the sincere pursuit of truth in favour of rhetoric, groundless assertion, exegesis or commentary, or some form of purely literary writing. Anthony Quinton, for example, states that existentialism, structuralism and critical theory "all, in varying degrees, rely on dramatic, even melodramatic, utterance rather than sustained rational argument."[53]

An initial reply may be to say: 'Tu quoque! It is not only Continental philosophers who write badly, but analytic philosophers also. The difficulty and inaccessibility of much analytic philosophy, resulting in large part from its endeavour to be logically rigorous, should not be overlooked. Consider, in this regard, the philosophical writings of Alfred Tarski, Rudolf Carnap, the early Wittgenstein, David Lewis, and Michael Dummett: hardly models of clarity and comprehensibility!'

To be sure, this charge, like all *tu quoque* charges, is somewhat irrelevant since whether analytic philosophers are guilty of the same, or a similar, wrong has no bearing on the truth of the original charge. Such a response, however, misses an important point in the above *tu quoque* criticism. For what this criticism indicates is that standards of clarity and rigour vary significantly from the one philosophical tradition to the other. In the eyes of a typical analytic philosopher, nothing could be more transparent and rigorous than Tarski's semantic conception of truth, or Davidson's truth-conditional theory of meaning, or Lewis' defence of modal realism: these projects might present difficulties to the beginning student, but with the requisite training and background knowledge their clarity and argumentative rigour can readily be appreciated. By contrast, a Continental philosopher not conversant with developments in the analytic tradition will find much of what passes as 'clear' and 'rationally defensible' in this tradition as barely intelligible and credible. This is illustrated well by Samuel Wheeler when he recounts: "I once gave Derrida a copy of Saul Kripke's *Naming and Necessity*, which I regard as a nearly transparent text, absolutely clear and brilliant. Derrida said he had tried to read this before but had not been able to understand what was going on. In contrast, he said, Heidegger was very clear."[54]

It seems, then, that analytic and Continental philosophers disagree quite radically as to what constitutes clear and cogent philosophical writing. In the analytic tradition, not surprisingly, it is the kind of clarity and rigour found in scientific and mathematical discources that is emulated. As W. D. Hart has pointed out, the emphasis on clarity in analytic philosophy is sometimes underwritten by substantive philosophical theses, one of which he calls 'the semantic ideal of rationalism': philosophy should be modelled on the mathematical style of exposition, which is typified by statements that are impersonal, unambiguous and impervious to context, and whose truth is intended to be timeless and without qualification.[55] In line with this ideal, Wittgenstein states in the Preface to his

Tractatus Logico-Philosophicus: "What can be said at all can be said clearly."[56] Further, as Hart notes, "it is no accident that the *Tractatus* is a sequence of separated and numbered theses; the *Tractatus* . . . embodies an extreme mathematical ideal of philosophy, perhaps even to the point of parody."[57]

Continental writings, on the other hand, embody very different ideals of clarity and rigour. The clarity sought by Continental philosophers, for example, is more closely tied to the kind of insight and understanding afforded by literary and narrative works than to that achieved by logical and scientific modes of reasoning. Also, despite the common caricature of the Continental philosopher as someone who flagrantly dispenses with truth and reason, I suggest it is far more accurate to say that philosophers in the Continental tradition do employ arguments and evidence, and by extension do accept the cognitive norms of truth, rationality and justification – it's just that their understanding as to what counts as a good or cogent argument, or what truth, rationality and justification amount to, often differs significantly from the views of analytical philosophers on these subjects. John Caputo, for example, does not do away with reason *in toto*, but puts forward a 'post-metaphysical' conception of reason that does not reduce rationality to merely calculative and rule-governed thinking.[58] There is, of course, an aversion within many quarters of the Continental tradition towards notions such as 'rationality' and 'justification'. But this is only because, as Merold Westphal has observed, such thinkers "are more likely to speak of understanding, or interpretation, or language, or even knowledge and truth than they are of rationality. It's almost as if they think modernity has spoiled the term and that it is now more misleading than illuminating to define humanity in terms of rational animality. Given contemporary 'modern' reductive analyses of rationality in terms of effective means-end calculation, it may be just as well (and more biblical)."[59]

In choosing, then, between competing philosophical perspectives, Continental philosophers do not simply make a baseless or merely instinctual decision. Unlike their analytic counterparts, however, they would not place considerable weight on the rules and techniques of formal logic and probability theory, or on the findings of the physical sciences, or on empirical criteria of theory evaluation such as verifiability, predictive power and simplicity, or even on the deliverances of intuition and common sense. Rather, if a choice for one philosophical perspective over another were to be made by a Continental writer, it would most likely be made on very different grounds, such as the ethical and socio-political implications of the perspective in question,[60] or the psychological motivations leading to the adoption of the perspective, or the degree to which the perspective promotes certain values (e.g., creativity, individuality) or is consonant with lived human experience and practices (e.g., personal freedom, authentic existence).

But if that is the case, then to understand the writings of Continental philosophers, to interpret them aright rather than to dismiss them as obscure and obscurantist, as analytic philosophers are wont to do, would demand a significant departure from the way in which philosophical texts are commonly read and engaged in the analytical tradition. The complaints of analytic philosophers who find Continental philosophy unreadable may therefore reside with the reader more than the text, as the reader may be bringing to the text an unrealistic or dubious set of assumptions as to how philosophy ought to be written and read. Consider in this context Derrida's response to those who complain about the difficulty of his works:

> You also asked me, in a personal way, why people are angry at me. To a large extent, I don't know. It's up to them to answer. To some small extent I know; it is not usually because people are angry at me personally (well, it happens in private, perhaps); but rather they are angry at what I *write*. They are angry at my texts more than anything else, and I think it is because of the *way* I write – not the content, or the thesis. They say that I do not obey the usual rules of rhetoric, grammar, demonstration and argumentation; but, of course, if they were simply not interested, they would not be angry. As it is, they start to get involved but feel that it's not that easy, that to read my texts they have to change the rules, to read differently, if only at another rhythm. They have to change the way they usually read and that's why they get angry; not because they are charging me with saying terrible things, I don't think.[61]

The tacit assumption made by Continental philosophers who argue in this fashion is that truth and rationality are not always, or even rarely, attained or furthered by means of the 'scientific' type of discourse constructed by analytic philosophers. More difficult truths, particularly those relating to the mystery of God, may well require more difficult language, language that is richer and more complex and subtle than the literal, fact-stating discourse of the sciences. Being faithful to the phenomena, in other words, may require a refusal to treat them as if they were transparent and thus able to be precisely expressed in a formalizable language. Not all phenomena, and especially aesthetic and religious phenomena, yield to this kind of treatment. This is why Continental philosophers like to think of themselves as phenomenologists of experience, respecting the ambiguous texture of lived experience by seeking to capture it in the kind of literary language employed by poets and novelists.[62]

Ultimately, then, the differences in the language and style of analytic and Continental philosophers are informed by divergent perspectives on the role and value of scientific forms of discourse and reasoning. The dispute over style, therefore, cannot be resolved independently of an assessment of the substantial philosophical differences dividing the two schools. It is some of these philosophical differences that I consider next.

3.2 Lack of content: the underlying commitments of Continental philosophy

As indicated in Sections 1 and 2 above, it is largely through its rejection of the scientific ideal of objectivity that Continental philosophy of religion differentiates itself from its analytic counterpart. The departure from this ideal involves, as we saw, the twin commitments of perspectivism and non-realist discourse about God. But why are analytic philosophers of religion generally reluctant to make any such commitments in their thinking?

3.2.1 Perspectivism
Perspectivism, particularly of the Nietzschean variety, typically arouses perplexity and hostility in analytic philosophers, whether they be of a secular or religious bent. The objection most commonly made against the doctrine of perspectivism relates to the doctrine's apparent self-defeating character. If, as Nietzsche holds, there are no facts but only interpretations, then how are we to understand this claim itself? Clearly, perspectivism must be construed either as a fact or as one further interpretation – but in the former case the doctrine is obviously self-refuting, while in the latter case the doctrine seems to become merely one interpretation among others, with no good reason or argument available for preferring it over its competitors.

In assessing this objection to perspectivism, two problems need to be distinguished. First, there is the issue of the internal consistency of the doctrine of perspectivism. And secondly, there is the problem of what we may call the 'dialectical impotence' of the doctrine, the presumed inability that anyone who espouses this doctrine has in supplying good reasons for taking up the doctrine.

Let's start with the objection that perspectivism is, in itself, incoherent or inconsistent.[63] Arthur Danto formulates the problem thus: "Does Perspectivism entail that Perspectivism itself is but a perspective, so that the truth of this doctrine entails that it is false?"[64] But this formulation will not do, for as Nehamas acknowledges, such a formulation assumes that if a view (in this case, perspectivism itself) is an interpretation it is *ipso facto* false. This is not the case. To call any view, including perspectivism, an interpretation is to say that it *may* be false (not that it *actually* is false), and that is not a sufficient refutation.[65] A more accurate rendering of the apparent problem of self-referential inconsistency is perhaps the following: If the thesis that all views are interpretations is true, then is there not at least one view that is not an interpretation, viz., the aforementioned thesis itself? Alternatively, according to perspectivism there are no objective truths – but is not this an objective truth?

Some commentators of Nietzsche's work have felt that it is rather facile to discredit Nietzsche's perspectivism by seizing upon his claim that there are no objective truths or facts. Perhaps such a procedure is indicative of nothing more than a failure to understand what Nietzsche means when he says that there are no facts. To claim that a statement of this sort must purport to be a factual statement (and thereby contradict itself) misses the mark entirely, for Nietzsche intends all statements – including his own – to be interpretations.[66] Thus, it is at least open to Nietzsche to say that the doctrine of perspectivism is true, but its truth is only relative to some perspective.

This, of course, is to adopt a global relativism with respect to truth, according to which one and the same proposition can be true relative to one perspective and false relative to another. Relativism of this sort, however, has traditionally been rejected as self-refuting. To see why, suppose we accept the kind of relativism in question, and suppose further that we must choose between one of these alternatives: either relativism has the same truth-value in all perspectives, or relativism is true in some perspectives and false in others.[67] Now, those who reject relativism may be called 'absolutists', according to whom there is at least one proposition which is true in all perspectives or (what perhaps comes to the same thing) is true independently of the specific perspective one has adopted. Let's begin, then, with the first alternative and assume that relativism is true in all perspectives. If we take this route, we must concede that there is a proposition – viz., that expressed by the thesis of relativism – which is true in all perspectives, in which case absolutism is true. Thus, if relativism is true in all perspectives, then absolutism is true – a clear contradiction.

In the face of such a stark contradiction, it is tempting to think that if relativism is true, its truth can only be relatively – not absolutely – true, that is to say, the truth of relativism may be thought to hold in some, but not in all, perspectives. Indeed, various commentators have been inclined to attribute this view to Nietzsche in order to rescue him from self-refutation.[68] Critics of relativism, however, often charge that the view that relativism is only relatively true is also self-refuting. Paraphrasing Steven Hales and Rex

Welshon, the paradoxical character of the relative truth of relativism can be brought out as follows: Suppose that relativism is true only in some perspectives, and suppose further that perspective Q happens to be one of those perspectives in which relativism is false and absolutism is true. Recall that absolutism is true only if there is some proposition that has the same truth-value in all perspectives. What we are meant to suppose, then, is that perspective Q contains at least one proposition p that is true (or false) in all perspectives. But what this entails is that, no matter what perspective we find ourselves in, we must concede that p has the same truth-value in that perspective as it has in Q. Relativism therefore cannot be true in Q or in any other perspective (since there is a proposition, viz., p, which is true in all perspectives). Thus, if relativism is true in some but not all perspectives, then relativism is false in all perspectives – another clear contradiction.[69]

I am sceptical of the soundness of this last criticism of relativism. The problem with the criticism is that it trades on an important ambiguity. The claim that Q contains some proposition that is true in all perspectives may receive either a strong reading:

> There exists a proposition p such that p is true in perspective Q and in every other perspective

or a weaker reading:

> From the standpoint of perspective Q, proposition p is true in all perspectives.

At most, it is only the harmless weaker reading that can charitably be attributed to the relativist. More generally, the claim that (global) relativism is relatively true may run into various difficulties, but self-refutation does not seem to be one of them. As Jack W. Meiland has stated, "That relativism is self-refuting . . . is a myth which must be laid to rest."[70]

But even if the charge of self-refutation were dropped, there are other and more forceful criticisms that could be made of the doctrine of perspectivism. One such criticism is that perspectivism (and hence global relativism) is dialectically impotent insofar as it relinquishes the power, traditionally thought to be the preserve of the philosopher, of offering non-question-begging reasons for the superiority of one perspective over another. Consider, for example, the hypothesis that relativism is true relative only to the relativist's perspective. If this hypothesis were accepted, what reasons could be offered to the absolutist to adopt the relativist's perspective? Put differently, if we assume that in some perspectives relativism is true while in others it is false, how is a neutral bystander to choose between relativism and absolutism? Indeed, the global relativist must forego the possibility of offering non-question-begging considerations in support of *any* change in perspective. Conversions from one perspective to another are thus rendered arbitrary, and global relativism itself is rendered dialectically impotent.

In response, it might be argued that the global relativist is not impotent to the extent of being unable to advance valid criticisms of competing perspectives. R. Lanier Anderson, for example, has argued that it is open to a Nietzschean perspectivist to launch an 'internal' or 'immanent' critique against some alternative perspective, where this involves offering reasons against the opponent's perspective that have force not only in the perspective within which they were developed, but also within the alternative perspective. For example, the Nietzschean perspectivist may develop a case against the metaphysical realist and the Kantian transcendental idealist by pointing out that the notion of the thing-in-itself (to which notion both the realist and the Kantian are committed) is incoherent. But since all of the perspectives in question accept coherence as a minimum standard for the acceptability of a theory, a non-question-begging case can be made in support of the relative superiority of the Nietzchean perspective (insofar as it eschews things-in-themselves).[71] And, of course, what goes for the perspectivist in this case also goes for the global relativist.

But consider the Nietzschean's claim that 'The notion of the thing-in-itself is incoherent'. The Nietzschean perspectivist is committed to the view that this claim is true within some perspectives and false within other perspectives. Whether the claim in question is true within the realist and Kantian perspectives is a moot point; but even if it were true within these perspectives there will clearly be other perspectives in which it is false. And the question can then be raised once more: How could a perspectivist offer any rational grounds in support of the claim in question to those who reject that claim (and who are correct in rejecting it, given the standards and values licensed by their perspective)? It has seemed to many, therefore, that a perspectivist can only preach to the converted or the near-converted. One may, as does R. Lanier Anderson, simply bite the bullet and accept the 'pluralist' position that, in some cases at least, two competing perspectives may both be true, as opposed to the commonsensical position that only one of them can be true.[72]

But I would suggest that the correct moral to be drawn is that, when evaluating the truth of an entire perspective or worldview, there will rarely (if ever) be neutral or non-question-begging territory from which to make such an assessment. Rather than the Enlightenment ideal of neutral, disinterested reason, all we have instead are images or narratives that help us make sense of the world and our place in it but which we may be unable to justify or substantiate to those who are not favourably disposed to our way of seeing things. This, indeed, is why proofs for the existence of God have been thoroughly unsuccessful in converting non-theists. One can always find fault with such proofs, if one is determined enough. But if one's 'heart' or will is 'correctly' predisposed (theologians will talk here of divine grace), then the force of the evidence might manifest itself – in that case one might find a good reason to convert to theism, but not a non-question-begging reason (since one was already looking upon the evidence in a 'prejudiced' manner). This is no objection, however, since there are no neutral, non-question-begging reasons to be had. Put otherwise, there is no view from everywhere – a God's-eye point of view – for that would be a view from nowhere and hence no view at all.

3.2.2 Non-realism

Apart from the doctrine of perspectivism, analytic philosophers of religion are also generally loathe to accept a non-realist account of religious language, according to which the language of religious believers must not be assimilated to the kind of fact-stating, physical-object discourse prominent in the natural sciences. (Thus 'non-real' is not meant to imply 'not real', but a reality of a radically different sort to that examined by the sciences.)[73] It is this account of religious language that is chiefly responsible for the division, as outlined in Section 2 above, between the God of the philosophers and the God of Abraham, Isaac and Jacob. For the central thesis in the latter conception of God is the claim that *God-talk is not fact-stating*. The other components in this conception – God is wholly other, God is not an existent or a being, belief in God is not a scientific belief, and God is a concrete, not an abstract, reality – either immediately follow from the claim that God-talk is not fact-stating or are naturally associated with this claim.

When discussing the non-factual account of religious discourse in Section 2, I pointed out that, although this account is common to both Wittgensteinian and Continental philosophers of religion, those in the Continental tradition usually attempt to support it by means of the doctrine of perspectivism. As I have already dealt with perspectivism, it might be instructive to see how Wittgensteinians go about defending their understanding of religious language. Given that the most prominent member of the Wittgensteinian school of philosophy of religion is undoubtedly D. Z. Phillips, in what follows I will restrict my comments to his perspective on religious language, and then to only one aspect of his perspective, viz., some of the reasons he has put forward for rejecting views of religious language which hold that such language is fact-stating.[74]

Phillips, following the later Wittgenstein, often describes religious beliefs as forming distinctive 'language games'. Occasionally, however, Phillips expresses some misgivings about this characterization.[75] For one thing, a 'game' suggests something frivolous or hobby-like, whereas religious beliefs have momentous significance and value, at least for those who accept such beliefs. More importantly, treating religious belief as a distinct language game has often raised the suspicion that any given religious tradition would then become a self-contained esoteric game having its own criteria of truth, rationality and intelligibility, thus rendering it immune from criticism 'from without'. Religious belief, on this view, becomes a form of fideism – 'Wittgensteinian fideism', to use Kai Nielsen's phrase.[76] In attempting to meet this criticism, Phillips points out that religious language games should not be thought of as being entirely cut off from non-religious language games and other aspects of human life. There are important connections between religious and non-religious forms of life, and these must be recognized if religious belief is not to degenerate into superstition. If, for example, a religious believer talks of death as if it were a sleep of long duration, one may accuse her of not taking death seriously; if, as we saw in Chapter 2, a believer were to attempt to rationalize or explain away the existence of suffering, one may accuse her of not taking suffering seriously – and these criticisms are drawn from what we already know and believe about such matters.[77] But despite these connections between the religious and non-religious domains, Phillips emphasizes that the distinctiveness of religious belief must not be overlooked. In particular, the language of religious believers must not be assimilated to the kind of fact-stating, physical-object discourse that characterizes the natural sciences.

Phillips's account of religious language can be understood by reference to the kind of view it stands in opposition to. The opposing view – accepted, incidentally, by the majority of contemporary analytical philosophers of religion – holds that religious beliefs purport to express 'facts' that are objective in much the same way that the facts accumulated by scientists are thought to be objective. This realist view can be broken down into a metaphysical thesis and an epistemic thesis:

(a) both God and physical objects exist objectively – i.e., they are and are what they are independently of what, if anything, we may think or say about them, and

(b) we human knowers are capable of acquiring objective knowledge of both God and physical objects, that is, we can come to know them as they are in themselves, without the distorting influence of (say) linguistic practices or conceptual schemes.[78]

Unfortunately, realism with respect to religious belief is often defined exclusively in terms of the above metaphysical component, (a). John Hick, for example, writes:

> Religious realism is the view that the existence or non-existence of God is a fact independent of whether you or I or anyone else believes that God exists. If God exists, God is not simply an idea or ideal in our minds, but an ontological reality, the ultimate creative power of the universe.[79]

But this gives the misleading impression that any non-realist or non-factual account of religious language reduces the reality of God to something like a mere fiction or projection. However, it is far from clear why a non-realist account of religious language, such as the one I am defending here, must be committed to this understanding of God. Non-realism, in other words, is more charitably viewed as a rejection of at least one of the two above theses, but not necessarily both of them. Indeed, the course taken by many religious non-realists involves a rejection of only the epistemic thesis, (b).[80] A non-realist of this sort would agree with the realist that the existence and nature of God, like that of physical objects, is independent of what any human being thinks or believes. Such a non-realist, however, would part ways with his realist colleague only over the epistemic question as to whether the reality of God (like that of physical objects) can be known in an objective way, that is to say, whether the truth or falsity of theism is something that can be discovered by the neutral and impartial assessment of evidence and arguments, as is typically done in natural theology.

The core of religious realism may thus be restricted to an understanding of religious knowledge as objective in nature. Such an epistemology, further, is usually tied to an account of religious language according to which God-talk is fact-stating. Like its non-factual counterpart, this factual account of religious discourse is often embedded in a particular conception of God, in this case that conception being what was earlier dubbed the 'God of the philosophers', a God who is largely comprehensible and definable, who either exists or does not exist, and who can be treated as an object of sorts, an explanatory hypothesis, and an inference from empirical data.

Phillips is adamant that this way of proceeding is entirely mistaken. In one of his early papers, for example, he writes:

> Because the question of divine reality can be construed as 'Is God real or not?' it has often been assumed that the dispute between the believer and the unbeliever is over *a matter of fact*. The philosophical investigation of the reality of God then becomes the philosophical investigation appropriate to

an assertion of a matter of fact. That this is a misrepresentation of the religious concept is made obvious by a brief comparison of talk about facts with talk about God.[81]

Fact-stating language, Phillips goes on to note, has the following characteristics. (1) When claiming something to be a 'fact', we typically presuppose that we are not entirely sure or certain that what we are stating is indeed the case:

> When do we say, 'It is a fact that . . .' or ask, 'Is it a fact that . . .?'? Often, we do so where there is some uncertainty. For example, if the police hear that a wanted criminal has died in some remote part of the world, their reaction might be, 'Check the facts'.[82]

(2) Fact-stating discourse, furthermore, has a contingent character, for it expresses truths that might have turned out to be false: "A fact might not have been: it is conceivable that the wanted criminal had not died."[83] (3) Given the contingent nature of facts, the language of facts is only appropriate when the subject-matter concerns contingent reality, such as physical properties or objects that come into being and pass away. (4) Finally, we have procedures in place for resolving disputes regarding matters of fact, and these procedures usually involve looking to the truth or falsity of other matters of fact. In all these respects, according to Phillips, the language of facts diverges from the language of religion.

In response to (1), Phillips states that believers are not tentative in, or uncertain of, their (religious) beliefs. They would not, for example, think of the reality of God as a conjecture or hypothesis that stands in need of proof or evidence. Phillips is therefore scathing of those, like Swinburne and Mackie, who like to apply the probability calculus to the question of the existence of God. He characterizes such philosophers as "the friends of Cleanthes," referring of course to Hume's character, Cleanthes, who also enquired into God's existence by asking whether God can be probabilistically inferred from the nature or existence of the world. Phillips counsels his readers to "give up bad philosophical friends, among them the friends of Cleanthes," for they distort the nature or underlying 'grammar' of religious belief:

> If religious beliefs are matters of probability, should we not reformulate religious beliefs so that the natural expressions of them become less misleading? Should we not say from now on, 'I believe that it is highly probable that there is an almighty God, maker of heaven and earth?'; 'I believe that it is highly probable that my Redeemer liveth'; 'I believe that it is highly probable

that God forgives sins'? Do these reformulations do justice to the nature of
religious beliefs? Hardly.[84]

The reality of God, rather, functions as a 'bedrock' belief in the religious
language game, a belief which informs an entire way of life without
itself being subject to confirmation, disconfirmation or doubt. Unlike
matters of fact, where we do not regard it wrong or bad to raise doubts,
doubt regarding God's existence is not merely out of place, but *sinful*
(analogously, faith is called a virtue).[85] Holding religious beliefs, then, "has
little in common with any kind of conjecture. It has to do with living by
them, drawing sustenance from them, judging oneself in terms of them,
being afraid of them, etc."[86]

In reply to (2), Phillips contends that, unlike facts, religious beliefs do
not express contingent truths. We might be prepared to say that it might
not rain tomorrow, but "the religious believer is not prepared to say that
God might not exist."[87]

As for (3), Phillips says that, if God is not something that might or might
not exist, then God cannot be thought of as an object, as one more thing,
as a being existing among other beings. Indeed, the life-transforming
impact that the reality of God is often said to have indicates that God
cannot properly be described as an object:

> Coming to see that there is a God is not like coming to see that an additional
> being exists. If it were, there would be an extension of one's knowledge of
> facts, but no extension of one's understanding. Coming to see that there is a
> God involves seeing a new meaning in one's life, and being given a new
> understanding. The Hebrew-Christian conception of God is not a conception
> of a being among beings.[88]

Discovering the existence of an object (say, a further planet in our solar
system) would result in an extension to our current body of knowledge,
but such a discovery – unlike a conversion to religious belief – would not
radically alter the character of one's personal life. Accepting God is quite
unlike accepting the existence of some physical object. Talk of God, then,
cannot to be modelled on talk about physical objects.[89] Phillips's point, as
Scott and Moore explain, is that "one cannot, by qualifying, explaining or
extending the forms of expression one uses with regard to physical objects,
reach an appropriate form of expression for talking about God."[90] It is
misleading, however, not only to speak of God as an 'object', but to even
speak of him as an 'existent', for our notion of existence carries with it
an implication of contingency: ordinarily, one cannot say that something
exists unless it makes sense to suppose that it might not have existed.

Phillips therefore prefers to say, along with Kierkegaard, that "God does not exist, He is eternal."[91] Since God does not belong to the order of contingent reality, our language about God should not be assimilated to our way of speaking about common (or contingent) objects, beings, or existents. The word 'God', Phillips states, "is not the name of an individual; it does not refer to anything."[92]

Finally, in response to (4), Phillips notes that disagreements between believers and unbelievers cannot be settled in the way in which we resolve factual disputes. Disagreements over facts usually take place against a background of shared beliefs, so that there is little or no disagreement as to (e.g.) what counts as a fact and what kind of evidence or investigation is relevant to settling a particular dispute over a matter of fact. If, for example, someone claims that there is a certain species of bacteria on the table when in fact there are none there, we can at least agree as to what kind of evidence or investigation would settle the issue. Disputes among believers and unbelievers, however, lack any such background of shared beliefs. As a result, there is no commonly accepted decision-procedure for adjudicating cases where, for example, one claims to perceive (or experience) God and another claims that the perception is illusory. As Phillips states,

> When the positivist claims that there is no God because God cannot be located, the believer does not object on the grounds that the investigation has not been thorough enough, but on the grounds that the investigation fails to understand the grammar of what is being investigated – namely, the reality of God.[93]

Putting together the above four points of divergence between factual discourse and religious discourse, Phillips concludes that religious beliefs are not statements of fact, but confessions of faith.[94]

Let's turn now to some of the reasons why philosophers, especially those in the analytic tradition, have thought that Phillips's position falls far short of a philosophically satisfying account of the nature of religious language.

Consider, to begin with, Phillips's claim that religious beliefs, unlike factual statements, are not tentative or conjectural in nature and do not require confirmation by way of proof or evidence. It is difficult to determine whether Phillips is here advancing a descriptive claim – this is just how religious beliefs are normally held – or a normative claim – this is how religious beliefs should be held – or both.[95] In any case, however, there lies trouble. For instance, it might be argued that Phillips's claim, when descriptively construed, stands refuted, or at least challenged, by the fact that there has always been a significant group of believers who have sought to construct a rational case in support of their religious beliefs. And normatively interpreted, Phillips's claim is countered by those who argue that, given the many challenges faced by religious belief (at the hands of Darwin, Marx, Freud, biblical scholars and various others), we *ought not* accept the existence of God without at least attempting to meet some of the objections levelled against theism, and perhaps also attempting to find some evidence in support of theism.[96]

In relation to the descriptive issue, it should at least be acknowledged that theistic religious traditions are complex phenomena allowing for a plurality of positions on such matters as the value and function of natural theology. There are strands within Christianity, for example, that have been favourable to the project of offering arguments in support of religious belief without recourse to divinely revealed truths (e.g., the apologists of the early Christian centuries and elements within scholastic theology in the Middle Ages). But at the same time one will also find within Christianity opposing streams of thought that are more sympathetic to Phillips's account of religious belief – the apophatic and mystical traditions are cases in point.[97] There is, furthermore, a tendency to read back into the 'proofs' of theologians such as Anselm and Aquinas the modern-day concern with substantiating the belief that God exists in an impartial and objective manner. It has been argued, however, that such readings are anachronistic insofar as they fail to take into account the confessional setting of medieval theology, where the goal is 'faith seeking understand-ing', this being the attempt to understand what is *already* believed as opposed to understanding *in order to* believe.[98] In short, Christianity, like any of the major world religions, is not a homogeneous entity, but displays an enormous variety of views about the nature and meaning of religious language. Any simple descriptive claim, such as 'religious believers do (or do not) base their beliefs on evidence', will therefore be misleading at best and patently false at worst.[99]

Turning from the descriptive to the normative, the evidentialist claim that we ought not accept religious belief without first possessing evidence in support of such belief is controversial even within analytic philosophy of religion. Reformed epistemologists as well as those influenced by James' 'will to believe' doctrine have argued that in certain circumstances it can be perfectly rational to accept belief in God without having (propositional or inferential) evidence. The worry, however, may be that if religious belief is not held in a tentative or conjectural way, as it would be if it were based upon evidence of some sort, then an important critical dimension would be lost: religious believers would be disinclined to subject their fundamental commitments to critical scrutiny and would adopt instead a dogmatic and intolerant attitude. Religious believers are, of course, regularly prone to fundamentalism: "these unhinged and impassioned lovers of the impossible," as Caputo says, "are also impossible people who confuse themselves with God and threaten the civil liberties and sometimes even the lives of anyone who disagrees with them, which they take to be equivalent to disagreeing with God."[100] But, clearly, the rejection of evidentialism need not lead to a fundamentalist outlook. For one thing, as Reformed epistemologists have emphasized, a theist for whom belief in God is basic (i.e., not held on the basis of evidence) may wish to strengthen his confidence in the truth of theism by seeking evidence in support of theism (a belief can thus have both inferential and non-inferential sources of justification or warrant). Also, beliefs held in the basic way are not immune from defeaters, and so the task of answering the objections of non-theists remains. In any case, the best antidote to fundamentalism may not be evidentialism, but perspectivism. Specifically, the recognition that our beliefs, including our religious beliefs, are thoroughly contextual and conditioned, affording us no privileged access to truth and reality, would be sufficient to instill the requisite degree of humility in our beliefs and practices.[101]

A further objection that could be raised against Phillips's non-realism concerns his claim that, whereas factual discourse is intended to refer to objects in the world, discourse about God is not intended to refer to any object or thing at all. As mentioned earlier, Phillips attempts to support this view by arguing that, if God could be thought of as an object, then 'discovering God' – as happens in religious conversions – would have the same effect as discovering some fact or the existence of some physical object; that is to say, there would merely be an extension to one's body of knowledge without any corresponding deepening in one's understanding of the value and meaning of life. It might be objected, however, that the discovery of a fact or an object can, and often does, radically alter one's worldview or way of life. Consider, for example, how any of the following could lead one to see life in an entirely different light: discovering one million dollars in your garden; discovering that your partner has died in a car accident; discovering that your partner has cheated on you; discovering that you have only ten years to live; discovering that you have been adopted, and so on. It appears, then, that the discovery of a fact can be an extension to one's knowledge *and* a life-changing experience.

But in the foregoing cases, involving the discovery of a large sum of money and so on, is it the increase in one's knowledge of facts that brings about the transformation in one's life? Or is this transformative effect the product, rather, of some new level of understanding or awareness that one has reached? It is difficult to see how factual knowledge, all by itself, can have any significant existential consequences. If I come to learn that I have an inoperable condition that will drastically shorten my life expectancy, then what effect (if any) this would have on how I lead my remaining years will depend on how this knowledge is assimilated with everything else I believe, desire and practise. I may fall to my knees and pray for a miracle. I may throw myself headlong into the pleasures of the flesh. Or I may continue pretty much as before. My newly acquired knowledge need not launch my life in any particular direction. The same holds with the countless mundane facts we stumble upon daily (e.g., it is raining in Chicago today, the library will be closed tomorrow): knowledge of such facts leaves open a range of responses. Knowledge of God, by contrast, is *always* life-transforming (or 'saving', to put it theologically), since it involves an awareness of God as the One who makes a total difference to our lives.

What, then, can we conclude about the current metaphilosophical division in the philosophy of religion? Given the interplay between metaphilosophical theory and philosophical practice, the prospects of unifying philosophy of religion, and philosophy generally, at the metaphilosophical level seem dim. No doubt, greater interaction between the analytic and Continental schools is to be encouraged, and this ought to be conducted in a spirit of charity and goodwill, so as to overcome the incomprehension and disparagement that has typified encounters between the two groups in the past. Each group has much to learn from the other, and it is difficult to disagree with Simon Critchley's view that, "There is something ultimately parochial and intellectually cowardly about identifying oneself with either side of a perceived philosophical divide, because it prevents the possible intellectual challenges that would be the consequence of a dialogue outside of one's professional entrenchments."[102] In this spirit, an increasing number of philosophers are now crossing and challenging the traditional boundaries, competently moving back and forth between the analytic and Continental traditions, and highlighting often unexpected connections and affinities between the two traditions.[103] As a result, many calls for *rapprochment* are being heard and proposals are being drawn for overcoming the analytic-Continental divide by synthesizing the best parts of each tradition and thus restoring the unity in philosophical practice that marked our pre-Kantian past.[104] Such a reunion, I suspect, would turn out be a false unity, as it can be achieved only at the cost of obliterating important philosophical differences that are integral to the metaphilosophical division. To unify, for example, the divergent approaches of analytic and Continental philosophy of religion would require, at a minimum, some way of harmonizing realist and non-realist conceptions of God and, more fundamentally, some way of bridging the scientific and 'prophetic' models of philosophical theology outlined earlier. Whether this can, or even should, be done is doubtful. But if we no longer wish to maintain the analytic-Continental divide, and we do not think it feasible to bridge it, then the only remaining option may be to overcome it by overcoming (traditional) philosophy itself – to kick the habit of philosophizing in the usual way, as Rorty encourages us to do, and thus move towards an inter-disciplinary, or even non-disciplinary or non-academic, way of philosophizing. This, it seems to me, would be a move in the right direction, and one which I take up in greater detail in the remaining chapters.

CHAPTER 5

KAZANTZAKIS' POOR MAN OF GOD: PHILOSOPHY WITHOUT PHILOSOPHY

Edmond Jabès opens his little book, *Desire for a Beginning, Dread of One Single End*, in characteristic style:

> "... a book – he said – that I'll never write because nobody can, it being a book:
> – against the book.
> – against thought.
> – against truth and against the word.
> – a book, then, that crumbles even while it forms.
> – against the book because it is incapable of thinking its totality, let alone nothing.
> – against truth because truth is God, and God escapes thought; against truth, then, which for us remains legendary, an unknown quantity.
> – against the word, finally, because the word says only what little it can, and this little is nothing and only nothing could express it."[1]

To write a systematic and coherently argued book against analytic philosophy while doing so using the very apparatus of such a philosophy (e.g., its vocabulary, style and methods) is clearly a performative contradiction. It might be suspected, and possibly with some justification, that the case I have developed and the way in which I have developed it in the foregoing chapters places me precisely in this invidious position. But that is not entirely correct. What preceded is more favourably viewed as analytic philosophy taken to its Wittgensteinian limits, where the ladder is thrown away after it has been used to scale the 'nonsense' of philosophy. It is time, therefore, to take a glimpse at what 'philosophy without philosophy' (to borrow Blanchot's turn of phrase) might look like, what form a 'weak philosophy' (to borrow from Vattimo) – one that chooses to go without the metaphysical support of objective, supra-perspectival truth and without the institutional backing of the academic establishment – could assume in practice. A philosophy of this sort is one which, in the manner of Jabès, produces books 'against the book', 'against the word' and 'against truth', and thus looks towards literary and artistic exemplars for its inspiration.

The exemplar I put forward here is Nikos Kazantzakis' novel, *The Poor Man of God* (first published in Greek in 1956).[2]

* * *

I hesitate to write, to add a single word or an iota more, as if anything needed to be added to this wonderful myth, "this legend, which is truer than truth itself" (3).

Kazantzakis frames his story with a short Prologue, and so will I.

Every so often we come across something or someone – a Gospel, a poem, a novel, a film, an extraordinary saint or an extraordinary sinner – that completely changes the course of our life. Some sixteen years ago, as a naïve first-year undergraduate student at university studying the great texts of philosophy and religion, I felt deeply unimpressed and alienated by the secular and materialistic culture of the academy, manifesting itself in an almost exclusive reliance on scientific modes of thinking with little appreciation for the dimensions of spirituality and faith. At least that's the way things struck me then. And so I returned to Kazantzakis, for I had already begun reading many of his writings in my last year of secondary school and, especially, over the summer break before the opening of the first university semester. But what I returned to was Kazantzakis' *The Poor Man of God*. I would skip lectures and tutorials, forget to have lunch and tea, miss my bus rides home, because I was totally enthralled and engrossed in this novel.

Sitting under the shade of a tree on a bright autumn day, surrounded by yellow and brown leaves and the wide green expanse of the campus lawns, almost on my own while everyone else was busily taking notes in the class-rooms and lecture theatres or playing cards and chasing boyfriends or girl-friends, I would be pouring over the pages of Kazantzakis' record of the life and times of this fool for Christ, Francis of Assisi. I must have appeared strange, if not mad, to my classmates, to my family and relatives, for the more I would feed upon and assimilate Francis' words, the more my soul would be nourished and grow aflame. I was gradually coming to life, and I knew things would never be the same again.

As I would read, I would imagine Kazantzakis in his Villa Manolita in Antibes, bent over his desk writing with a Giotto reproduction of Francis behind him.[3] This was to be the last novel he completed, assuming that the semi-autobiographical *Report to Greco* – his last major work, finished the year before his death – does not count as a novel. The seventy-year-old author of *The Poor Man of God* was by then a widely travelled as well as a widely acclaimed writer, with a store of novels, travelogues, essays and plays behind him that had already begun to attract an international following. He had also begun to attract the ire of the religious authorities. In the same year he wrote *The Poor Man of God* (1953), the Orthodox Church in Greece sought to prosecute him for sacrilege owing to the content of *Freedom or Death* and *The Last Temptation*, while the following year the Vatican placed *The Last Temptation* on the Index of Forbidden Books. Ironically, in the midst of such ecclesiastical opposition, Kazantzakis would reignite his love for Francis, one of the most venerated saints of the church.[4] With his wife, Eleni, he would spend the summer of 1952 in Italy, retracing the steps of his beloved *Poverello* in Assisi, where the couple "wandered in shady lanes singing the *Fioretti*."[5] On his return home to Antibes, Kazantzakis would write in a letter to Börje Knös:

> In Assisi I lived once more with the great martyr and hero whom I love so much, Saint Francis. And now I'm gripped by a desire to write a book about him. Will I write it? I don't know yet. I'm waiting for a sign, and then I'll begin. Always, as you know, the struggle within me between man and God, between substance and spirit, is the stable leitmotif of my life and work.[6]

The sign, as happened often in Francis' life, appears to have come by way of illness and suffering. Kazantzakis was soon beset by various physical ailments requiring hospitalization, including a severe eye infection, perhaps like the one that afflicted Francis (323). Although he had already begun writing the novel on Francis in late 1952 from Antibes, he left the manuscript half-finished in order to undergo medical tests in Holland for a prior condition. In the months that followed, however, Kazantzakis experienced a harrowing series of medical problems, particularly with his right eye (which he was eventually to lose altogether). It was during this time that the novel on Francis took an entirely new shape:

> Now, in the course of my illness, this work has been growing steadily richer inside me. I took notes, wrote Franciscan songs, created scenes, and the work kept constantly expanding with the great wealth [of new material]. I shall rewrite it from the beginning with new impetus . . . As much as I could, I've tried to take advantage of the illness to rewrite it inside of me; and so I hope that I transformed the illness into spirit. (Letter to Börje Knös, written from Paris on 12 June 1953.)[7]

But it was not *in spite of* his illness that Kazantzakis created this powerful work, but *because* of it. As he himself pointed out some years later to his long-time friend, Pandelis Prevelakis, who was bedridden at the time: "This immobility may prove fruitful. Whatever is best in *The Poor Man of God*, I dictated to Eleni at the time of the fever."[8]

> Creativity does not come from well-planned and efficiently run think-tanks, seminar workshops, conferences or projects headed by professional, highly-trained academics and business leaders. Creativity comes, like an unmerited gift of divine grace, to the 'loser' relentlessly working away at some obscure problem, hidden from view and derided by all.
>
> It is only the creative genius who has 'poetic license', and this because such a person has suffered more than any other for what they have accomplished.
>
> Critics have not failed to notice connections between Albert Camus' apparently dispiriting thoughts about 'the absurd' and his recurrent physical illnesses. But attempts to 'psychologize away' Camus' philosophy of the absurd are misguided, for what they overlook is the fact that it is primarily through pain and suffering that the truth of the world is revealed – something known to artists of all times.
>
> The best philosophy is always borne out of great suffering, not comfortable and relaxed armchair theorising. Wittgenstein recognized this well, and also embodied this principle in his own life and thought, as Norman Malcolm has highlighted:
>
> "As he [Wittgenstein] struggled to work through a problem one frequently felt that one was in the presence of real suffering. Wittgenstein liked to draw an analogy between philosophical thinking and swimming: just as one's body has a natural tendency towards the surface and one has to make an *exertion* to get to the *bottom* – so it is with thinking. In talking about human greatness, he once remarked that he thought that the measure of a man's greatness would be in terms of what his work *cost* him. There is no doubt that Wittgenstein's philosophical labours cost him a great deal."[9]

I look into those black, beady and piercing eyes of Kazantzakis that are painfully strained over his manuscript, and notice large tears blurring his sight and smudging the ink on the pages. Just as Brother Leo, when recounting the life of Francis, would be guided by the tender hand of his spiritual father, so Kazantzakis tells us that "everywhere about me, as I wrote, I sensed the saint's invisible presence" (3). And we, too, when reading this work, feel that whispering to us in one ear is Brother Leo, whispering in another is Kazantzakis, while right before our very eyes stands a pale and emaciated figure, with bare, bloodstained feet, wearing a dirty coat that has been patched and repatched a thousand times, and who is joyfully dancing and singing in a rapturous voice: Francis, God's sweet little pauper.

I have never met another person such as him, no matter how hard I have looked since I first laid eyes on him.
Tears would also roll down my cheeks as his great humility and gentle kindness would transform whatever they touched, both friends and (especially) enemies, the poor as well as the rich, the wicked as well as the righteous, both humans and animals, from the most fearsome snake to the least significant ant.

The truth is, though, that the truth about Francis, the truth that is Francis cannot be described and explained in a way that adequately captures his 'essence', that which makes him utterly unique. "Francis runs in my mind like water," admits Brother Leo. "He changes faces; I am unable to pin him down . . . How can I ever know what he was like, who he was? Is it possible that he himself did not know?" (25, 30).

Truth is like that. And the ultimate truth, Truth Itself, that is, God, always evades neat and accurate formulations, much to the consternation of philosophers and theologians.

Indeed, I have never heard a philosopher or theologian describe God as precisely and clearly as Francis:

> "Brother Francis, how does God reveal himself to you when you are alone in the darkness?"
> "Like a glass of cool water, Brother Leo . . . I'm thirsty, I drink it, and my thirst is quenched for all eternity." (26)

Other times, Francis would say:

> "God is a conflagration, Brother Leo. He burns, and we burn with him." (27)

And Francis would indeed catch fire: "Put yourself out, Brother Francis," poor Leo would cry, "put yourself out before you burn up the world!" (26)

> These metaphors and images are immediately understood by the heart, but are reluctantly admitted, if they are at all, into the intellect.

Hence Francis' advice: "The heart is closer to God than the mind is, so abandon the mind and follow your heart: it and it alone knows the way to paradise," (209, cf. 356) advice not easily accepted by the more learned brothers of Francis' group, such as Ruffino and Elias.

> Pascal, *Pensées*:
> "Le coeur à ses raisons que la raison ne connaît point."

> All of his works, Anselm Kiefer explains, "are but aspects or traces of a theme that in human concepts, in language, is not representable. All of painting, but also literature and everything that is connected to it, is always but a circling around something unsayable, around a black hole or a crater, whose centre one cannot penetrate. And whatever one takes up for themes has only the character of pebbles at the foot of the crater – they are path markers in a circle that one hopes gradually closes in around the centre."[10]

The mind, with its sophisticated proofs and refutations, wishes to augment its authority, to "spread itself out and conquer the world not only by means of heaven but also by force" (300), whereas the simple, illiterate heart has no such ambitions, but desires only love and peace.

'But isn't this taking things too far?' protests the scholar. The same question could be asked about virtually anything Francis does. The path of learning, however, is not necessarily rejected outright, but nor is it advocated as a path that is as valid as any other.

> *Man's knowledge is nothing but ashes.* (361)

> Francis, therefore, angrily seizes a book he sees a young novice poring over and throws it into the flames, telling the novice that the only Easter day on which his (Francis') congregation did not see the Resurrection was when a visiting theologian from the University of Bologna came to deliver the sermon. (357)

>> The learned Germans, Kazantzakis wrote in one of his travelogues, if presented with the choice between two doors, on the one written 'Paradise' and on the other

written 'Lecture about Paradise', would unhesitatingly
rush to the latter.[11]

Francis: "Instead of being crucified, I simply think about
crucifixion" (211).

The same novice is given permission (by Brother Giles) to
preach a sermon, but on one condition: "You must mount the
pulpit and start crying Baa! Baa! like a sheep. Nothing else –
just Baa! Baa!" (358)

Had he followed this advice, Francis no doubt would have
said to him what he had said some time earlier to Brother
Leo, after the latter had risen to speak during a meeting of
the brethren. Some of the brothers had already spoken elo-
quently against the Rule that Francis had drawn up, but
when Brother Leo rose to speak he could only stammer a
few words, became completely confused and then burst
into tears:

"No one else spoke with such skill, such strength," Francis
said. "Brother Leo, you have my blessing." (305)

> . . . and it won't do harm if your words are
> broken with weeping – tears on occasion
> carry the weight of speech.
> – Ovid, *Epistulae ex Ponto* 3.1.158

The loquaciousness of the scholastic brethren compared to the
silent, wordless communication between Francis, Bernard and
Pietro (404): the difference between the God of the philosophers
and scholars and the God of Abraham, Isaac and Jacob.

When Francis breaks the silence, he does not reach for lengthy
tomes and tractates, but for the lute: song and dance.

Music: the greatest and most mysterious force in this world;
no other form of expression or communication even comes
close in potency and poignancy.

Music as the most important source of religious experience.

It has often been said that music provides the most cogent
proof of the existence of God. But nothing could be further
from the truth *in the case of much music*. No greater truth,
however, could be told of music at its best.

God is a fire that burns but also purifies. Like the scorched landscapes in Anselm Kiefer's paintings, the destruction is never entirely negative, but always holds out the promise of renewal and re-creation.[12]

The God of Kazantzakis – a philosopher's God? In light of the recent proliferation of attempts to interpret Kazantzakis' fiction through the lens of Whiteheadian process theism (led by Daniel Dombrowski and Darren Middleton[13]), it should be recalled that Kazantzakis was consistently opposed to the kind of 'logocentric' language found in much process theology. The writings of leading process philosophers and theologians, including A. N. Whitehead, Charles Hartshorne and David Ray Griffin, read like most other works in speculative metaphysics: the language is abstract and propositional, there is an emphasis on precise definitions and distinctions as well as on dense and rigorous argumentation, and in short the aim is the systematic elaboration in as literal a way as possible of a worldview in consonance with the latest findings of science. But all this is foreign to Kazantzakis: his works (particularly his novels and plays) are passionate narratives infused with poetry and paradox, analogies and parables, dreams and symbols, thus yielding multiple and sometimes contradictory meanings. Even his most overtly philosophical work, *Salvatores Dei*, resembles a lyrical poem more than a metaphysical tractate. It is not so much that Kazantzakis chose to express himself in this way, but that he felt compelled to do so: the deepest reaches of reality, and the reality of God above all, could not be expressed otherwise without distortion. There is a danger, therefore, in speaking of "Kazantzakis' narrative fiction as a mythopoesis of process thought," as Middleton does.[14] For this gives the impression that the literary fiction of Kazantzakis can be 'translated', 'formalized' and indeed 'purified' without remainder into the system of process philosophy. Middleton is too astute a reader of Kazantzakis to succumb to this fallacy: "process theology," he notes, "may not with impunity be spoken of as the kernel trapped inside the husk of Kazantzakis's fiction."[15] Others, however, have not been as careful, and it is unfortunately not uncommon to find philosophers using works of literature as nothing more than sources for abstract principles or doctrines. But this is reductionism of a very crude kind, attempting to still the dance and song of a Zorba or a Francis into something mechanical and monotonous.

There is, in addition, that famous letter Kazantzakis wrote in January 1908, soon after arriving in Paris to pursue postgraduate studies:

> At present I am studying philosophy and literature at the Sorbonne, the Collège de France, and the Ecole des Hautes Etudes.
> I want to formulate an individual, personal conception of life, a theory of the world and of human destiny, and then, in accord with this, systematically and with a specific purpose and program, to write – whatever I write.[16]

As is well known, Kazantzakis found just such a "theory of the world and of human destiny" in Bergson's account of evolution as the product of a dynamic impulse, the *élan vital*. However, as Bien points out, Kazantzakis' attraction to scientific rationalism did not last long: "His [Kazantzakis'] mystical temperament, his aestheticism, and his intellectual quarrel with science [as expressed in his 1909 essay, 'Has Science Gone Bankrupt?'] all kept impelling him increasingly toward intuitional rather than scientific language, faith rather than proof."[17] And so, although Kazantzakis initially (i.e., up till 1913) sought to buttress Bergson's speculations with empirical evidence, he quickly came to think of Bergsonian vitalism in more mystical fashion whose 'truth' is not amenable to scientific confirmation and disconfirmation. Indeed, it was the anti-intellectualist tendencies in Bergson's own philosophy that influenced Kazantzakis to elevate art above both science and philosophy, to think of art (as he put it in an interview in 1935) as "the only 'human method' that can . . . suddenly reveal life's mystery to human eyes."[18] The mature Kazantzakis, then, would have repudiated the kind of 'rational' philosophical system developed by process theists, and to 'translate' Kazantzakis' fiction into such a system is to attempt to do what that very fiction claims cannot be done.

A disparity therefore exists between literature and theology (or at least the sort of theology that seeks to systematize, explicate and precisify the language of faith), as Middleton highlights when comparing the theologies of process thinkers with the fictional works of Kazantzakis. The discourses of literature and theology represent, in Middleton's view, "competing" and "conflicting" voices, "they appear to trespass upon one another's ground."[19] But these two ways of thinking and writing, adds Middleton, can be brought together into a mutually enriching, albeit uneasy, alliance. Like Apollo and Dionysius in Nietzsche's *The Birth of Tragedy*, literature and theology may represent "the dynamic collusion of two complementary yet antagonistic forces or activities, with each being responsible for creating, destroying, and re-creating the other."[20] In this dialectical relationship, each discipline needs and feeds off the other. For one thing, literature cannot do without theology, for "without 'theology's' disciplined ordering of experience, fiction has no guard against the dangers of practicing a ludic randomness by which it is impossible for us to live."[21] There is much to be said for this view. The quest for discipline, however, has a habit of arresting the play of our structures of signification and succumbing to our craving for the kind of stability and security that can only be supplied by a transcendental signified. This is not necessarily an objection, at least if a creative imagination requires the very tension produced by placing the desire for coherence, order and rational systematization in opposition with the desire to trespass these constraints.

The visible as the surest sign of the invisible. "The only way we can divine the appearance of God's face," says Francis, "is by looking at beautiful things" (60). God condescends to our material limitations, appearing to us in the form of a beautiful night sky, a glass of refreshing water, or a consuming fire.

But do we have any material limitations? We are given to believe that nothing is more real than the matter we are enclosed within: the stars, mountains and rivers, our bones, hair and skin. We are imprisoned in this world of matter, and there may well be no escape. We are given over to doubt as to whether there truly is any such thing as 'the spirit' or 'the soul', these being remnants of medieval metaphysics and psychology that have been overturned by the investigations of science. But what if, at least for a moment, we were to consider something utterly heretical: nothing material exists, everything is spirit!

> Francis whispers to us, as he did to his constant companion, Brother Leo: "The canary is like man's soul. It sees bars round it, but instead of despairing, it sings. It sings, and wait and see: one day its song shall break the bars." (69)

It is as flame that God appears to Francis's mother, Lady Pica, a flame that once burned within, making her feel like bursting into tears, dancing in the middle of the yard and rushing into the street, taking to the road and never returning to her parents' house (62–63).

When Francis would pray, a great flame would lick his face. (184)

Abba Joseph said to Abba Lot: "You cannot be a monk unless you become like a consuming fire."[22]

Anselm Kiefer, the alchemist, knows this well. He shows how creation and destruction are one and the same in bringing forth powerful symbols and imagery by cracking, breaking apart and scorching the canvas and other materials; seeking and liberating the spirit within matter by applying the fire of purification.

Aperiatur terra[23]
"Let the earth be opened
and bud forth a saviour and let justice spring up at the same time." (Isaiah 45:8)

> Destruction and re-creation
> violent upheaval and spiritual renewal
> Fire
> apocalyptic and redemptive

> haunted by memories of the past . . . the tragic in history . . . time, history, and memory . . . celestial metaphysics . . . mythic journeys . . . charred landscapes . . . struck with wonder at the horrors we are capable of inflicting upon each other . . . heavy, daunting, uncomfortable, grandiose, melancholic, deeply disturbing . . .

Like the alchemists of old, Kiefer searches for the philosopher's stone which transmutes the basest metals into gold and gold into spirit. Kiefer attempts to achieve this transmutation through the use of lead, one of his favourite materials: "I feel closest to lead because it is like us. It is in flux. It's changeable and has potential to achieve a higher state of gold."[24] Lead, he adds elsewhere, "has a life of its own. It's a quite spiritual material. Indeed, I would go as far as to say that lead has a spirit. Whatever material I work with, I feel I'm extracting the spirit that already lives within it."[25]

The living God, the eternal flame that scorches the earth and lights people's souls on fire. Francis' painful 'nights of fire' – shivering with a raging temperature and wrestling at night with all manner of demons and saints – were to deliver him from his prodigal past and set him on an extraordinary new path. This fiery experience would be consummated with the words that Francis asked his mother to write on the back of a painting of the Crucified:

> On Sunday,
> the twenty-fourth day of September
> in the year 1206 after the birth of our Lord,
> my son Francis was reborn. (75)

I am reminded of another great soul, Blaise Pascal, a remarkably gifted man who lived only to the age of 39 but made many important contributions to mathematics and the physical sciences. Like Francis, Pascal was both deeply human, often succumbing to frivolous and worldly pursuits, and deeply religious: always struggling to reform his ways, suffering terribly from physical ailments (and from persecution by civil and religious authorities) but convinced that suffering is the natural state of the Christian. Most memorable, however, was his 'night of fire'. After narrowly escaping death from a horse-carriage accident on 23 November 1654, Pascal underwent an intense religious experience ("light flooded his room", according to some accounts). He would not breathe a word of what happened to anyone, but instead recorded the experience on a piece of parchment and had the note sown into the lining of his coat, thus keeping it close to his heart wherever he went. The note began with the following words:

> The year of grace 1654.
> Monday, 23 November, feast of St. Clement,
> pope and martyr and others in the martyrology.
> The eve of Saint Chrysogonus martyr and others.
> From about half-past ten in the evening
>   until about half-past midnight.
>   FIRE
> The God of Abraham, the God of Isaac, the God of Jacob.
> Not of the philosophers and scholars.
> Certitude, certitude, feeling, joy, peace.

From then on Pascal renounced mathematics and science, devoting himself passionately to religious contemplation and writing. He would on occasion slide back into the study of mathematics, but whatever he wrote during this time he chose to write anonymously, employing pseudonyms so as to avoid the reprehensible desire for reputation that marked the life of the scientist even in his own day.

Francis' burns, the effects of his intimate contact with God, were nevertheless painful and the cause of much suffering. Francis' body would become one open wound as a result of his ascetic struggles. Brother Leo, himself no

stranger to the harsh realities of a beggar's life, was astounded by the
lengths Francis would go to. In reference to Francis' feet, for example,
Brother Leo states: "Never in my life had I seen feet so distressed – so
melancholy, feeble, gnawed away by journeys, so full of open wounds – as
his. Sometimes when Father Francis lay sleeping I used to bend down
stealthily and kiss them, and I felt as though I were kissing the total
suffering of mankind" (27).

> *The Two Ways.* One is to suffer; the other is to become a
> professor of the fact that another suffered.
> – Søren Kierkegaard, journal entry for 1854.[26]

Francis not only patiently endures suffering, but also *seeks it out*: he incites
people to attack him by telling them that the more stones they throw at
him, the more blessed by God they will be (110); tormented by demonic
thoughts, he beats his flesh mercilessly all night long with a knotted
cord while sprawled out on top of bitterly cold snow (340); and he implores
Christ: "Let me feel thy sufferings and holy passion in my body and soul;
let me feel them as intensely as is possible for a sinful mortal" (496). But
he is not driven by vanity or arrogance to attain new heights (as the bishop
and others claimed: 118, 242), nor is he driven by an inhuman masochistic
temperament, as some contemporary critics have thought.[27] Rather,
Francis is motivated by the conviction that only through suffering can
redemption be found. For Brother Leo and the common man, pain is
nothing more than a physical sensation to be avoided: "I was a man," Leo
reflects, "a reasonable man, and a wretched one. I felt hunger; and
the stones, for me, were stones", while "the stones that people threw at
[Francis] were like a sprinkling of lemon flowers" (155). For Francis, in
other words, pain and suffering are a providential sign that one is on the
road towards fulfilling the supreme obligation to "transubstantiate the
matter that God entrusted to us, and turn it into spirit" (4). Tom Doulis, in
an article on "Kazanztakis and the Meaning of Suffering", put it well:

> Whereas for the ancient tragedians suffering meant wisdom, and for
> Dostoyevsky it meant pity and love, for Kazantzakis suffering means
> certitude in being chosen for salvation by the love of a compassionate
> and interested Creator. It exhibits to man the strength and resiliency of
> his nature by showing him how little he needs comfort and security.[28]

However, this is not to engage in theodical 'justifications' of suffering, a
project I argued against in Chapter 2. Rather, it is to point to a practical
response that can be made to the vicissitudes of life, one in which it is the
sufferer himself who confers meaning onto his suffering, snatching victory

from the jaws of defeat, as it were (as opposed to attempting to decipher the 'objective' value or meaning of his suffering).

> Ascent. To climb a series of steps. From the full stomach to hunger, from the slaked throat to thirst, from joy to suffering. God sits at the summit of hunger, thirst, and suffering; the devil sits at the summit of the comfortable life. Choose.[29]

However, pain, in Francis' view, also affords an opportunity to identify with the sufferings of Christ and of every human being: he takes their sufferings upon himself, not to lighten their load (or not merely for this reason), but as an expression of a profound sense of solidarity and responsibility. Francis recognizes, as did Father Zosima (in Dostoevsky's *The Brothers Karamazov*, part 2, bk 6) that, "In truth we are each responsible to all for all, only people don't realize it, but if they did, we should all instantly be in paradise!" This is why, when Francis' brotherhood fell into disarray, Francis could sincerely say, "It is my fault. I am the one who sinned, who craved women, food, a soft bed, and who filled his mouth with the goat's flesh" (278). And when Brother Leo confesses his sins to Francis, Francis punishes *himself* (484). That is also why, according to Francis, paradise cannot exist as long as hell exists, for "how can anyone be completely happy when he looks out from heaven and sees his brothers and sisters being punished in hell?" Therefore, if one is saved all are saved, and if one is lost all are lost (390).

Francis' logic is impeccable.
Solidarity in suffering, solidarity in sin.

> God is the great companion – the fellow-sufferer who understands.
> – A. N. Whitehead, *Process and Reality*[30]

And then
that great little sparrow from Assisi arrived
playing his lute merrily
and seeing me
immediately shrunk to the ground with a sigh.
He did not tell me
what to do and what not to do
where to go and where not to go
how to do this and how to do that
– he just sighed and sat next to me.

Identification with
the defeated
the forgotten
the excluded
and reverence for all life
was also the legacy of Albert Schweitzer
– "the Saint Francis of our era" (in Kazanztakis' dedication).

Contrary to the common perception of Kazantzakis as an otherwise progressive thinker who was unfortunately unable to come to terms with the modern egalitarian ideal of women as having equal value and status to men, Kazantzakis has Francis furthering the aspirations of his mother, not father (172); he has Francis overcoming his initial reservations in welcoming Clara into the life of poverty, and then helping her find a hermitage (353–54, 359); and, most of all, he has Francis conversing lovingly with Sister Clara and the other sisters at the convent of San Damiano's in an atmosphere "overflowing with sweetness and compassion," making Francis' heart "blossom luxuriantly in the feminine air," and giving outsiders the impression that the convent had gone up in flames. "It was the first time," we are told, "the sisters had felt what an infinitely divine gift it was to be a woman, and also what a responsibility" (384–95).[31]

Closer to the divine than the masculine, is the feminine.

Another heretical hypothesis: By the time Kazantzakis had completed this last novel of his, he was well on his way towards making a radical departure from the philosophical theories of his past. To be sure, the Nietzschean and Bergsonian ideas that informed much of his earlier work remain present in *The Poor Man of God*, but the concepts and slogans have now been emptied and are filled with new content, this time the content not coming from a preconceived and systematically worked-out philosophy, but from the flesh and bones of Francis himself. The vision that Francis, the Lamb of God, dictates to his biographer is one of perfect love and peace, a love that prays for the forgiveness even of Satan (391), and a love infused with a humility and gentleness that runs counter to the 'Life is war, toil, violence!' doctrine often espoused by Kazantzakis in the past (cf. 280–81).[32] Francis, not surprisingly, had a deep effect on Kazantzakis, and it appears that Kazantzakis had begun in the final years of his life to move away from the 'heroic nihilism' of *Salvatores Dei* – "We come from a dark abyss, we end in a dark abyss"[33] – even though this nihilism was always tempered by a Bergsonian activism that challenges us to fashion meaning in an otherwise meaningless world (hence the qualifier 'heroic' in 'heroic nihilism').[34] Kazantzakis, in other words, was making steps towards a more optimistic vision, though perhaps one that continued to be tinged with the tragic in light of the blood-drenched ascent that it involved. This is rarely recognized by commentators who persist in taking Kazantzakis at his word when he wrote to Max Tau in 1951 that *Salvatores Dei* "is my credo, the core of my work, and even more, the core of my entire life."[35]

> Note that the nightmare of absolute nihilism comes to Brother Leo one night only after he had deserted Francis and spent the evening with the bandit, Captain Wolf, greedily eating food and guzzling wine. (473–80)

> Despite the above comment to Max Tau, Kazantzkis did not view his novels as simply variations on the one theme, but as successive attempts to reach further and break new ground: *aperiatur terra*.

>> Letter to Börje Knös, 30 January 1952:
>> I am obliged to see to it that each book of mine will be one step further ahead and higher. *The Last Temptation* took such a step. The new book must advance yet another stride. And this responsibility is a very heavy one . . .[36]

> And after *The Poor Man of God* was completed, the author himself was surprised at what he had given birth to. In a letter to Prevelakis, dated 6 December 1953, Kazantzakis wrote:

>> [*The Poor Man of God*] is one of the works you won't like, and I'm puzzled as to how I wrote it. Well, is there a religious *mystique* inside me? Because I felt great emotion when I wrote it . . .[37]

Brother Leo, like Nietzsche's madman, spends his life searching for God. But the fact of the matter is that God is also searching for us. Francis cries out towards the heavens:

> "All day long I search desperately for You;
> all night long, while I am asleep, You search for me;
> when, O Lord, when, as night gives way to day, shall we meet?" (28)

But the search for God is not open to just anyone. Special qualities are required, the most important of which is *laziness*. Yes: laziness! Forget about what you've heard and been taught by well-intentioned but ignorant priests and theologians, the route to God is laziness. And here's the proof, if proof is needed:

> "The labourer who lives from hand to mouth returns home each
> night exhausted and famished. He assaults his dinner, gobbles up his

food lickety-spit, then quarrels with his wife, beats his children without rhyme or reason simply because he's tired and irritated, and afterward clenches his fists and sleeps. Waking up for a moment he finds his wife at his side, couples with her, clenches his fists once more, and plunges back into sleep . . . Where can he find time for God?" (39)

But the lazy person, as Brother Leo goes on to explain, has all the time in the world. He doesn't bother looking for a job, he doesn't bother looking for a wife, and so he avoids all the troubles that come with work, marriage and children. Instead, he can simply sit in the sun during winter, lounge in the shade during summer, and at night stretch out on his back on the roof of his house, gazing at the moon and the stars, while wondering: Who made all this? And why? (39).

Inevitably, however, curiosity turns to anguish, and the search for God takes on the importance of life and death. Upon this search hangs the salvation of one's soul.

But where do we start? What road should we take in our search? In fact, as Augustine (following Plato) noticed, how can we search for something if we do not *know* what we are searching for? And how, if we do not know what we are searching for, can we be said to be *searching* for it at all? Self-proclaimed spiritual guides are not troubled by these questions, as they confidently claim to know the surest path to God. According to Brother Leo, however, it was only an obscure holy man living in a cave and blinded by weeping who could give the answer that was "both most correct and most frightening":

"Holy ascetic, I have set out to find God. Show me the road," Brother Leo asked.
"There is no road", he answered, beating his staff on the ground.
"There is no road! What then is there?" Brother Leo asked, seized with terror.
"There is the abyss. Jump!"
"Abyss!? Is that the way?"
"Yes. All roads lead to the earth. The abyss leads to God. Jump!" (41)

This is the only way to God.
The divine descent.

We don't wish to admit that this is the only way to God, for we always try to take the easy way out. But there is a simple way to determine which is the way to God: the one that's most difficult, the one that both descends and rises.

Initially, Francis recognized this, and sighed (129). Later, with experience that only suffering could bring, he would make the same point, but fervently and without dejection (325).

Trans-descendance:
> turning flesh into spirit.

There are two paths available to us, one entirely different from the other but perhaps both leading to the same destination. There is the straight and reasonable path of the respectable man, where God is found in marriage and children, in good food and wine, in cleanliness and health. And there is the crooked and incomprehensible path of the disreputable saint, where God is found in homelessness and poverty, in sickness and solitariness. Which path to take? (165–66)

Francis' answer:
"Good God, to marry, have children, build a home – I spit on them all!" (165)
Few ears would wish to listen.
One winter morning, Francis creates seven snow statues, each representing a member of his would-be family (including a wife with "huge pendulous breasts", two sons and two daughters), and when the sun rose he commanded it to "beat down upon my family and melt them!" (341)
> Ordinary happiness: *the last temptation.*
"To have nothing, absolutely nothing: that is the road that leads to God. There is no other," Francis says to his bishop. (220)

> "The kingdom of heaven is at hand . . .
> Take no gold nor silver nor copper in your belts, no sack for your journey, nor an extra tunic, nor sandals, nor a staff . . ." (Matthew 10:7, 9–10)

Absolute poverty: to have nothing – not even God?
Meister Eckhart: "Therefore I pray to God that he may make me free of 'God'."
Brother Francis: "Lord, give me the strength to enable me one day to renounce hope, the hope, O Lord, of seeing thee." (244)
(Poverty as a matter more of metaphysics than economics.)
From *being* to *nothingness.*

> But to have nothing, to become nothing is at the same time to have everything, to be everything (and anything), because absolute poverty brings absolute freedom. (242)

> Augustine: "Love, then do what you will."
> From *nothingness* to *being*.
>> The ascent: from one abyss to another,
>> and dancing and weeping in between. (284)

But it is the uphill path that brings *perfect joy*.
A constant 'No!' to the small, insignificant joys (or temptations), so as to
be able to reach the 'Great Yes!'.
And what does this 'Yes!' look like? Well, take a look for yourself:
Hungry and cold, Francis and Brother Leo find themselves caught in a
rainstorm during one of their nightly sojourns, and so they rush towards
a nearby monastery to seek temporary shelter. They are met, however,
by a gigantic doorkeeper who not only refuses them entry, but also beats
both of them to a pulp, leaving them half-dead. They lie asleep near the
gates of the monastery till dawn, when they hear the doorkeeper
approaching. The door is opened. They now have the opportunity to go in,
to find a place to warm up a little and eat, but instead they decide to head
off once more on their journey. "Francis was so happy, he flew". (160)
Herein lies genuine freedom, the 'Great Yes!'.[38]
A hard lesson, and so it is not surprising to find a reviewer of Kazantzakis'
novel passing the following judgement:
"Recommendation: Beware of Nikos Kazantzakis bearing gifts."[39]

> Look at me, I am without a country, without a home, without
> possessions, without a slave; I sleep out on the ground; I have
> no wife, no children, no fine residence, but only earth and
> heaven and one sorry cloak. And what do I lack? Am I not
> without sorrow, without fear? Am I not free?
> – the Cynic, as quoted by Epictetus[40]

But there is always something, no matter how trifling it may seem, that
prevents us from embarking upon this uphill path. For some it might be the
weight of books and theological questions that prevent us from ascending
(187–88). For others it might be some prized possession that one cannot let
go, whether it be a house, a car, a wife, or even a small, richly decorated
pitcher (200).
Unless these idols are smashed into a thousand pieces, one can never
see God.

> "Name your idol, and you will know who
> you are."
> – Jean-Luc Marion[41]

Francis dares to do what he finds most difficult to do: He finds a leper, embraces him and kisses him on the lips. (135)
He then carries the leper in his arms, covering him with his robe. When he later draws the robe aside, the leper has disappeared. It was Christ himself all along.

"For I was hungry and you gave me something to eat, I was thirsty and you gave me something to drink, I was a stranger and you invited me in, I needed clothes and you clothed me, I was sick and you looked after me, I was in prison and you came to visit me." (Matthew 25:35–36)
"This, Brother Leo, is what I understand: all lepers, cripples, sinners, if you kiss them on the mouth – they all become Christ." (138)

Searching for God high and low, by day and by night, we soon forget what we were looking for, and then a flash of insight: "Who knows, perhaps God is simply the search for God" (43). God in all his fullness was always there, the voice within, closer to us than we are to ourselves. "It is unnecessary for us to run to the ends of the earth in his pursuit. All we have to do is gaze into our own hearts" (148, cf. 434).

This hidden and abysmal God that is sought but never found should not be confused with the garden-variety gods we are taught to believe in from childhood.

In a delightful book, entitled *Kids' View of God*, Candice Dunn and Rebecca Mann present many interesting, humourous and even insightful perspectives on God and religion that are had by children from four to nine years of age.[42] What is most interesting, however, is how closely some of the childrens' quotes resemble the thoughts found in the dense and technical writings of highly trained philosophers of religion: "If you're naughty God curses you with a punishment from your mum" (Vivien, aged 7); "God knows everything that you do before you do it 'cause he's hiding behind the door" (Alex, aged 5); "God has a special tracking device that beeps when you're naughty and he knows who's done it" (Jonathan, aged 9); "You know when God is around because you get a nice feeling in your heart" (Saskia, aged 9). I am afraid that many philosophers have not grown out of the religion they were taught as children.

This is the very religion we find practised by many of Francis' family and friends. Before setting out on one of his expeditions to sell various goods at a nearby city, Francis' father, Pietro Bernardone, would customarily attend Mass and attempt to strike a deal with the local saint, Saint Ruffino.

"You protect my merchandise," he would haggle with the saint, "and I'll bring you a silver lamp from Florence, a heavy embossed one that will make you the envy of the other saints, who have nothing but tiny lamps made of glass" (33).

> This calculative, means-end rationality is widespread in moral thinking today, but was also not unknown in Francis' time. 'Why shouldn't I eat, drink and be merry', a villager challenges Francis, 'for if I don't get into heaven, I will have lost only one life, while if you don't get into heaven you will have lost two' (458). How can one argue with that?

One more remarkable quote from *Kids' View of God*. Children were asked to put a question to God, and along with some typical responses (e.g., "Can you help my grandpa get better?"), there is this gem from Eve, aged 4: "Dear God, I haven't thought of a question yet. I will probably think of it when I'm dead." That is precisely what Francis would say.

The impoverished doctrinal gods of the philosophers and the living God who grabs his followers by the scruff of the neck, and tosses them from peak to peak until they break into a thousand pieces (73). Initially, however, the demands are small and seemingly easy to fulfill. Later, more difficult and arduous demands are placed on one, and eventually nothing less than the impossible becomes one's mission (84). "Go there where you cannot go, to the impossible, it is indeed the only way of going or coming" (Derrida).[43]

To begin with, Francis is given the task of rebuilding the dilapidated chapel of San Damiano. But afterwards he understood that much more was demanded of him: he was now to rebuild himself: "Francis, Francis – make Francis firm, rebuild the son of Bernardone!", the voice commanded him (102). But how was he to rebuild himself? By demolishing his self, the self that was preventing the union with the divine; by kenotically emptying his self of pride, making a fool of himself, for Christ's sake.

> "If anyone would come after me, he must deny himself and take up his cross and follow me." (Matthew 16:24, Luke 8:34; cf. Luke 9:23)

> Absolute poverty: not so much having no possessions, but not being possessed by anything, above all, not being possessed by the 'ego' and its hopes and fears. As Lewis Owens explains,

>> "This 'perfect poverty'. . . is in fact the only road that leads to 'God' and is achieved by overcoming an attachment to the ego.

> Self-overcoming and consequent self-realization therefore leads to 'God'. This self-realization is achieved via a process of detachment from inauthentic attachment to the individual self-will, which harbors hopes and fears for immortality or extinction after death."[44]

There once was an ascetic, Francis tells his brothers, who upon dying, ascended to heaven and knocked on the gates. 'Who is there?' came the reply. 'It's me!' answered the ascetic. 'There isn't any room for two here', said the voice. 'Go away!' (309–310)

> To forget who you are and what your name is, not to have any will and not to say 'I' – that is true freedom! (427)

And so, at the very place where he grew up and where everyone knew him well, at the heart of Assisi, in the middle of the town square, on a Saturday evening when the citizens were beginning to gather outside, Francis rises up and shouts: "Come one, come all! Come to hear the new madness!" (109). And what was 'the new madness'? "Love! Love! Love!" Francis would proclaim, while dancing and jumping, and covered in blood from the stones and other missiles thrown at him by the jeering crowd (111).

Humiliation as the path to humility.

Each step in the ascent is one more attachment loosened, if not completely severed. Francis begins with the most powerful ties that bind us to earth, those of mother and father, lover and wife, friends and acquaintances. Having divested himself of these attachments, Francis removes the very clothes he is wearing and returns them to his father. Standing "naked as the day his mother brought him into the world," in front of his father, the local bishop and a throng of curious citizens, he says to the bishop: "Until now I called Sior Pietro Bernardone my father. Henceforth I shall say: 'Our Father who art in heaven'." (117)

> "Reading the texts of the early ascetics, I have come to realize that perhaps the most essential lesson learned in life is the lesson of surrender, of letting go. It is a hard lesson, and one that is only reluctantly embraced by most of us. But I am convinced that this life is given to us in order to learn how to lose."
> – John Chryssavgis[45]

But as Bernardone himself wonders: What kind of God is it who separates sons and daughters from their fathers and mothers? (168)

An unfathomable abyss: a *mysterium tremendum et fascinans.*

> the Insatiable
> the Merciless
> the Indefatigable
> the Unsatisfied
> . . . the bottomless Abyss (173)

Love of God: divine madness.

> Intoxicated with God
> He would pray and pray
> but every now and again
> he would reach a dead-end
> and what he could not pray
> he would sing
> and what he could not sing
> he would dance
> and what he could not dance
> he would cry
> but what he could not cry
> would only die.

To those on the outside looking in, sanctity is indistinguishable from madness (122). Consider, for example, the comments of Kazantzakis scholar, Morton Levitt: "The ascetic strictures he [i.e., Francis] offers are so opposed to normal living that they are bound to repel us; we suspect that no sane man would follow such a fanatic and that no sane age could produce one."[46]

Abba Antony said: "A time is coming when men will go mad, and when they see someone who is not mad, they will attack him saying, 'You are mad, you are not like us'."[47]

Francis, God's beloved buffoon.

2 + 2 = 22 (Kazantzakis' formula for Francis[48])

"If you think that you are wise in this age, you should become fools so that you may become wise," wrote Paul in 1 Corinthians 3:18. And the fools for Christ's sake followed the apostle's exhortation to the letter. The holy fool would pretend to be mad or immoral, doing things that would be regarded as incompatible not only with an ascetic life, but with a Christian life in general. Thus, that wonderful holy fool from Emesa in Syria, Symeon, would do such things as take on the blame for the pregnancy of a young girl, even pretending to be ashamed of what he had supposedly done; and visiting a prostitute, giving everyone the impression that he had slept with her, when in fact he had only brought her food

since he knew that she was starving. (One can imagine this prostitute react-
ing in the same way the prostitute in Damietta reacted after her failed
attempt to seduce Francis [326–27].) During the day, Symeon would roam
the streets, playing the madman, the fornicator, the glutton, the drunkard,
the fool – and he would be treated accordingly. But after dark he would
completely disappear from view, praying to God all night long in total
secrecy and silence.

Abba Macarius said, "If slander has become to you the same as praise,
poverty as riches, deprivation as abundance, you will not die."[49]

All this, nonetheless, is *not enough*. It is never enough.
We protest, 'Enough is enough! I can't go any further!'
But God demands: 'You can! You must!'

> Our body is the bow, God is the archer, and the soul is the
> arrow.
> There are three kinds of souls, three kinds of prayer:
>> 'I am a bow in your hands, Lord. Draw me, lest I rot.'
>> 'Do not overdraw me, Lord. I shall break.'
>> 'Overdraw me, Lord, and who cares if I break!' (270)

You are the crucified who crucifies
– Geoffrey Hill, "Lachrimae"[50]

The perpetual ascent. Francis realizes that we are to save not only our
souls, but also the souls of our fellow brothers and sisters – in fact, we cannot do the former without doing the latter. Francis therefore sets out to go
from town to town, preaching to his fellow Christians to return to Christ,
for "the kingdom of heaven is at hand!". (178–79)

> But even this is not enough: Always attentive to the voice (or
> Cry) within, Francis casts his net wider as he is called to save the
> infidel Muslims, and he therefore sails to Damietta and preaches
> fearlessly to the Sultan. (315–19)

But this too is not enough: Francis fears that he is still not on the
right road (332). He realizes, with much sorrow, that he must
surrender the reigns of the brotherhood he established to other
hands (370–73), and he must even surrender the hope that after
he has departed the brothers will continue in the path of total
poverty and simplicity (399–400).

>> "But a time is coming, and has come, when you will be
>> scattered, each to his own home. You will leave me all
>> alone." (John 16:32)

> The journey upward is lined with Judas kisses.
> Francis exemplifies "the transformation of mate-
> rial defeat into spiritual victory"[51]: success breeds
> satisfaction and stagnation, whereas Francis' fail-
> ures (in converting the Sultan, in preaching to the
> crusaders, in keeping the friars united) spurs a rest-
> less but liberating struggle that enables him to
> remain faithful to the Cry within.

> God calls us to go beyond our selves.

> Ultimately, however, God calls us to go beyond God:
> "Brother Leo, to be a saint means to renounce not only
> everything earthly but also everything divine" (20).

It is terrifying to see how quickly the divine ascent can turn into
a descent. Francis briefly leaves his brothers in order to travel to Rome
to seek papal approval for his new order, and in no time the brothers
are quarrelling, rebelling against Francis' teachings, visiting houses of
plea-sure, eating and drinking to their heart's content, even going so far as
hunting down a goat on Good Friday, tearing it limb from limb and greed-
ily devouring it: "They chewed hurriedly, swallowed, grabbed a new
mouthful; then, as though they had become drunk, they began to dance
round the severed head and twisted horns, blood and fire dripping from
their mouths" (277). The human soul is a battleground between light and
darkness, divinity and bestiality, and even one who has reached the heights
of divinity – especially such a one – can, like a flash of lightning, fall into
the mire of the inferno.

> "I saw Satan fall like lightning from heaven." (Luke 10:18)

The ascent continues. Obedient to the Cry within, Francis decides to marry.
His bride? Lady Poverty.
The borders are being overrun: hungry but full and rich in poverty,
the brothers cheerfully celebrate a wedding feast without a wedding, a
bridegroom without a bride.
The new divine madness. (225–26)
Love is never 'rational', how much more an excess of love.

The new divine madness: Francis talks and communes with nature, conversing with birds, swallows and doves as though he were talking with his
own biological brothers and sisters (290–91; cf. 522–23). And he can hear
what the birds have to say to him in return.

In Francis' heart, an old chronicler has it, the whole
world found refuge: the sinner, the poor, the sick,
the birds, the wolves, the flowers.

> "The swallows beat their wings happily, the doves cooed, and
> the sparrows came close to Francis and began to peck tenderly at
> his robe." (292)

>> Before heading off, Francis makes the sign of the cross
>> over the birds, blesses them, and then bids them
>> farewell.

> A tender and overflowing love for every living and breathing
> thing, for everything that suffers and even for everything that
> doesn't:

> "God bless Brother Water," Francis says as he sips a cup of water
> (367). One is reminded of his 'Canticle of Brother Sun', where he
> sings the praises of the Lord for creating Brother Sun ("radiant
> with great splendour"), Sister Moon and the stars ("precious and
> fair"), Brother Wind, Sister Water ("humble and dear and pure"),
> Brother Fire ("strong and merry"), Sister Mother Earth ("who
> sustains us and holds us to her breast, and produces abundant
> fruits, flowers, and trees"), and even Brother Death ("whom no
> living person can escape"). (563–64, 575)

Communion with nature is communion with God.

Spinoza: "*deus sive natura*".[52]

Australian newspaper cartoonist and artist, Michael Leunig, in a "Confession" published on his website, describes his sudden impulse one Saturday morning in the midst of the Vietnam War in 1969 to depart from serious political commentary in his drawings and instead to present his editor with "an absurd, irresponsible triviality" in the form of a man riding towards the sunset on a large duck and with a teapot on his head. This was to change Leunig's approach forever:

> In the wake of this drawing I at once began to express my most
> personal self with less embarrassment; to play with my ideas more
> freely; to bring warmth into my work; to focus on modest, everyday
> situations and nature as sources of imagery and to see my work as
> nourishing rather than mocking or hurtful.[53]

This turn to personal expression and the free play of ideas, to a spirit of warmth and modesty, to a natural style that seeks to sustain and uplift rather than to outdo or defeat – why have philosophers been unable to make such a turn?

What are these quirky characters and animals that Leunig draws all about? What does a picture of a teapot-wearing duck-riding man mean? Like Francis' ravings, this is just stupid sentimentalism, childish and immature, even dangerous for a rational and intelligent person. Thus speaks the modern mind.

From an interview with Andrew Denton on the ABC show, "Enough Rope" (aired on 8 May 2006):

> *Andrew Denton:* Now once more for the beginners, what was the duck about?
>
> *Michael Leunig:* Well, I don't know. I thought everybody would understand what a duck is about, and it's just, there is the duck. And suddenly the whole nation seems perplexed about what does a duck mean? I think a nation is in trouble that cannot accept a duck.[54]

Out of touch with the world of nature, out of touch with themselves and their humanity, people must now be reminded of who they really are and where they really belong. Leunig therefore sees it as his duty to not so much point out the absurdities in contemporary social and political affairs, as may have been the duty of a cartoonist in days gone by, but to point out what is human. And as he notes, "it's rather odd that I would have to do that, or feel compelled to do that. It's as if I feel we're losing our humanity all the time, and so you've got to keep trying to rescue bits of it to the extent you can, and that's odd when you think about it."[55]

Camus' description of New York during a trip to the United States in 1946 – "the hundreds of thousands of high walls," a "desert of iron and cement," "a hideous, inhuman city"[56] – brings to mind my first impressions of central Melbourne as I was being led by my father through the city streets as a seven- or eight-year-old. I recall the feeling of being surrounded by enormous buildings that block out the sunlight, casting a gloomy, greyish haze around the thousands of pedestrians and cars. I can relate to Camus, then, when he writes in his journal: "Impression of being trapped in this city, that I could escape from the monoliths that surround me and run for hours without finding anything but new cement prisons, without the hope of a hill, a real tree, or a bewildered face . . . Terrible feeling of being abandoned. Even if I hugged all the beings of the world to my breast, I would remain unprotected."[57] (One of my recurrent dreams is exactly as Camus describes it: entrapment within the cement city walls.)

Michael Leunig presents a similar picture when describing his departure from his farm house, where he would feel rested and hopeful, to an inner-city hotel room in preparation for his television interview with Andrew Denton: "Soon I am funnelled away from my pastures of doddering wombats and installed in a cell in a concrete tower overlooking a Sydney expressway." Later in the same article Leunig recounts how, immediately prior to the interview, he felt his memory "dismantled by expressways and sleepless nights in concrete towers."[58] Such dehumanizing buildings are a regular feature of major cities, and even the outer-city suburbs – with their nameless neighbours, giant shopping malls, polluted roads and artificial lawns – are often inimical to a life of spirituality and reflection. Leunig summarized the matter perfectly when he said,

> The city to me is developing problems which I can't much deal with anymore. I feel too cramped and violated somehow when I see these great monuments to a kind of crass commercial greed. Life's just becoming too hard in the city for me and for many others. I think we haven't made our cities very well at all. I don't think we know how to take care of ourselves as well as we perhaps once did.[59]

A brilliant idea from Camus, which occurs to him upon entering his room at a small inn located "a thousand miles from everything":

> During a business trip a man arrives, without any preconceived idea, at a remote inn in the wilderness. And there, the silence of nature, the simplicity of the room, the remoteness of everything, make him decide to stay there permanently, to cut all ties with what had been his life and to send no news of himself to anyone.

The ascent continues,
the long ascent of a wild, inaccessible mountain,
at the summit of which,
amidst cold, rain and snow,
awaits God. (443–44)

> "To increase by nothings.
> Lightweight. Lightweight," he said.
> "What nothings are you talking about?" asked, one day, a disciple.
> And the sage replied: "The mind sets its goal ever farther.
> O vertiginous push upward; but what is up unless a perpetual denial of down?"
> And he added: "Down here was nothing and up there is nothing – but *between*, light strains through."[60]

> . . . I wretch lay wrestling with (my God!) my God.
> – Gerard Manley Hopkins, "Carrion Comfort"[61]

at the summit
of the holy mountain
after sleepless nights and incessant struggles
to transmute darkness into light
Francis is consumed by fire
Mount Alvernia is ablaze
hands and feet bleeding profusely
a deep open wound in his side
gasping for breath
crucified
and resurrected
at the same time
for crucifixion and resurrection
are one and the same (498–503)

> Like Brother Leo, I too peer out of my window, feeling despondent and sad, and then notice a sparrow making its way towards me:

"And it was you, Father Francis, it was you dressed as a tiny sparrow." (598)

CHAPTER 6

AFTER THE END OF PHILOSOPHY OF RELIGION

Analytic philosophy, although dominant in philosophy departments across the Anglo-American world and increasingly elsewhere too, is experiencing a deep crisis. The discipline has reached an impasse that has largely gone unnoticed by its practitioners: it has become heavily institutionalized and dogmatically beholden to a narrow platform of scientific rationality to the extent that it has little to offer those seeking answers to the most significant questions, questions concerning the Why, Whence and Whither of life. "Where do we come from? Where are we going? What is the meaning of this life? That is what every heart is shouting, what every head is asking as it beats on chaos," writes Kazantzakis.[1] Analytic philosophy, however, has given itself over to the search for *knowledge*, a purely scientific or objective understanding of the world, while abandoning the search for *wisdom*, a way of thinking that (like much ancient philosophy) integrates theoretical knowledge with practical issues such as the nature of a good and happy human life.[2] One can hardly imagine, for example, an analytic philosopher beginning a book or journal paper in the same vein as the powerful opening in Albert Camus' *The Myth of Sisyphus*: "There is but one truly serious philosophical problem, and that is suicide. Judging whether life is or is not worth living amounts to answering the fundamental question of philosophy."[3] Existentially pressing questions such as 'the meaning of life' are instead pushed to the periphery of analytic philosophy, if they are raised and discussed at all.

In an essay entitled, interestingly enough, "Has Philosophy Lost Contact with People?", W. V. Quine expresses very well this conception of philosophy:

> What I have been discussing under the head of philosophy is what I call scientific philosophy . . . By this vague heading I do not exclude philosophical studies of moral and aesthetic values. Some such studies, of an analytical cast, can be scientific in spirit. They are apt, however, to offer little in the way of inspiration or consolation. The student who majors in philosophy primarily for spiritual comfort is misguided and is probably not a very good student anyway, since intellectual curiosity is not what moves him.
>
> Inspirational and edifying writing is admirable, but the place for it is the novel, the poem, the sermon, or the literary essay. Philosophers in the professional sense have no peculiar fitness for it. Neither have they any peculiar fitness for helping to get society on an even keel, though we should all do what we can. What just might fill these perpetually crying needs is wisdom: *sophia* yes, *philosophia* not necessarily.[4]

Elaborating on this metaphilosophy, Scott Soames has recently written:

> In general, philosophy done in the analytic tradition aims at truth and
> knowledge, as opposed to moral or spiritual improvement. There is very little
> in the way of practical or inspirational guides in the art of living to be found,
> and very much in the way of philosophical theories that purport to reveal
> the truth about a given domain of inquiry. In general, the goal in analytic
> philosophy is to discover what is true, not to provide a useful recipe for
> living one's life.[5]

This demarcation between 'sophia' and 'philosophia' in analytic philosophy
has contributed to what Simon Critchley aptly describes as "an experiential gap between the realms of knowledge and wisdom, truth and meaning,
theory and practice, causal explanation and existential understanding."[6]
The creation of such a divide is an almost occupational hazard of the
philosopher, as Kierkegaard emphasized when he stated:

> In relation to their systems most systematisers are like a man who builds an
> enormous castle and lives in a shack close by; they do not live in their own
> enormous systematic buildings. But spiritually that is a decisive objection.
> Spiritually speaking a man's thought must be the building in which he lives –
> otherwise everything is topsy-turvy.[7]

Strangely, having just emerged from a century marked by unprecedented
levels of human suffering (caused in part by the two world wars, the Holocaust and many other genocides) and by unparalleled degradation of the
natural environment, one would have thought that any dissociation of
knowledge from wisdom would be particularly difficult to sustain. And
yet, the gulf between theoretical speculation and existential commitment
continues to hold sway in analytic philosophy, even though it has become
in the eyes of many (and, increasingly, analytic philosophers too) too high
a price to pay. In particular, the relentless pursuit of a scientific conception
of the world at the expense of the everyday moral, practical and existential
problems people face can only "clip an angel's wings," to use John Keats'
words – it will fail to provide the kind of enlightenment and spiritual nour-
ishment that, since at least Socrates and Plato, have been thought necessary
for leading a fulfilled life.[8]

This may help explain why philosophy departments in the English-
speaking world, where analytic philosophy flourishes, have recently come
under heavy criticism. Robert Solomon, for example, bemoans the state of
much contemporary philosophy. In his book, *The Joy of Philosophy: Thinking Thin versus the Passionate Life*, he contends that philosophy has largely

lost its way, replacing the joys of imaginative speculation, passionate engagement, vision and openness, with a tribal mentality that seeks to preserve its legitimacy by means of inaccessible jargon, an adversarial style of proof and refutation, and a narrow focus that invariably excludes the 'perennial problems of life'. Solomon even goes so far as to say that "philosophy has all but disappeared in the best universities in America."[9] "The 'best' philosophy departments," he adds, "have become those that are the most technically brilliant and have the least to say to most students."[10] Not finding their most urgent questions addressed in the academic philosophy journals and lecture theatres, students inevitably look elsewhere. And one can hardly blame them, in Solomon's view: "For a great many intelligent people these days, better the libidinal fantasies of Shirley MacLaine than the tedium of the professional skepticism that finds fault with every argument, confusions in every insight, foolishness in every good feeling, an intractable paradox hiding beneath every figure of speech."[11] Solomon therefore exhorts his colleagues to go "beyond the thinness of arguments to the richness that is philosophy, trying to add to our experience rather than to 'prove a point'."[12]

The situation is no different in analytic philosophy of religion. Indeed, the situation here is arguably more serious, for religion is one area where the existential and lived dimension cannot be neglected or reduced to purely abstract concerns without doing violence to the very object of inquiry. To many religious believers, particularly those belonging to non-Western religious traditions, analytic philosophy of religion would appear to be a philosophy of anything but *religion*. There is, as was pointed out in the discussion on the problem of evil in Chapter 2, a disconnection in analytic philosophy of religion between the investigator and what they purport to be investigating, a disconnection that parallels that between knowledge and wisdom and which is felt to be particularly acute in the overly abstract and theoretical way in which analytic philosophers deal with religious questions. What is needed, therefore, is *a completely fresh start*, doing away with the tired and stale institutions, dogmas and vocabularies, and rediscovering in their absence new forms of religious thinking – or, more accurately, rediscovering old forms of religious thinking that have become buried in the sophisticated technical discourse of scientific-minded philosophers.

The value of myth, for example, needs to be retrieved. Although a fountain of wisdom in ancient cultures, myth is routinely ignored or dismissed by academic philosophers today, especially those working in the analytic tradition. As Bruce Wilshire points out in *Fashionable Nihilism*, the denigration of myth in analytic philosophy is motivated by a rampant scientism that diminishes the weight and fullness of life, thus leading inexorably to nihilism and despair. In Wilshire's words:

> Recall how Socrates in *Phaedo* concludes his arguments for the immortality of the soul. He and his friends conclude that they had at least done their best in engaging a greatly difficult question. But the dialogue doesn't end there. Socrates launches into an extending recounting of ancient myths of the journey of the soul after death, its passage through underground rivers, and so on. Try this yourself with the typical graduate student analytically trained: Ask him or her why Socrates (and Plato) end the dialogue this way. *See if you get any intelligent discourse on the immemorial role of myth in the development and constitution of human beings.* Typically you will get, at best, a logician's response to the validity of Socrates' earlier arguments, and that's about all. *In hearing nothing but the latest in "scientific" philosophy, they have been cheated by their professors.*[13]

In his recent and insightful book, *The Spirituality Revolution*, David Tacey also advocates a transformation in our language, particularly when we begin to speak about God. Tacey observes

> . . . that all symbolic representations of the divine die, and society has to set about to renew and remake its sacred images. The new images must carry weight, significance, beauty and conviction, and they cannot simply be invented by human reason, but must well up from the spirit of the people and from the mythopoetic imagination.[14]

Tacey thus calls for *a new image of God* in the wake of the death of the rationalistic and moralistic God, and he entrusts the poets, artists and philosophers to fashion this new image. He likewise calls for a fresh spirituality to renew and transfigure the spirit, the spirit that has been crushed by institutionalized religion. At the centre of this spiritual revolution stands a God who is not "remote, detached, interventionalist and supernatural," as is the God of old-style religion, but a God who is "intimate, intense and immanent."[15] God is not to be conceived, Tacey explains, as "an extrinsic or outside super-reality, but as a mystery at the core of ordinary reality. In other words, transcendence is not imagined literally as an other world 'on top' of or above this world, but as a deeper dimension of the real that transcends our normal perception."[16] On this view, atheism, doubt and nihilism are a dialectical necessity, necessary prolegomena to a new vision of God that "rises up phoenix-like after conventional forms have been melted down."[17] The new vision, however, must be expressed in a new language, one in which the existence of God is neither a matter of philosophical demonstration nor a matter of irrational experience or feeling, but a matter of 'reasoned trust' (in Hans Küng's words[18]) or 'mystical faith' (to borrow from David Tacey[19]).

Religious language that does not undergo this (painful) transfiguration will only be suitable for expressing *a paper God* that gets blown about by the winds. The following comments from Gilles Deleuze, originally published in 1968, are still pertinent today:

> The time is coming when it will hardly be possible to write a book of philosophy as it has been done for so long: 'Ah! the old style . . .'. The search for new means of philosophical expression was begun by Nietzsche and must be pursued today in relation to the renewal of certain other arts, such as the theatre or the cinema.[20]

An essential but neglected ingredient in this "search for new means of philosophical expression" is *contamination*. The writings of Derrida, to the chagrin of analytic philosophers, constantly 'contaminate' philosophical ideas and concepts with sex, psychoanalysis and personal details and fantasies. This is as it should be: the transcendental needs to be penetrated by the empirical, and vice versa. Analytic philosophers of religion, however, have failed to learn this lesson. Each clear and precise statement about God must be upset and subverted, contaminated with paradox and metaphor, in order to be true to the reality it seeks to express. This, indeed, is the practice enjoined by apophatic (or negative) theology, which consists in an endless dialectic of saying and unsaying, or 'saying-away', so that the God of faith is never imprisoned or immobilized in human language.

But what is typically forgotten is the advice of the Nobel-prize winning poet and playwright, Derek Walcott: "To change your language you must change your life."[21] Any transformation in the way in which we write and read philosophy presupposes changes in our way of life, beginning with changes in our political or institutional life.

This means that philosophy must be released from its current institutional shackles, or else it is destined to wither away. It is in and through the university, of course, that we have institutionalized philosophy and, more broadly, reason and rationality. As John Caputo has pointed out, "we have put reason away, put it in a safe place, confined it in closed quarters in order both to keep it safe and to keep the existing order safe from it."[22] And we have done this by creating within the university a culture of professionalism and scientism, with teams of experts and professionals who determine what counts as 'rational discourse' and who restrict themselves to the methods and standards of science in making such determinations. In an incisive passage that is worth quoting in full, and in terms that would be familiar to most academics, Caputo explains how this institutionalization of reason has taken place:

> Debates about reason are debates conducted by university professors in journals and books, at symposia and public lectures, by men and women who aspire to tenure, promotion, and support for more research. What is rational and what is not are very often a function of the powers that be within the academy, of those who hold the senior faculty positions in a more or less identifiable number of elite institutions. It is they who set the style and tone of the discourse in the profession. They define the "right questions" and the right way to go about addressing these questions. They set the standards for, and determine the selection of, the kinds of articles that can be published in the journals, the sorts of books that the best university presses publish, the kinds of proposals that can be supported by the foundations. They review one another's books, discuss one another's articles, invite one another to the colloquia and seminars they sponsor, recommend one another for foundational support, hire one another's doctoral students, invite one another to serve as visiting professors, nominate one another for distinguished chairs and lectureships and offices in professional societies – in a self-validating, self-congratulating circle which controls the profession.[23]

Inevitably, when philosophy is institutionalized in this way, we forego both the experimental spirit (where, for example, the free play of ideas and unorthodox forms of thinking and writing are encouraged) and the spirit of dissent and protest against the status quo (especially the status quo within the discipline and the university at large). One can hardly imagine, as Caputo goes on to say, a Kierkegaard or a Nietzsche (or, I would add, a Kazantzakis) surviving, let alone flourishing, in an oppressive institutional atmosphere such as this. These thinkers "do not bend their knee to what the university calls reason. They reject the etiquette, the style, the discourse, the good manners of the university which keep everything safe, which preserve decorum at all costs, including the cost of repressing dissent."[24]

But the problems that beset philosophy are not only generated from within the discipline or the university, but also (and especially) from without – in particular, from the wider socio-economic environment. Consider, for example, the ethos of managerialism and the drive towards corporatization sweeping through universities and academic life. An article recently published in *The Times Higher Education Supplement* summarized the situation well. Entitled, "Academia Has Sold Out, 72% Believe," in reference to a survey of academics in the United Kingdom,[25] the author outlined some of the key findings of the study, which included the following:

> Higher education is "selling its soul" as managerialism, regulation and the drive to get "bums on seats" replace the wider human good of academe, according to explosive new research.
>
> The study . . . says that 72 per cent of academics think higher education has lost its role as the "conscience and critic of society". Some 85 per cent agreed that the "humanity and excitement" have been lost, while 77 per cent said the "joy of learning" once associated with higher education has been lost to targets and performance measures.[26]

These results reflect the mounting pressures faced by academics to conduct and publish research merely in order to attract funding or to advance their career prospects. As in the commercial world, 'targets' (or should I say 'sales targets'?) have become an integral part of life in today's academy: measuring performance against standards relating to such things as the number of grants secured and the number of articles and books published over a prescribed period of time. And so the pressure is on to win more and more grant money, and to publish, publish, publish, no matter how undeveloped one's work may be, or how unsatisfied one may feel with the work – it's publish or perish! In such circumstances the quality of one's work is unavoidably diminished. This hectic rat-race is world's away from the approach of Wittgenstein, who wrote: "In philosophy the winner of the race is the one who can run most slowly. Or: the one who gets there last."[27] Philosophy, done properly, takes time – often, a great amount of time. It is therefore becoming difficult to pursue a genuinely philosophical life in the increasingly corporatized climate of the academy.

In creating – whether it be by way of writing, painting or even praying – the bureaucratic world of 'targets' and 'key performance indicators' must disappear. Indeed, the very world of time must be transcended, so that it is no longer restricted to the geometric subdivisions into which, as Kazantzakis puts it, "it has been so humiliatingly jammed by the sober, lucid mind of the West." Echoing Bergson, Kazantzakis points to an alternative world where "time is released from its mathematical, firm-set confines; it becomes a substance that is fluid and indivisible, a light, intoxicating vertigo which transforms thought into reverie and music."[28]

These words, however, seem to be wasted on the present ambitious generation of graduates and young academics. In another recent article from *The Times Higher Education Supplement*, headlined "Young Guns Ditch Old Values,"[29] we are informed that scholars in the early stages of their careers have imbibed, and indeed embraced, the corporate model of the university promulgated by government ministers and university chancellors. Those entering the academic profession, in other words, are not led by a 'higher calling' to seek knowledge and wisdom, but are driven by 'performance targets' to climb the professorial scale. What matters most, then, are research ratings, student (or consumer) satisfaction, numbers of enrolled students and so on. The outcome, as one commentator aptly put it, is "a culture of research audits that promote instrumental knowledge, teaching audits designed to promote 'skills' rather than specific content, and various league tables pitting colleagues and institutions against each other in a form of academic Darwinism."[30] This emphasis on productivity, utility and ambition stands in stark contrast to the attitude of the Desert Fathers and Mothers of the early Christian centuries, who have always appeared counter-cultural, but no more so than today. In the desert, the values dominant in contemporary culture are simply inverted: noise and endless chatter are replaced with silence, action and instant change give way to inaction and patience, publication and fame are superseded by obscurity and humility.

Philosophy, in short, must become *a way of life*. Pierre Hadot has emphasized that this is how philosophy was conceived in the ancient world. "In Antiquity," he writes, "the philosopher regards himself as a philosopher, not because he develops a philosophical discourse, but because he lives philosophically." The philosopher, therefore, need not have been "a professional or a writer. He was first of all a person having a certain style of life, which he willingly chose, even if he had neither taught nor written."[31]

One is reminded of Henry David Thoreau's famous words: "There are nowadays professors of philosophy, but not philosophers." Thoreau goes on: "To be a philosopher is not merely to have subtle thoughts, nor even to found a school, but so to love wisdom as to live according to its dictates, a life of simplicity, independence, magnanimity, and trust. It is to solve some of the problems of life, not only theoretically, but practically."[32]

Far from being a way of life, philosophy has degenerated, like most disciplines in the modern university, into just another job, a technical field concerned with working out in a detached and mechanical manner what follows from what, or who said what and why, a nine-to-five occupation from which one may take leave in the evenings and weekends, or else an ambitious career move motivated by titles, honours and promotions. The philosopher then becomes no different from the local plumber or businessman. And the annual philosophy conference begins to look indistinguishable from the trade conventions of the Association of Furniture Manufacturers and the Association of Hotel Managers, where one goes to catch up with old colleagues, exchange obscure and specialized information and make valuable business deals (or, in the case of academic conferences, seek out the best new talent for hire).[33]

Nietzsche repeatedly warned of the dangers of this kind of professionalization and commodification of reason and knowledge that turn the finest minds into factory fodder. For example, as part of his renowned critique of the ascetic ideal in the third treatise of his *Genealogy of Morality*, Nietzsche states:

> Where it is not the most recent manifestation of the ascetic ideal – there it is a matter of cases too rare, noble, select to overturn the general judgment – science today is a *hiding place* for every kind of ill-humor, unbelief, gnawing worm, *despectio sui* [self-contempt], bad conscience – it is the very *unrest* of being without an ideal, the suffering from the *lack* of a great love, the discontent in an *involuntary* contentedness. Oh what does science today not conceal! How much it is at least *supposed* to conceal! The competence of our best scholars, their mindless diligence, their heads smoking day and night, their very mastery of their craft – how often all this has its true sense in preventing something from becoming visible to oneself! Science as a means of self-anesthetization: *are you acquainted with that?...*[34]

Similarly, in an earlier work, *Untimely Meditations*, Nietzsche wrote:

> Now, Pascal believes quite generally that men pursue their business and their sciences so eagerly only so as to elude the most important questions which would press upon them in a state of solitude or if they were truly idle, that is to say precisely those questions as to Whither, Whence and Why. Amazingly, the most obvious question fails to occur to our scholars: what is their work, their hurry, their painful frenzy supposed to be for?... But if you, as men of science, treat science in the way a worker treats the tasks that are to furnish his means of life, what will become of a culture condemned to await the hour of its birth and redemption in the midst of such excitement and breathless confusion? No one has time for it – and yet what is science for *at all* if it has no time for culture? At least reply to this question: what is the Whence, Whither, To what end of science if it is not to lead to culture? To lead to barbarism, perhaps?[35]

Barbarism is indeed the outcome when the goals of the university are no longer directed towards the search for truth in a socially and morally engaged fashion, inspiring students and scholars to transform themselves and their communities. But if many religious believers have succeeded in finding sustaining sources of spirituality beyond the excessively institutionalized confines of the church, then the question becomes unavoidable: Why must philosophy and philosophers be confined to the university?

Indeed, why are *philosophy departments* required anyway? The compartmentalization of the humanities into highly specialized departments has created cliques of academics, with each group largely estranged from the other. Someone employed by the Princeton philosophy department would typically know more about the research being carried out in the Harvard philosophy department than about the work being done in the Princeton sociology or politics department, which may well lie just across the hall. How can education flourish in such a climate of artificial disciplinary division? Unfortunately, as Theodore Roszak pointed out many years ago,

> It would be difficult for many academics to imagine higher education taking place without the departmental arrangement. They forget how newly hatched both department and profession are – and how intellectually flimsy were many of the motives that originally spawned the various departments that are now often revered as though, indeed, God himself had designed them on the second day of creation.[36]

Bruce Wilshire has, in fact, proposed an overhaul of the departmental university system as a remedy for the nihilistic consequences of the scientism that has taken hold of analytic philosophy and higher education more broadly. Specifically, Wilshire proposes:

(1) The closure of philosophy departments. Since nearly every discipline in the sciences and humanities involves, at some level, philosophical assumptions and commitments, philosophers should align themselves with whatever departments are closest to their interests and accomplishments. Philosophers of religion, for example, could move into Religious Studies or Theology departments, and by doing so they may be less tempted to ignore the history and practices of the world's great religious traditions.

(2) The requirement that, every five years, each member of the university delivers a presentation addressed to the entire academic community of their university, thus encouraging communication across artificially imposed disciplinary boundaries.

(3) "In the end, we should proceed to a completely decompartmentalized and deprofessionalized university as rapidly as we wisely can. That is, to a *university* that lives up to the literal meaning of the name: that which has a center and turns around it – the creation of meaning, the discovery and husbanding of truth, and the development of centered and expansive persons. What would remain would be a very few general fields, defined in greatly overlapping terms, and headed by universal minds who appear now and again in the strangest places. Consider Isaiah Berlin, Albert Einstein, James Conant, Susanne Langer, or William James himself."[37]

If such proposals were taken up, that would effectively mean the end of academic philosophy as pursued in most parts of the Anglo-American world. But putting an end to the current institutional practice of philosophy demands a corollary reconsideration of the ends (functions and aims) of philosophy and indeed of the institution of the university as a whole.

Universities, indeed, have had a checkered history that many academics, and philosophers especially, like to overlook. C. G. Estabrook observes in an interesting article on this subject that "the first universities arose spontaneously in the optimistic and rationalistic culture of the High Middle Ages, when it was thought that the world could be remade by logic and law."[38] Informal associations or guilds of students and teachers began to form, but "the danger of unregulated critical discussion was apparent to the authorities in feudal society, so they took a step that cleverly controlled this potentially dangerous but apparently necessary activity: they made it official and licensed it."[39] Estabrook goes on to say, "Now teaching had of course been going along swimmingly without licenses, but the introduction of a licensing system had the happy effect from the point of view of those wishing to control teaching that licenses could be lifted."[40] Estabrook then makes an insightful comment that is no doubt lost on much of the present academic establishment:

> One of the best historians I know says that the first thing to ask about any human situation is "Cui bono?" – "Who profits?" Whose interests are being served? If we ask this question about the almost millennium-long history of the university, the answer is monotonously the same: the political elite of each successive society, who – liking to have tame intellectuals about – license the universities and turn them to their purposes.[41]

Universities, like any other institution, are never 'pure' or entirely exempt from the influence of the various networks of power that operate in society. As mentioned earlier, in today's market-driven world universities are expected to perform much like businesses, with the aim of being profitable and productive, especially productive in servicing the technical and vocational needs of industry and government. The value of the university is therefore increasingly viewed in pragmatic terms, so that its importance resides primarily in its capacity to produce lawyers, accountants, doctors, computer specialists and of course scientists and engineers who can be recruited to help build the state's military defence system. No academic, then, works in a political vacuum, but instead of being aware of this and assuming the necessary degree of vigilance, the ahistorical nature of the analytic tradition has made many philosophers from this tradition blind to the wider implications and connections of their work.

In conclusion, then, if philosophy and the institutional structures in which it is embedded are to be renewed, then philosophers themselves have a responsibility to help bring this about. Philosophers can no longer rest content with specialized academic writing, with mechanically producing journal papers and books in conformity to the (largely unwritten) laws enforced by the gate-keepers of the Academy so as to ensure that what is published is as far removed from passion, emotion, wisdom and understanding as possible. As philosophers, we need to find our voice again, to loosen our tongues, as Caputo has done so effectively, and to follow the great poets and visionaries such as Kazantzakis in writing and speaking in impossible languages. "Only write here what is impossible, that ought to be the impossible-rule."[42]

NOTES

Chapter 1

1. Chris Dercon, "Foreword," in Stephanie Rosenthal, *Black Paintings: Robert Rauschenberg, Ad Reinhardt, Mark Rothko, Frank Stella* (Munich: Hatje Cantz Verlag, 2006), p. 7.
2. I do not mean to impugn Reinhardt's black paintings with this comparison, for these paintings have great positive and spiritual worth. As Alfred Barr, Jr., founding director of the Museum of Modern Art, noted: "We believe that Reinhardt's 'black' paintings are among the memorable works of art produced in this country during the 1960s. Painted with exacting craftsmanship, extraordinarily subtle in color, they reveal themselves slowly. They are objects of contemplation, serene events of the spirit, elegant in their mystery. They invite meditation . . .". Quoted in Rosenthal, *Black Paintings*, pp. 35–36.
3. See, for example, John Passmore, "The End of Philosophy?", *Australasian Journal of Philosophy* 74 (1996): 1–19.
4. Friedrich Nietzsche, *Thus Spoke Zarathustra*, trans. Walter Kaufmann (New York: Penguin, 1978), II:19 (pp. 133–34), III:8 (pp. 178–82).
5. Friedrich Nietzsche, *The Gay Science*, trans. Walter Kaufmann (New York: Vintage Books, 1974), §108, p. 167.
6. Interview with Richard Kearney (Paris, 1981), published in Richard Kearney, *Debates in Continental Philosophy: Conversations with Contemporary Thinkers* (New York: Fordham University Press, 2004), p. 84.
7. Robert Nozick, *Philosophical Explanations* (Cambridge, MA: The Belknap Press, 1981), p. 1, emphasis in the original.

Chapter 2

1. Irving Greenberg, "Cloud of Smoke, Pillar of Fire," in John K. Roth and Michael Berenbaum (eds), *Holocaust: Religious and Philosophical Implications* (Minnesota: Paragon House, 1989), p. 315.
2. See, for example, Trakakis, "On the Alleged Failure of Free Will Theodicies: A Reply to Tierno," *Sophia* 42 (2003): 99–106; "Evil and the Complexity of History: A Response to Durston," *Religious Studies* 39 (2003): 451–58; "God, Gratuitous Evil, and van Inwagen's Attempt to Reconcile the Two," *Ars Disputandi: The Online Journal for Philosophy of Religion* [www.Ars Disputandi.org], vol. 3, 2003; "What No Eye Has Seen: The Skeptical Theist Response to Rowe's Evidential Argument from Evil," *Philo* 6 (2003): 263–79; "Second Thoughts on the Alleged Failure of Free Will Theodicies," *Sophia* 43 (2004): 83–89; "Is Theism Capable of Accounting For Any Natural Evil At All?" *International Journal for Philosophy of Religion* 57 (2005): 35–66; "Does Hard Determinism Render the Problem of Evil even Harder?", *Ars Disputandi: The Online Journal for Philosophy of Religion* [www.Ars

Disputandi.org], vol. 6, 2006; and *The God Beyond Belief: In Defence of William Rowe's Evidential Argument from Evil* (Dordrecht: Springer Publishing, 2007).

3. Much of this Section has been distilled from ch. 9 of my *The God Beyond Belief: In Defence of William Rowe's Evidential Argument from Evil*.

4. See John Milton, *Paradise Lost*, ed. John Leonard (London: Penguin, 2000 [originally published in 1667]), Book I, v.26.

5. See Rowe, "Evil and Theodicy," *Philosophical Topics* 16 (1988): 131.

6. Richard Swinburne takes on this ambitious aim when describing the overall goal of his book *Providence and the Problem of Evil* thus: "I am certainly committed to, and sought to argue for, the strong version of the strong thesis: For every instance of evil, God is justified in allowing it" ("Reply to Richard Gale," *Religious Studies* 36 (2000): 221).

7. However, another species of 'greater goods', defended vigorously by Roderick Chisholm and Marilyn Adams, are 'defeater goods', goods which are made up of an organic unity of good and bad elements, with the bad elements somewhat paradoxically rendering the whole better than it would otherwise have been. See Chisholm, "The Defeat of Good and Evil," in Marilyn Adams and Robert Adams (eds), *The Problem of Evil* (Oxford: Oxford University Press, 1990), pp. 53–68, and Marilyn Adams, *Horrendous Evils and the Goodness of God* (Melbourne: Melbourne University Press, 1999), ch. 8.

8. See Alvin Plantinga, "The Free Will Defence," in Max Black (ed.), *Philosophy in America* (London: George Allen & Unwin, 1965), pp. 204–20.

9. A view of this sort is endorsed by Peter van Inwagen, "The Argument from Particular Horrendous Evils," *Proceedings of the American Catholic Philosophical Association* 74 (2000): 66–67, though van Inwagen thinks of stories that might well be true for all we know as 'defences' rather than theodicies, and puts them forward in the context of a sceptical theist outlook.

10. See, for example, Paul Draper, "The Skeptical Theist," in Daniel Howard-Snyder (ed.), *The Evidential Argument from Evil* (Bloomington: Indiana University Press, 1996), pp. 182–87. Cf. the adequacy conditions for theodicy specified by John Hick in "An Irenaean Theodicy," in Stephen T. Davis (ed.), *Encountering Evil: Live Options in Theodicy*, second edition (Louisville: Westminster John Knox Press, 2001), p. 38.

11. For a more detailed account, see ch. 10 of my *The God Beyond Belief*.

12. Hick develops his soul-making theodicy in Part IV of *Evil and the God of Love*, first edition (London: Macmillan, 1966). Apart from this work, other important presentations of his theodicy occur in "God, Evil and Mystery," *Religious Studies* 3 (1968): 539–46; the revised edition of *Evil and the God of Love* (New York: HarperCollins, 1977), which includes an extra chapter where Hick responds to some of his critics; "An Irenaean Theodicy," originally published in Stephen T. Davis (ed.), *Encountering Evil* (Edinburgh: T & T Clark, 1981), pp. 39–52, and republished with some minor amendments in the new edition of Davis' collection issued in 2001 (both editions also contain interesting discussions between Hick and the other contributors); and *Philosophy of Religion*, fourth edition (Englewood Cliffs: Prentice-Hall, 1990), pp. 44–48.

13. Hick, *Evil and the God of Love*, first edition, p. 362.

14. See Hick, *Evil and the God of Love*, first edition, pp. 317–18.

15. Many theists, of course, do not accept libertarianism, but adopt a compatibilist conception of freedom. It is commonly thought, however, that determinism, whether of the hard or soft variety, renders the problem of evil intractable for theism. See, for example, Antony Flew, "Compatibilism, Free Will and God," *Philosophy* 48 (1973): 231–44, Bruce Reichenbach, "Evil and a Reformed View of God," *International Journal for Philosophy of Religion* 24 (1988): 67–85 and Robin Le Poidevin, *Arguing For Atheism: An Introduction to the Philosophy of Religion* (London: Routledge, 1996), pp. 91–96. For an opposing view, see my paper, "Does Hard Determinism Render the Problem of Evil even Harder?".

16. For Swinburne's free will theodicy for natural evil, see his *Providence and the Problem of Evil* (Oxford: Clarendon Press, 1998), pp. 176–92.

17. Hick, *Evil and the God of Love*, revised edition, p. 375. On Hick's eschatology, see also Part V of his *Death and Eternal Life* (Glasgow: Collins, 1976). Hick likes to capture the importance of the afterlife for theodicy with the slogan, 'No theodicy without eschatology' (see, for example, Hick's "Transcendence and Truth," in D. Z. Phillips and Timothy Tessin (eds), *Religion without Transcendence?*, London: Macmillan, 1997, p. 48).

18. See the works listed in note 2 above.

19. One point to note in the meantime is that much of the trouble, as Rowan Williams explains, seems to be caused by the theodicist's overly anthropomorphic conception of divine action. The theodicist's God, Williams writes,

> . . . is (like us) an agent in an environment, who must 'negotiate' purposes and desires in relation to other agencies and presences. But God is not an item in any environment, and God's action has been held, in orthodox Christian thought, to be identical with God's being – that is, what God does is nothing other than God's being actively real. Nothing could add to or diminish this, because God does not belong in an environment where the divine life could be modified by anything else.
> (Williams, "Redeeming Sorrows," in D. Z. Phillips (ed.), *Religion and Morality*, London: Macmillan, 1996, p. 143)

What this indicates is that one's theology (particularly one's conception of God) should begin with, and be informed by, the problem of evil, rather than (as usually happens) attempting to conform one's views on evil and suffering to an already established theology. For an elaboration of this view, see Stewart R. Sutherland, *God, Jesus and Belief: The Legacy of Theism* (Oxford: Basil Blackwell, 1984), ch. 2.

20. One cannot overlook, however, the important contributions to anti-theodicy made by modern Jewish theologians in the wake of the Shoah. See, for example, Zachary Braiterman, *(God) After Auschwitz: Tradition and Change in Post-Holocaust Jewish Thought* (Princeton: Princeton University Press, 1998), where the idea of 'anti-theodicy' receives its first systematic development.

21. See Kenneth Surin, *Theology and the Problem of Evil* (Oxford: Basil Blackwell, 1986), Terrence W. Tilley, *The Evils of Theodicy* (Washington, D.C.: Georgetown University Press, 1991) and D. Z. Phillips, *The Problem of Evil and the Problem of God* (London: SCM Press, 2004).

22. See Phillips, *The Problem of Evil and the Problem of God*, ch. 3.
23. Ibid., ch. 3, §§6–7, pp. 63–71.
24. Ibid., ch. 2, §3, pp. 33–44.
25. As R. F. Holland points out in his paper "On the Form of 'The Problem of Evil'" (collected in his *Against Empiricism: On Education, Epistemology and Value*, Oxford: Basil Blackwell, 1980, pp. 229–43), without the idea of God as a member of a moral community, one cannot speak of God as having or not having morally sufficient reasons (pp. 238–39). Holland, interestingly, goes even further to argue that, even if God were a member of a moral community, it is false that God must have some good reason for what he does (pp. 239–40).
26. Phillips, *The Problem of Evil and the Problem of God*, p. 40, emphasis his.
27. Ibid.
28. Albert Camus, *The Rebel*, trans. Anthony Bower (Harmondsworth: Penguin, 1971), p. 57.
29. William Styron, *Sophie's Choice* (London: Corgi Books, 1980), p. 642.
30. Phillips, *The Problem of Evil and the Problem of God*, p. 43.
31. Ibid., ch. 3, §§3–4, pp. 56–60.
32. Quoted in Phillips, *The Problem of Evil and the Problem of God*, pp. 58–59.
33. Phillips, *The Problem of Evil and the Problem of God*, p. 57, emphases in the original.
34. Ibid., p. 57.
35. Ibid., p. 59.
36. Ibid., p. 60. Note, however, Swinburne's response:

> I am *not* saying that a world with a lot more choice and a lot more opportunity to be of use, together with the bad states which would be needed for that, would be better than our world. There certainly does come a point where additional bad states make things overall worse, and a point at which it would be quite wrong of a creator to create a world with so much bad in it.
> (*Providence and the Problem of Evil*, p. 243, emphasis in the original)

But if the level of suffering in our world is not excessive in the sense of providing more opportunities to be of use than is necessary, then with what confidence can we say that *doubling* the current levels of suffering will be excessive and counter-productive in the relevant respect?

Furthermore, if God subscribes to the 'do evil that good may come' ethic, then should not we do the same? Swinburne's response has been to argue that God, as our creator and benefactor, may have the right to allow us to endure abuse and murder for the sake of some greater good, whereas we do not have those sorts of rights over each other (*Providence and the Problem of Evil*, ch. 12). But see David McNaughton's reply, "Is God (Almost) a Consequentialist? Swinburne's Moral Theory," *Religious Studies* 38 (2002): 265–81, where it is argued that, from a deontological framework, what God has the right to do to us must be tempered by our basic human rights, such as the right not to be sexually abused regardless of any good that may result.

37. Phillips, *The Problem of Evil and the Problem of God*, p. 71, emphasis in the original.
38. Another critic worth mentioning in this context is Michael Levine, who characterizes the responses of Swinburne and (especially) van Inwagen to the problem of evil as "terrible solutions to a horrible problem". With much poignancy, Levine writes:

> If van Inwagen and Swinburne were political figures, there would be protesters on the street. I mean this literally and not polemically. After all, what they have done is to offer not just a prima facie, but an ultimate justification for the holocaust and other horrors. What should be explained is how this has gone virtually unnoticed in the literature.
> ("Contemporary Christian Analytic Philosophy of Religion: Biblical Fundamentalism, Terrible Solutions to A Horrible Problem, and Hearing God," *International Journal for Philosophy of Religion* 48 (2000): 107)

    Levine goes on to suggest that the proposals of Swinburne and van Inwagen are "indicative of the lack of vitality, relevance and 'seriousness' of contemporary Christian analytic philosophy of religion" (p. 112).
39. See the papers by Swinburne and Phillips in Stuart C. Brown (ed.), *Reason and Religion* (Ithaca: Cornell University Press, 1977).
40. Swinburne, "The Problem of Evil," in Brown (ed.), *Reason and Religion*, p. 92.
41. Phillips, "The Problem of Evil," in Brown (ed.), *Reason and Religion*, p. 115.
42. Swinburne, "Postscript," in Brown (ed.), *Reason and Religion*, p. 130, emphasis in the original.
43. Surin, *Theology and the Problem of Evil*, p. 84, emphases in the original. Interestingly, in a more recent paper Swinburne evinces some sympathy with such moral criticisms. After writing that "if the long term is very long, the short term may not be very short" – meaning by this that, if it is an eternity in heaven we stand to gain, then our short-term or temporal sufferings may justifiably be greater than they would be if there were no afterlife – Swinburne adds: "I must admit that whenever I write sentences like the above and then watch some of the world's horrors on TV, I ask myself, 'Do I really mean this?' But in the end I always conclude that I do" ("Response to My Commentators," *Religious Studies* 38 (2002): 305). Some defendants cannot help but indict themselves.
44. Surin, *Theology and the Problem of Evil*, p. 84. The quote is from Adorno's *Negative Dialectics*, trans. E. B. Ashton (London: Routledge & Kegan Paul, 1973), pp. 17–18.
45. Surin, *Theology and the Problem of Evil*, pp. 84–85. Surin notes that he is referencing Stanley Cavell's analysis of the 'grammar' of the refusal to acknowledge the humanity of the other, particularly as found in Cavell's *The Claim of Reason: Wittgenstein, Skepticism, Morality, and Tragedy* (Oxford: Clarendon Press, 1979), pp. 329–496.
46. A further problem with the teleology of suffering which should not go unmentioned relates to its assumption that there can be an 'outweighing' relation between goods and evils, so that (e.g.) the evil of child abuse can be outweighed by the good of free will and the goods free will makes possible (e.g., the ability to enter into relationships of love with others). The problem

here is twofold. First, in order for there to be a scheme of outweighing goods and outweighed evils, it must be possible to isolate, quantify and then compare our multifarious experiences. But does this even make sense? Where, for example, does the experience of child abuse start and end, and how is its degree of badness to be measured and compared against the mere existence of human free will (or the free will of the assailant)? But secondly, even if talk of a particular good outweighing a certain evil made sense, should we be so ready to adopt such a language? Theodicists, unfortunately, never stop to ask whether the language of the marketplace is suited to express moral realities, particularly the horrific moral realities we encounter. Instead, they go about attaching a 'fixed price' to goods and evils (where the value of one good might be +7, while the disvalue of some evil might be –5) and then weighing the one against the other, blithely unaware of the dehumanizing effects of such language. I express my indebtedness here to Rowan Williams's excellent essay, "Redeeming Sorrows."

47. Stewart R. Sutherland, *Atheism and the Rejection of God: Contemporary Philosophy and 'The Brothers Karamazov'* (Oxford: Basil Blackwell, 1977), p. vii.

48. A. Boyce Gibson, *The Religion of Dostoevsky* (London: SCM Press, 1973), p. 176.

49. Gibson, *The Religion of Dostoevsky*, p. 179. The exchange between Ivan and Alyosha occurs in book 5, chapter 4 (entitled 'Mutiny') of *The Brothers Karamazov*.

50. This is how Ivan sarcastically describes his compilation – see Dostoyevsky, *The Brothers Karamazov*, trans. David McDuff (London: Penguin, 1993 [originally published in Russian in 1880]), p. 274.

51. For Ivan's account of these and other instances of horrific evil, see Dostoyevsky, *The Brothers Karamazov*, pp. 274–79. At least some of Ivan's stories are actual incidents that Dostoyevsky had culled from Russian newspapers. For some of the sources Dostoyevsky was relying upon, see Victor Terras, *A Karamazov Companion: Commentary on the Genesis, Language, and Style of Dostoevsky's Novel* (Madison: University of Wisconsin Press, 1981), p. 224 (items 151, 153 and 158).

52. Dostoyevsky, *The Brothers Karamazov*, p. 278.

53. Surin, *Theology and the Problem of Evil*, pp. 52–53, emphasis in the original. Cf. Surin's statement in his paper, "Theodicy?" *Harvard Theological Review* 76 (1983): 243, that "Theodicy is inherently flawed: it requires us to be articulate in the face of the unspeakable." I should also point out that on pp. 96–105 of his *Theology and the Problem of Evil*, Surin provides an excellent analysis of Ivan Karamazov's critique of theodicy.

54. I register my indebtedness here to Robert Solomon's penetrating exploration of tragedy in ch. 5 of his *The Joy of Philosophy: Thinking Thin versus the Passionate Life* (New York: Oxford University Press, 1999). See also James Wetzel, "Can Theodicy Be Avoided? The Claim of Unredeemed Evil," *Religious Studies* 25 (1989): 1–13, who admits that "the vice of speculative theodicy is that it cannot accept the possibility of irredeemable evil" (p. 8), even though he goes on to argue, against Surin, that traditional theodicy cannot be avoided.

55. Dostoyevsky, *The Brothers Karamazov*, p. 281.
56. Stump, "Suffering and Redemption: A Reply to Smith," *Faith and Philosophy* 2 (1985): 433, emphasis hers. Similar sentiments are recorded by William Alston, "The Inductive Argument from Evil and the Human Cognitive Condition," *Philosophical Perspectives* 5 (1991): 48, Marilyn Adams, *Horrendous Evils and the Goodness of God*, pp. 29–31, and Michael Tooley, "The Argument from Evil," *Philosophical Perspectives* 5 (1991): 113.
57. Michael Scott expresses an objection to theodicies raised by Kenneth Surin as follows:

> It is one thing to claim that moral evil is justified as the inevitable consequence of human beings being free and responsible; it is quite another to suggest to a person who has been raped that the suffering involved in that experience is in some way balanced out by God's gift of free will to human beings. The failure of the practice of theodicy in connecting with the practical realities of evil seems to leave the theodicist vulnerable to the charge of moral insensitivity.
> (Scott, "The Morality of Theodicies," *Religious Studies* 32 (1996): 2)

It should be noted, however, that the general practice of free will theodicists nowadays is to abide by the adequacy condition identified above so as to avoid the kind of problems mentioned by Scott. Whether such a move can meet all the difficulties raised by the anti-theodicist is another matter.

58. Children occupy a special place in Dostoyevsky's novels, which often highlight (but without idealizing) the innocence and unquestioning love of children. The precious character of childhood, and of the memories it leaves behind, are also frequently stressed by Dostoyevsky. It is not surprising, then, to find that Dostoyevsky enjoyed an especially close relationship with children. His second wife, Anna Grigorievna, recalls in her memoirs that,

> He [her husband, Fyodor] had a special ability to talk with children, to enter into their world, win their trust (and this even with strange children he met by accident) and get the child so interested that he would become gay and obedient at once. I account for this in his unflagging love for little children, which told him how to behave in a given situation.

(Anna Dostoevsky, *Dostoevsky: Reminiscences*, trans. and ed. Beatrice Stillman, New York: Liveright Publishing, 1975, p. 283.) I explore some of the distinctive characteristics of childhood, and what they have to teach us, in "Becoming Children: The Hidden Meaning of the Incarnation," *Theandros: An Online Journal of Orthodox Christian Theology and Philosophy* [www.theandros.com], vol. 3, no. 3, Spring/Summer 2006.

59. Dostoyevsky, *The Brothers Karamazov*, p. 281.
60. Phillips, *The Problem of Evil and the Problem of God*, pp. 85–86. An additional difficulty in the idea of evil as something that can be compensated for or redeemed is that this view naturally leads to a denial of the reality of

evil or to the belief that evil is not as bad as it initially seems. Consider, for example, Alexander Pope's infamous lines:

> All Discord, Harmony, not understood;
> All partial Evil, universal Good:
> And, spite of Pride, in erring Reason's spite,
> One truth is clear, 'Whatever IS, is RIGHT.'
> (*An Essay on Man*, Epistle I, vv. 291–94, in John Butt (ed.), *The Poems of Alexander Pope*, London: Methuen & Co., 1963, p. 515)

To be sure, theodicists vehemently deny that they are committed to the unreality of evil. They would argue that, in describing, say, the everlasting post-mortem beatific vision of God as a good which 'redeems' or 'defeats' the evils in one's life, the evils continue to be thought of as evil. However, the theodicist adds, viewed *sub specie aerternitatis* the evils one suffers can no longer be seen as destroying the value and meaning of one's life, for they will then be seen as somewhat trivial in comparison to the glorification experienced in heaven (see, for example, Romans 8:18) and as providing various benefits not otherwise obtainable (e.g., character growth). But this, I suggest, is to effect a change in our perspective on evil that is so radical as to deaden our moral sensibilities, particularly our sense of horror and disgust aroused by much evil. Stewart Sutherland develops this view in response to Marilyn Adams, who appeals to the experience of the beatific vision as an incommensurable good that both outweighs and defeats all evils, even evils of the worst or horrific kind, that one may have undergone in one's temporal life. Sutherland replies that "at its minimum the defeat of horrendous evil requires a significant qualification of the initial moral perceptions and commitments which lead to the classification of evils as horrendous evils. That is to say, the individual must, in the end, come to the view that viewed in a proper light horrendous evils are not so bad after all!" (Sutherland, "Horrendous Evils and the Goodness of God," *The Aristotelian Society Supplementary Volume* 63 (1989): 317). See also Brice R. Wachterhauser, "The Problem of Evil and Moral Scepticism," *International Journal for Philosophy of Religion* 17 (1985): 167–74, where it is argued that the very condition of having a *moral* perspective is the ability to recognize at least some instances of evil as unjustifiable.

61. Dostoyevsky, *The Brothers Karamazov*, p. 282, emphasis in the original. One is reminded here of the following exchange between Dr Bernard Rieux and the Jesuit priest, Father Paneloux, in Albert Camus' novel, *The Plague*:

> 'I understand,' Paneloux said in a low voice. 'That sort of thing [the death of a child resulting from a plague] is revolting because it passes our human understanding. But perhaps we should love what we cannot understand.'
>
> Rieux straightened up slowly. He gazed at Paneloux, summoning to his gaze all the strength and fervour he could muster against his weariness. Then he shook his head.
>
> 'No, Father. I've a very different idea of love. And until my dying day I shall refuse to love a scheme of things in which children are put to torture.'

Camus, *The Plague*, trans. Stuart Gilbert (London: Penguin, 1960), p. 178.

62. Dostoyevsky, *The Brothers Karamazov*, p. 282. Dostoyevsky, particularly in his younger days, was heavily influenced by the work of Schiller (in a letter to his brother Mikhail in 1840, Dostoyevsky wrote: "I have learned Schiller by heart, spoken Schiller, raved Schiller," quoted in Kenneth Lantz, *The Dostoevsky Encyclopedia*, Westport: Greenwood Press, 2004, p. 385). This influence is evident in Ivan's famous phrase of 'returning my entry ticket', which is borrowed from Zhukovsky's Russian translation of Schiller's poem, "Resignation" (1784), specifically lines 3–4 of the third stanza: "The entrance letter to an earthly paradise / I return to Thee unopened" (see Victor Terras, *A Karamazov Companion*, p. 16).

63. Surin, *Theology and the Problem of Evil*, p. 98. I strongly recommend Stewart Sutherland's insightful analysis of Ivan's atheism. Sutherland detects three strands in Ivan's subtle form of atheism, the first of which is the rebellion against God mentioned above, the second consists of viewing God in terms that are "profoundly and intentionally blasphemous", while the third involves a denial of the validity and intelligibility of the religious way of life. See Sutherland, *Atheism and the Rejection of God*, ch. 2.

64. Dostoyevsky, *The Brothers Karamazov*, p. 282.

65. It might be objected that Kant's categorical imperative as formulated here (the so-called 'humanity formulation') does not rule out using people as means to our ends – something, in fact, we regularly do – but using people *merely* as means to our ends. I do not wish to dispute this. My point, however, is that theodicists do tend to picture God as treating human creatures as mere means to his ultimate ends.

Consider, for example, Swinburne's suggestion that, as long as God grants you a life that is overall good, he has the right to treat you as a means to some end, or more specifically, he has the right to allow you to suffer so as to provide opportunities to others to respond well to that suffering (*Providence and the Problem of Evil*, p. 233). But, going by the kinds of calculations theodicists (Swinburne included) like to make, it is relatively easy for God to ensure that you have a life that is good overall. For it should be noted that, in this context, 'life' denotes one's entire (pre- and post-mortem) life, and that the value of the heavenly afterlife is thought to be an incommensurable good, or at least a good that far outweighs any merely temporal good or evil. In that case, God can deliberately inflict serious harm on someone for the good of others, but then ensure that the sufferer has a life that is good overall by simply offering them a heavenly afterlife as compensation. It is doubtful that God, in violating the basic dignity of a person in this way, is treating them as an end in themselves or setting great store on their humanity.

For a helpful discussion of Kant's 'formula of humanity', see Thomas E. Hill, Jr., "Humanity as an End in Itself," *Ethics* 91 (1980): 84–99, where Hill argues that, for Kant, to treat human persons as ends in themselves is to view the humanity in persons as having an unconditional and incomparable worth that cannot be traded off for something of greater value.

66. But if theodicy is rejected, how should the theist respond to the problem of evil? This is an important question, deserving a chapter in its own right. Briefly put, the kind of response I would favour is that offered by Dostoyevsky

himself, who sought to (indirectly) counter Ivan's rebellion by juxtaposing it with the Christian form of life embodied by Alyosha and, especially, Father Zosima. For further details on this kind of strategy, see Sutherland, *Atheism and the Rejection of God*, chs. 6–8.

67. David Ray Griffin, *God, Power, and Evil: A Process Theodicy* (Philadelphia: The Westminster Press, 1976), p. 16.
68. Tilley, *The Evils of Theodicy*, p. 231.
69. Tilley, *The Evils of Theodicy*, p. 231. The tendency to fatalism, or to a sense of passivity, is created by the theodicist's view that no evil is gratuitous, from which it may be inferred that there is little point in attempting to prevent a particular evil from occurring since the evil, even if it were to occur, would only help to serve some purpose ordained by God. Some, indeed, have thought that this exposes a fundamental incoherence in the project of developing 'greater-good' theodicies. See, for example, William Hasker, "The Necessity of Gratuitous Evil," *Faith and Philosophy* 9 (1992): 23–44.
70. Surin, "Theodicy?" p. 230. The footnote quoted is from note 10, p. 230 of Surin's paper.
71. Surin, *Theology and the Problem of Evil*, p. 50. For an excellent illustration of this premise, see the essays in Part II of John K. Roth (ed.), *Genocide and Human Rights: A Philosophical Guide* (Basingstoke: Palgrave Macmillan, 2005), these essays showing the various ways in which philosophy has been complicit in genocide.
72. Surin, *Theology and the Problem of Evil*, p. 51.
73. Ibid.
74. See Richard T. McClleland, "Normal Narcissism and the Need for Theodicy," in Peter van Inwagen (ed.), *Christian Faith and the Problem of Evil* (Grand Rapids: William B. Eerdmans Publishing Company, 2004), pp. 185–206. In this perceptive essay on the (pathological) psychological motivations lying behind theodicy, McClleland speaks of the abstractions of theodicists as producing an "Echo effect." The reference here is to the myth of Narcissus, as recounted by Ovid, where the nymph Echo is deprived of her powers of speech by Hera (the wife of Zeus and goddess of marriage), and is consequently unable to express any thoughts of her own, but can only repeat (or echo) the last words that she hears from others. But Echo is best known for falling in love with the beautiful Narcissus, who shuns her advances and as a result she gradually wastes away in grief until she is nothing more than an answering voice. McClleland explains that the nymph Echo "has ceased to be a real character at all, so lacking in psychological depth and solidity as finally to be nothing but a disembodied and depersonalized voice" (p. 194). Theodicies, McClleland goes on to add, have a similar (Echo) effect when they fail to give the sufferer a voice, and instead treat their sufferings in an abstract and hence psychologically shallow manner (pp. 202–04).
75. Plantinga, *God, Freedom, and Evil* (Grand Rapids: Eerdmans, 1977), pp. 28–29, emphases in the original.
76. Ibid., pp. 63–64, emphasis in the original.
77. David O'Connor, "In Defense of Theoretical Theodicy," *Modern Theology* 5 (1988): 64. On the previous page of his paper (p. 63), O'Connor draws the distinction between the conceptual and the ministerial problems as follows: "In the domain of the [conceptual problem of evil] success and failure are

measured by rules of logic and sufficiency of evidence, that is, by making the
right distinctions and by having good arguments . . . while in the [domain of
the ministerial problem of evil] the measures of success and failure are subjective, existential, and pragmatic. In the former, we succeed to the degree we
come out with a good explanation, while we succeed in the latter to the degree
we cope."

78. See Scott, "The Morality of Theodicies," p. 3.
79. Ibid., p. 5.
80. O'Connor, "In Defense of Theoretical Theodicy," p. 68.
81. See Scott, "The Morality of Theodicies," p. 6.
82. Surin, *Theology and the Problem of Evil*, p. 50.
83. Sutherland, in *Atheism and the Rejection of God*, pp. 141–42, points out that
    theodicy offers a set of emotions or emotional responses to the world which is
    intended to appease and placate sufferers, and to therefore sanction evil
    (echoes of Marx's 'opium of the people'). By way of contrast, consider the
    emotional response to the world's atrocities exemplified by Ivan Karamazov:
    anger, bitterness, protest and rebellion. As Sutherland notes, to seek to alter
    these emotions or to question their appropriateness would amount to rede-
    scribing the situation facing Ivan, and in that sense it would be to falsify the
    facts concerning evil – this is precisely what Ivan believes is asked of him by
    the theodicist.
84. Greenberg's test, it might be objected, would have the effect of reducing us all
    to a position of *silence* in the face of evil. I do not think this is right. Responses
    other than silence to the problem of evil are available, as indicated in note 66
    above. Nevertheless, the importance of silence is usually overlooked by
    analytic philosophers, who rush in where angels fear to tread, as it were, by
    not hesitating to tell us God's reasons for permitting suffering or why such
    reasons cannot be known by us. This attitude can be contrasted with the
    reticence of Holocaust survivors to write and talk about their experiences,
    many waiting ten to twenty years before breaking their silence. "They were
    afraid," Elie Wiesel explains, "that, in the very process of telling the tale, they
    would betray it . . . So we didn't speak about it because we were afraid of
    committing a sin" ("Richard L. Rubenstein and Elie Wiesel: An Exchange," in
    Roth and Berenbaum (eds), *Holocaust: Religious and Philosophical Implica-
    tions*, p. 367). To be sure, the only credible *immediate* response to evil is not
    talk, but *action*. As John Roth explains, in an essay which also takes
    Greenberg's statement as its epigraph, "Talk about a theodicy of protest or
    about antitheodicy would not be much more credible in the literal presence of
    the burning children. Efforts to rescue the children and to resist the powers
    that took their lives would be the only statements that could fully approach
    credibility in those dire straits" ("Theistic Antitheodicy," *American Journal of
    Theology and Philosophy* 25 (2004): 277).
85. Voltaire, *Candide, or Optimism*, trans. John Butt (London: Penguin, 1947),
    ch. 6, p. 37.
86. This prioritization of the 'objective' over the 'subjective' illustrates that the
    theodicist (like many in the analytical tradition of philosophy) fails to see that
    someone who has suffered some painful loss or illness may have acquired an
    insight or understanding of suffering not available to one who has not gone
    through such an experience (much like people who have lived in poverty or

under oppression may be aware of social realities that those in positions of power and wealth cannot but be oblivious to).

87. See Emmanuel Levinas, "Useless Suffering," trans. Richard Cohen, in Robert Bernasconi and David Wood (eds), *The Provocation of Levinas: Rethinking the Other* (London: Routledge, 1988), p. 163. For further discussion of Levinas' rejection of theodicy, see Richard A. Cohen, *Ethics, Exegesis and Philosophy: Interpretation after Levinas* (Cambridge: Cambridge University Press, 2001), ch. 8, and Richard J. Bernstein, "Evil and the Temptation of Theodicy," in Simon Critchley and Robert Bernasconi (eds), *The Cambridge Companion to Levinas* (Cambridge: Cambridge University Press, 2002), pp. 252–67.
88. Williams, "Redeeming Sorrows," p. 148.
89. Ibid., p. 147, emphasis in the original.

Chapter 3

1. Georges Bataille, "Un-knowing and Its Consequences," *October* 36 (1986): 80.
2. Ayer does not mention this meeting in his second autobiography, *More of My Life* (first published in 1984), where he recounts his post-WWII movements. However, in his first autobiography, *Part of My Life*, which covers the first thirty-five years of his life (i.e., 1910–1945), Ayer recalls an earlier and similar encounter with Bataille in 1945:

> Isabel [Delmer] had many friends in Paris and introduced me to them. It was through her that I met the writer Georges Bataille, whom I vainly tried to persuade that time was not merely a human invention.

A. J. Ayer, *Part of My Life: The Memoirs of a Philosopher* (New York: Harcourt Brace Jovanovich, 1977), p. 288. Given the similarities between Ayer's account and that provided by Bataille, it is possible that Ayer has mistakenly placed the 1951 meeting in 1945. Consider also Ayer's comments on his friendship with Maurice Merleau-Ponty:

> Though it is often conducted in terms of which it is difficult to make much sense, the investigation of concepts by Husserl and his followers bears some affinity to the sort of conceptual analysis that G.E. Moore engaged in, and it might therefore have been expected that Merleau-Ponty and I should find some common ground for philosophical discussion. We did indeed attempt it on several occasions, but we never got very far before we began to wrangle over some point of principle, on which neither of us would yield. Since these arguments tended to become acrimonious, we tacitly agreed to drop them and meet on a purely social level, which still left us quite enough to talk about. (*Part of My Life*, p. 285)

3. See Carnap, "The Elimination of Metaphysics Through Logical Analysis of Language," originally published in German in 1932, published in English with

translation by Arthur Pap in A. J. Ayer (ed.), *Logical Positivism* (Glencoe: The Free Press, 1959), pp. 60–81, esp. pp. 69–73. A similar assessment has been provided more recently by Paul Edwards in *Heidegger's Confusions* (Amherst: Prometheus Books, 2004), where Edwards writes that "sober and rational persons will continue to regard the whole Heidegger phenomenon as a grotesque aberration of the human mind" (p. 47). These uncharitable readings of Heidegger may be compared with Gilbert Ryle's generous, though not uncritical, review of Heidegger's *Sein und Zeit*, in *Mind* 38 (1929): 355–70, though Ryle too became increasingly hostile towards Continental philosophy (phenomenology especially) in the latter part of his career.

4. Derrida's essays in this exchange are collected in *Limited Inc* (Evanston: Northwestern University Press, 1988). For Searle's contribution to this 'debate', see his "Reiterating the Differences: A Reply to Derrida," *Glyph* 1 (1977): 198–208.

5. Letter to the London *Times*, 9 May 1992. Reprinted in Jacques Derrida, *Points . . . Interviews, 1974–1994*, ed. Elisabeth Weber, trans. Peggy Kamuf *et al.* (Stanford: Stanford University Press, 1995), pp. 419–21.

6. Quoted in Simon Glendinning, "Analytic Philosophy," in John Protevi (ed.), *A Dictionary of Continental Philosophy* (New Haven: Yale University Press, 2006), p. 27.

7. William Charlton, *The Analytic Ambition: An Introduction to Philosophy* (Oxford: Blackwell, 1991), p. 3. An important exception worth mentioning are the biannual conferences convened by the European Society for Philosophy of Religion, which are attended by both analytic and Continental philosophers. (Thanks to Marcel Sarot for bringing this to my attention.)

8. Quoted in Glendinning, "Analytic Philosophy," in John Protevi (ed.), *A Dictionary of Continental Philosophy*, p. 27.

9. Gilles Deleuze and Félix Guattari, *What Is Philosophy?*, trans. Hugh Tomlinson and Graham Burchell (New York: Columbia University Press, 1994), p. 1, emphasis in the original.

10. In talking about 'Continental philosophy' I realize that I am contradicting the very practice of many philosophers who fit into this category, especially those on the Continent, who do not like to identify themselves as 'Continental philosophers'. As Simon Glendinning points out, "It is arguable that the construction of the category of continental philosophy has been the *sine qua non* of the formation of the analytic movement: calling a work by that name has enabled self-styled analytic philosophers to render inaccessible to themselves whatever they have been interested in underestimating" ("Analytic Philosophy," p. 28). It should be borne in mind, however, that the term 'Continental philosophy' is now increasingly used as a positive self-designation by many (see, for example, the change in the title of the influential journal *Man and World* to its current *Continental Philosophy Review*, and the publication of such reference works as *A Dictionary of Continental Philosophy*). This development, however, is mainly restricted to the Anglophone world.

11. I therefore disagree with Simon Glendinning's view (in "Continental Philosophy," in John Shand (ed.), *Fundamentals of Philosophy*, London: Routledge, 2003, pp. 408–42) that the category of 'Continental philosophy' ought to be shunned on the grounds that it overlooks the diversity of work produced by

thinkers who are said to fall within that tradition. I also disagree with those who argue that the distinction between analytic and Continental philosophy has little to recommend it. Stephen Priest, for example, contends that this distinction "enshrines several confusions and considerable historical naïveté" and that it "can be exposed methodologically, geographically, and historically" ("'Continental' and 'Analytic'," in Ted Honderich (ed.), *The Oxford Companion to Philosophy*, second edition, Oxford: Oxford University Press, 2005, pp. 172–74). See also the "Introduction" in Brian Leiter (ed.), *The Future For Philosophy* (Oxford: Clarendon Press, 2004), esp. pp. 11–17.

12. Manoussakis, "Religion, Philosophy of," in John Protevi (ed.), *A Dictionary of Continental Philosophy*, p. 492.

13. See Caputo's intellectual autobiographies, "Of Mystics, Magi, and Deconstructionists," in James R. Watson (ed.), *Portraits of American Continental Philosophers* (Bloomington: Indiana University Press, 1999), pp. 25–33, and "Confessions of a Postmodern Catholic: From Saint Thomas to Derrida," in Curtis L. Hancock and Brendan Sweetman (eds), *Faith and the Life of the Intellect* (Washington D.C.: The Catholic University of America Press, 2003), pp. 64–92.

14. John Caputo, *Demythologizing Heidegger* (Bloomington: Indiana University Press, 1993), and *Against Ethics: Contributions to a Poetics of Obligation with Constant Reference to Deconstruction* (Bloomington: Indiana University Press, 1993).

15. Alvin Plantinga, *The Nature of Necessity* (Oxford: Clarendon Press, 1974), p. 198.

16. For an excellent recent example of this penchant for formalization, see Jordan Howard Sobel, *Logic and Theism: Arguments For and Against Beliefs in God* (Cambridge: Cambridge University Press, 2004).

17. Plantinga construes warrant as "that property – or better, quantity – enough of which is what makes the difference between knowledge and mere true belief," which he then goes on to define in terms of proper function: "A belief has warrant just if it is produced by cognitive processes or faculties that are functioning properly, in a cognitive environment that is propitious for that exercise of cognitive powers, according to a design plan that is successfully aimed at the production of true belief" (*Warranted Christian Belief*, Oxford: Oxford University Press, 2000, p. xi).

18. Plantinga, *Warranted Christian Belief*, pp. 188–89, emphases in the original.

19. Plantinga, *The Nature of Necessity*, p. 185, emphasis in the original.

20. Caputo, *On Religion* (London: Routledge, 2001), p. 2.

21. Ibid., p. 132.

22. Caputo, *The Prayers and Tears of Jacques Derrida: Religion without Religion* (Bloomington: Indiana University Press, 1997), p. 332.

23. The extracts that follow are taken from pp. 283–95 in Caputo's *The Weakness of God: A Theology of the Event* (Bloomington: Indiana University Press, 2006). The in-text page references refer to this work.

24. David E. Cooper, "Analytic and Continental Philosophy," *Proceedings of the Aristotelian Society* 94 (1994): 3, where he writes: "We know where Quine or Derrida belongs, before grasping what he is saying, from the way he says it."

25. In fact, literary forms of discourse are often seen in Continental thought as superior to (or encompassing all) other forms of discourse, including scientific

ones. See, for example, Roland Barthes, "Science Versus Literature," *The Times Literary Supplement*, 28 September 1967, pp. 897–98.

26. Caputo has not always written in this fashion, as he himself points out: "I have always been writing about the intersection of religion and philosophy, but in the beginning I undertook a more scientific, a more exegetical interpretation of the relationship between Heidegger and the religious tradition. Those first texts – *Heidegger and Aquinas* [published in 1982] and *The Mystical Element* [published in 1978, revised edition published in 1986] – were written with a kind of traditional academic propriety, a calm, professional style. My own personal voice was muted there. Then, in *Radical Hermeneutics* [published in 1987], I found my own voice." Quoted in B. Keith Putt, "What Do I Love When I Love My God? An Interview with John D. Caputo," in James H. Olthuis (ed.), *Religion with/out Religion: The Prayers and Tears of John D. Caputo* (London: Routledge, 2002), pp. 150–51. In a subsequent interview, Caputo attributed this change to the influence of Derrida: "Derrida loosened my tongue, that is to say, he gave me the nerve to write like Kierkegaard" ("Loosening Philosophy's Tongue: A Conversation with Jack Caputo," with Carl Raschke, *Journal of Cultural and Religious Theory* [www.jcrt.org], vol. 3, no. 2 (April 2002), §8.

27. Jeremy Biles, "Review of Slavoj Zizek, *The Puppet and the Dwarf: The Perverse Core of Christianity*," *The Journal of Religion* 86 (2006): 501.

28. Ibid.

29. Ibid., p. 502. Cf. a reviewer's description of another recent Žižek book: "Audacious and vertiginous, this book is everything one expects from him [i.e., Žižek], a heady mix of psychoanalysis, politics, theology, philosophy, and cultural studies that will leave the reader both exhausted and exhilarated" (Marcus Pound, "Review of *Conversations with Žižek* by Slavoj Žižek and Glyn Daly," *The Heythrop Journal* 47 (2006): 680).

30. Analytic philosophy, to be sure, has also taken an interdisciplinary turn of late, but of a very different kind, one that overlaps with the scientific inquiries pursued in fields such as biology, physics, computer science, linguistics, economics and empirical psychology.

31. A. W. Moore, "Arguing with Derrida," in Simon Glendinning (ed.), *Arguing with Derrida* (Oxford: Blackwell, 2001), p.79.

32. Engel, "Analytic Philosophy and Cognitive Norms," p. 222.

33. Frank P. Ramsey, *The Foundations of Mathematics and Other Logical Essays*, ed. R. B. Braithwaite (London: Routledge & Kegan Paul, 1931), p. 263, note 1.

34. P. M. S. Hacker, "The Rise of Twentieth Century Analytic Philosophy," in Hans-Johann Glock (ed.), *The Rise of Analytic Philosophy* (Oxford: Blackwell, 1997), pp. 51–76.

35. Michael Beaney, "Analysis," §9, in Edward N. Zalta (ed.), *The Stanford Encyclopedia of Philosophy (Summer 2003 Edition)* URL = http://plato.stanford.edu/archives/sum2003/entries/analysis/.

36. A. P. Martinich and David Sosa (eds), *Analytic Philosophy: An Anthology* (Malden: Blackwell, 2001), p. 3.

37. Ordinary language philosophers, in particular, would not have viewed their investigations in line with the broadly scientific model by which I characterize

the analytic enterprise. Rather, their conception of philosophy, derived in large part from Wittgenstein's *Philosophical Investigations*, was the deflationary one of showing how philosophical problems are not genuine problems to be resolved through the construction of elaborate theories, but pseudo-problems arising solely from the misuse of language.

38. Scott Soames characterizes the contemporary practice of analytic philosophy as 'the era of specialisation', and comments that, "In my opinion, philosophy has changed substantially in the last thirty or so years. Gone are the days of large, central figures, whose work is accessible and relevant to, as well as read by, nearly all analytic philosophers. Philosophy has become a highly organized discipline, done by specialists primarily for other specialists" (Soames, *Philosophical Analysis in the Twentieth Century*, vol. 2, Princeton: Princeton University Press, 2003, p. 463).

39. In the heyday of positivism, the conceptual adequacy test would have included, or been supplemented by, a test for meaningfulness which would rely on some form or other of the verificationist theory of meaning.

40. See, for example, the analyses provided in Edward R. Wierenga, *The Nature of God: An Inquiry into Divine Attributes* (Ithaca: Cornell University Press, 1989), Joshua Hoffman and Gary S. Rosenkrantz, *The Divine Attributes* (Oxford: Blackwell, 2002), and Daniel J. Hill, *Divinity and Maximal Greatness* (London: Routledge, 2005).

41. The programme of offering a coherent account of the nature of God and providing cogent arguments for the existence of God is today widely associated with the work of Richard Swinburne, who carries out this programme in *The Coherence of Theism* (Oxford: Clarendon Press, 1977; revised edition: 1993) and *The Existence of God* (Oxford: Clarendon Press, 1979; revised edition: 1991, second edition: 2004). Swinburne describes and defends his programme in "Philosophical Theism," in D. Z. Phillips and Timothy Tessin (eds), *Philosophy of Religion in the 21st Century* (Basingstoke: Palgrave, 2001), pp. 3–20.

42. Some of these criticisms are nicely summarized and defended by William Wainwright in "Philosophical Theology at the End of the Century," in D. Z. Phillips and Timothy Tessin (eds), *Philosophy of Religion in the 21st Century*, pp. 21–30. For an excellent critique of modern treatments of Anselm's ontological argument, see John Clayton, "The Otherness of Anselm," in Orrin F. Summerell (ed.), *The Otherness of God* (Charlottesville: University Press of Virginia, 1998), pp. 14–34.

43. See Norman Kretzmann, "Abraham, Isaac, and Euthyphro: God and the Basis of Morality," in Donald V. Stump, James A. Arieti, Lloyd Gerson and Eleonore Stump (eds), *Hamartia: The Concept of Error in the Western Tradition. Essays in Honor of John M. Crossett* (New York: Edwin Mellen Press, 1983), pp. 27–50.

44. Hick has defended this position in a number of places, but perhaps most thoroughly in *An Interpretation of Religion: Human Responses to the Transcendent*, second edition (Basingstoke: Palgrave, 2004; first edition published in 1989).

45. It is interesting to note the optimism of many analytic philosophers of religion on the issue of how much progress, if any, has been made in their field. Consider, for example, the following assessment by Robert Adams, where he

looks back to the mid-1950s when he took up the formal study of philosophy: "Despite the formidable obstacle posed by the arguments and concerns surrounding the verifiability theory [of meaning], we hoped that the methods of analytical philosophy might be used to achieve some progress with regard to theological questions – and I believe these hopes have been realized in significant measure over the last forty years" ("Reflections on Analytical Philosophical Theology," in William J. Wainwright (ed.), *God, Philosophy and Academic Culture: A Discussion Between Scholars in the AAR and the APA*, Atlanta: Scholars Press, 1996, p. 80).

46. Levy, "Analytic and Continental Philosophy: Explaining the Differences," *Metaphilosophy* 34 (2003): 300–01.
47. There are, however, some important affinities between modernist art and analytic philosophy, as John Skorupski points out in "The Legacy of Modernism," *Proceedings of the Aristotelian Society* 91 (1991): 17–18.
48. It is indeed this push towards novelty and iconoclasm that has contributed to many of the criticisms voiced against Continental philosophy. Gary Gutting, for example, has noted that the emphasis on novelty and iconoclasm is "responsible for the continentalists' characteristic weakness of pretentious obscurity. When the effort to move creatively beyond old categories fails, as it usually does, the result may well be little more than self-important gibberish or, marginally better, an excruciating restatement of the obvious." ("'Rethinking Intuition': A Historical and Metaphilosophical Introduction," in Michael R. DePaul and William Ramsey (eds), *Rethinking Intuition: The Psychology of Intuition and Its Role in Philosophical Inquiry*, Lanham: Rowman & Littlefield, 1998, p. 10.)
49. Gilles Deleuze and Félix Guattari state that "philosophy is the art of forming, inventing, and fabricating concepts" (*What Is Philosophy?*, p. 2).
50. Cooper, "Analytic and Continental Philosophy," p. 4.
51. Ibid. This is, however, a trend on the wane within analytic philosophy, particularly with the recent rise of 'applied ethics', where issues of general public concern (such as the justification of war and our treatment of animals and the natural environment) are discussed in a way that is integrated with broader philosophical research in areas such as political and moral theory, and even metaphysics and epistemology.
52. Levy, "Analytic and Continental Philosophy: Explaining the Differences," p. 301. On the prominence given to critique and emancipation in the Continental tradition, see Simon Critchley, *Continental Philosophy: A Very Short Introduction* (Oxford: Oxford University Press, 2001), ch. 4. But as Critchley points out (on pp. 99–100), analytic philosophy also at times takes on an overtly political programme of social change. Critchley cites the example of the Vienna Circle, where the left-leaning factions liked to draw connections between the overthrow of metaphysics and the establishment of a radical democracy. However, one could also point to recent work being done in areas such as feminism and environmental ethics within analytic circles, which is sometimes integrated with more traditionally analytic subjects such as logic and metaphysics (the contribution of Richard Routley, who later changed his name to Richard Sylvan, to non-standard logics and environmental philosophy is one among many examples of this tendency).

53. Cooper, "Analytic and Continental Philosophy," p. 9. Cooper is quoting from Kant's *Political Writings*, trans. H. Nisbet (Cambridge: Cambridge University Press, 1991), p. 54.

54. As Simon Critchley puts it, "for the Continental tradition, philosophical problems do not fall from the sky ready-made and cannot be treated as elements in some ahistorical fantasy of *philosophia perennis*. One's reading of a classic philosophical text from the tradition does not so much take the form of a college dinner conversation, as much as a meeting with a stranger from a distant land whose language one is only beginning to understand, and with difficulty" (*Continental Philosophy*, p. 59).

Chapter 4

1. Merold Westphal, "Prolegomena To Any Future Philosophy of Religion Which Will Be Able To Come Forth As Prophecy," *International Journal for Philosophy of Religion* 4 (1973): 129–50. Many of the themes of this paper subsequently received further treatment by Westphal, particularly in the light of postmodern critiques of Western philosophy. See especially Westphal's *Overcoming Onto-theology: Toward a Postmodern Christian Faith* (New York: Fordham University Press, 2001).

2. Westphal, "Prolegomena," p. 141.

3. Ibid., p. 142.

4. Ibid., pp. 143–44.

5. Ibid., p. 144.

6. Ibid., p. 147.

7. Ibid., p. 148.

8. Ibid., p. 149.

9. Ibid.

10. Caputo, "The Poetics of the Impossible and the Kingdom of God," in Philip Goodchild (ed.), *Rethinking Philosophy of Religion: Approaches from Continental Philosophy* (New York: Fordham University Press, 2002), p. 45.

11. In this respect, Caputo is even in conflict with some members of the Continental camp, such as Westphal and Marion, who advocate a 'religion *with* religion'. See, for example, the criticisms of Marion's ecclesiology in Caputo's "How To Avoid Speaking of God: The Violence of Natural Theology," in Eugene Thomas Long (ed.), *Prospects for Natural Theology* (Washington, D.C.: The Catholic University of America Press, 1992), pp. 143–47, and Caputo's critique of Westphal's views in "Methodological Postmodernism: On Merold Westphal's *Overcoming Onto-theology*," *Faith and Philosophy* 22 (2005): 284–96.

12. Caputo notes that his attempt in *The Prayers and Tears of Jacques Derrida* to portray Derrida as a deeply religious thinker was received with much surprise and chagrin, first from religious believers who could not see how deconstruction could be made compatible with religious faith, but also from "secularizing deconstructionists, who on the question of religion repeat deeply modernist critiques of religion with perfect loyalty." See Caputo, "Messianic Postmodernism," in D. Z. Phillips and Timothy Tessin (eds), *Philosophy of Religion in the*

21st Century, pp. 158–59. Cf. Caputo's comment in *The Prayers and Tears of Jacques Derrida*: "Deconstruction: a *skandalon* to Derrida's right-wing critics and a stumbling block to his securalist defenders" (p. 212).

13. For a lucid discussion of these themes, see Caputo's *Deconstruction in a Nutshell: A Conversation with Jacques Derrida* (New York: Fordham University Press, 1997), chs 5 and 6. Indeed, Caputo often notes that the most religiously interesting dimension of Derrida's thought is its reclamation of the voice of prophetic Judaism, rather than its apophatic side.

14. Derrida, "Faith and Knowledge: The Two Sources of 'Religion' at the Limits of Reason Alone," in Jacques Derrida and Gianni Vattimo (eds), *Religion* (Stanford: Stanford University Press, 1998), p. 17.

15. Caputo, "Messianic Postmodernism," p. 160.

16. Ibid., p. 161.

17. Westphal, "Prolegomena," p. 141.

18. Ibid., pp. 131–32.

19. Ibid., p. 133.

20. Ibid., pp. 132–33.

21. Ibid., pp. 137–39.

22. Ibid., p. 139.

23. There is, then, a close connection between metaphilosophy and first-order philosophical views. On this matter, see also Richard Rorty, "Analytic and Conversational Philosophy," in C. G. Prado (ed.), *A House Divided: Comparing Analytic and Continental Philosophy* (New York: Humanity Books, 2003), pp. 20–25, where Rorty relates divergent metaphilosophical outlooks to particular philosophical views on concepts and meaning.

24. Nietzsche, *The Will to Power*, trans. Walter Kaufmann and R. J. Hollingdale, ed. Walter Kaufmann (New York: Vintage, 1967), §481.

25. E. E. Sleinis, *Nietzsche's Revaluation of Values: A Study in Strategies* (Urbana: University of Illinois Press, 1994), p. 24.

26. As Nietzsche puts it, "As if a world would still remain over after one had deducted the perspective!" (*Will to Power* §567; cf. §560).

27. In some Continental writers, Westphal in particular, there is only a commitment to an attenuated form of perspectivism, according to which there is in fact a perspective that simply and finally gets everything right, but such a perspective can only be had by God, not by any human knower. See, for example, Westphal's "Appropriating Postmodernism," collected in his *Overcoming Onto-theology*, pp. 75–88. Caputo criticizes this 'watered-down' perspectivism in "Methodological Postmodernism: On Merold Westphal's *Overcoming Onto-theology*."

28. Caputo, *More Radical Hermeneutics: On Not Knowing Who We Are* (Bloomington: Indiana University Press, 2000), p. 1. Cf. Caputo's discussion of 'the Secret' on pp. 17–24 in *On Religion*, where he states: "The secret is that there is no Secret, no capitalized Know-it-all Breakthrough Principle or Revelation that lays things out the way they Really Are and thereby lays to rest the conflict of interpretations" (p. 21). On Caputo's hermeneutics, see also his *Radical Hermeneutics: Repetition, Deconstruction, and the Hermeneutic Project* (Bloomington: Indiana University Press, 1987).

29. Caputo, *On Religion*, p. 63.

30. Ibid., p. 59. Caputo's description of the Enlightenment critique of religion as "unvarnished reductionism" occurs on p. 63 of *On Religion*. Cf. Caputo, *Philosophy and Theology* (Nashville: Abingdon Press, 2006), p. 49.

31. In his recent book, *The Weakness of God*, Caputo develops a weak theology centred around the notion of 'the weakness of God', which rejects the classical theistic doctrines of divine omnipotence and sovereign power in favour of a conception of divinity as 'a weak force'. The origins of such a theology lie in part with Gianni Vattimo's 'weak thought', where the metaphysical sense of reality and being is weakened or dissolved, making possible the rise of hermeneutics and secularization, this being the precise fulfillment of the Christian message of kenosis. See Santiago Zabala (ed.), *Weakening Philosophy: Essays in Honour of Gianni Vattimo* (Montreal and Kingston: McGill-Queen's University Press, 2007). Caputo, however, also draws upon Derrida's notion of a 'weak force', Benjamin's 'weak messianic force', and the apostle Paul's proclamation of the weakness of God in 1 Corinthians 1:25 (see Caputo, *The Weakness of God*, p. 7).

32. These two elements of the Continental critique of the scientific ideal in philosophy of religion correspond very roughly to two strands within postmodern thought, labelled by Caputo as 'Dionysian postmodernism', which draws upon the Nietzschean themes of perspectivism and difference as plurality, and 'messianic postmodernism', which is inspired by the Kierkegaardian and Levinasian notion of difference as radical alterity and transcendence. See Caputo, "Messianic Postmodernism," pp. 153–66, where Caputo displays a preference for the messianic form of postmodernism while also acknowledging "the porousness of this distinction, the way these two bleed into and communicate with each other" (p. 165).

33. Richard Messer, *Does God's Existence Need Proof?* (Oxford: Clarendon Press, 1993), pp. 18–29.

34. Swinburne, *The Existence of God* (1979 edition), p. 8.

35. Messer, *Does God's Existence Need Proof?*, p. 19.

36. Ibid.

37. See Richard Swinburne, *The Existence of God*, rev. ed. (Oxford: Clarendon Press, 1991), and Michael Martin, *Atheism: A Philosophical Justification* (Philadelphia: Temple University Press, 1990).

38. Quoted in Messer, *Does God's Existence Need Proof?*, p. 21.

39. Caputo, *The Prayers and Tears of Jacques Derrida*, p. 336.

40. See Messer, *Does God's Existence Need Proof?*, pp. 22–29.

41. Caputo, "God Is Wholly Other – Almost: 'Différance' and the Hyperbolic Alterity of God," in Summerell (ed.), *The Otherness of God*, p. 190. However, as the title of his paper suggests, Caputo cautions against an absolute alterity that knows no bounds, as this would run the risk of dissolving God into "an ominous anonymity" (p. 191). Similarly, Caputo elsewhere states that, "The biblical God . . . is not simply 'wholly other'. Clearly God is beyond us and we do not grasp God. There is an incomprehensibility about God, but God also makes Godself vividly known to us. But the notion that God is simply, transcendentally remote and wholly other does not capture the biblical experience of God." Quoted in B. Keith Putt, "What Do I Love When I Love My God? An Interview with John D. Caputo," pp. 168–69.

42. Caputo, *On Religion*, p. 25, emphases in the original.

43. As Caputo explains, the denial that I have the authority to pronounce myself a 'believer' (or 'non-believer') is also based on the rejection of a unitary conception of the self: "Every time I say *'credo'* there is a voice within me that contradicts that faith and insists it does not believe a thing. Even so, those who say they disbelieve or do not believe must confess that they are haunted from within by another voice, one that fears that unbelief has forever closed itself off from the depth of things, from a wisdom both ancient and beautiful" ("Methodological Postmodernism," p. 294). See also Derrida's doubts regarding the believer/non-believer divide, in "Epoché and Faith: An Interview with Jacques Derrida," in Yvonne Sherwood and Kevin Hart (eds), *Derrida and Religion: Other Testaments* (New York: Routledge, 2005), pp. 37–38, 46–47.

44. David Burrell, *Faith and Freedom: An Interfaith Perspective* (Oxford: Blackwell, 2004), p. 220.

45. See Jean-Luc Marion, *God Without Being: Hors-Texte,* trans. Thomas A. Carlson (Chicago: University of Chicago Press, 1991 [originally published in French in 1982]).

46. See Richard Kearney, *The God Who May Be: A Hermeneutics of Religion* (Bloomington: Indiana University Press, 2001).

47. Caputo, *The Weakness of God,* p. 12.

48. See Caputo, *The Weakness of God,* pp. 121–24.

49. Caputo, *On Religion,* pp. 114–15.

50. Ibid., p. 116. Caputo therefore rejects the very idea of there being a 'one true religion' not so much on the grounds of religious pluralism (as does John Hick), but because that notion commits a category-mistake, treating a 'poetics of experience' (i.e., religious language) as though it were a cognitivist or propositional discourse.

51. Heidegger, *Identity and Difference,* trans. Joan Stambaugh (New York: Harper & Row, 1969), p. 72.

52. Hans Küng, "Rediscovering God," in Philip Hillyer (ed.), *On the Threshold of the Third Millenium* (London: SCM Press, 1990), p. 87. See also Brian Davies' penetrating critique of some trends within recent American philosophy of religion, in "Letter from America," *New Blackfriars* 84 (2003): 371–84.

53. Quinton, "Continental Philosophy," in Honderich (ed.), *The Oxford Companion to Philosophy,* second edition, p. 170. For similar criticisms, see Dagfinn Føllesdal, "Analytic Philosophy: What Is It and Why Should One Engage In It?" in Hans-Johann Glock (ed.), *The Rise of Analytic Philosophy,* pp. 1–16; Jacques Bouveresse, "Why I Am So Very unFrench," in Alan Montefiore (ed.), *Philosophy in France Today* (Cambridge: Cambridge University Press, 1983), pp. 9–33; and Pascal Engel, "Analytic Philosophy and Cognitive Norms," *The Monist* 82 (1999): 218–34. Bouveresse and Engel are speaking as defenders and exponents of analytic philosophy, but from within the setting of French academic philosophy. This makes for interesting reading, and Bouveresse in particular does a good job in highlighting the difficulties of alienation and intolerance faced by practitioners of analytic philosophy in France – this, of course, mirroring the situation faced by many Continental philosophers in Anglo-American philosophy departments.

54. Samuel C. Wheeler III, *Deconstruction As Analytic Philosophy* (Stanford: Stanford University Press, 2000), p. 2.

55. See W. D. Hart, "Clarity" in David Bell and Neil Cooper (eds), *The Analytic Tradition: Meaning, Thought and Knowledge* (Oxford: Blackwell, 1990), pp. 197–222. Hart states that the commitment to clarity in analytic philosophy is also motivated by what he dubs 'the epistemic thesis of rationalism' (which formed part of Descartes' doctrine of clear and distinct ideas): clarity is itself the strongest, if not the sole, guarantee of knowledge. Hart goes on to show, by way of a comparison between Carnap and the later Wittgenstein, that the ideal of clarity has been understood and justified in quite different ways within analytic philosophy. As Hart summarizes the matter, "On Carnap's conception of clarity as exactness, rigour and precision, clarity paves the way for the mathematical methods of natural science. On Wittgenstein's later conception of clarity as perspicuity, clarity paves the way of understanding" (p. 219).
56. Ludwig Wittgenstein, *Tractatus Logico-Philosophicus*, trans. C. K. Ogden (London: Kegan Paul, Trench, Trubner & Co., 1922), p. 27.
57. Hart, "Clarity," p. 204.
58. See Caputo, *Radical Hermeneutics*, ch. 8.
59. Westphal, "Of Stories and Languages," in Myron B. Penner (ed.), *Christianity and the Postmodern Turn: Six Views* (Grand Rapids: Brazos Press, 2005), p. 231.
60. Consider, for example, Vincent Descombes' observation that, "In France, the development of a political position remains the decisive test, disclosing as it does the definitive meaning of a mode of thought" (*Modern French Philosophy*, trans. L. Scott-Fox and J. M. Harding, Cambridge: Cambridge University Press, 1980, p. 7). In a similar vein, Walter Lowe comments that "a *press toward the ethical* . . ., and more specifically a press toward the praxiological empowerment of the ethical, functions for non-T as the crucial philosophic test within religion," where 'non-T' roughly designates the kind of philosophy of religion typically pursued in Continental philosophy and in Religious Studies departments in the United States (Lowe, "Two Types of Philosophy of Religion," in Wainwright (ed.), *God, Philosophy and Academic Culture*, p. 32, emphasis in the original). As Lowe goes on to point out, questions of truth, rationality and morality are usually converted in the Continental tradition to questions of the form, 'Whose truth? Truth in what interest?'.
61. Derrida, "Following Theory," in Michael Payne and John Schad (eds), *life. after.theory* (London: Continuum, 2003), p. 17, emphases in the original. Similarly, Carl Raschke says of Derrida's notoriously difficult style of writing that

> You're not supposed instantly to "understand it" or "even get it". Just like you don't wolf down a fine filet, you don't swallow in one gulp a great piece of literature or philosophy. Anyone who whines that a philosopher should "just say straightforwardly" what he or she means is sort of like the guy who douses ketchup on his beef Wellington. You've got to learn to appreciate what you're eating – or reading.
> ("The Difference That Faith Makes," *Church and Postmodern Culture* 2.1, Spring 2007)

See also Ralph Humphries' perceptive comments on the difficulties in understanding a philosophical work, in "Analytic and Continental: The Division in

Philosophy," *The Monist* 82 (1999): 262, 268 (and the accompanying note 22 on p. 277).

62. See Henryk Skolimowski, "Quine, Ajdukiewicz, and the Predicament of 20th Century Philosophy," in Lewis Edwin Hahn and Paul Arthur Schilpp (eds), *The Philosophy of W. V. Quine* (La Salle: Open Court Publishing, 1986), pp. 466–69.

63. Much of what follows is taken from Nick Trakakis, "Nietzsche's Perspectivism and Problems of Self-Refutation," *International Philosophical Quarterly* 46 (2006): 91–110, though I have changed my mind on some crucial points since the publication of this article.

64. Arthur Danto, *Nietzsche as Philosopher* (New York: Macmillan, 1965), p. 80.

65. See Nehamas, *Nietzsche:Life as Literature* (Cambridge, MA: Harvard University Press, 1985), pp. 66–67.

66. Cf. Martin Heidegger, *Nietzsche*, ed. D. F. Krell, trans. J. Stambaugh, D. F. Krell and F. A. Capuzzi (San Francisco: Harper, 1991 [originally published 1961]), vol. 3, pp. 26–28.

67. Clearly, these may not be the only possible alternatives. There may, for instance, be perspectives in which relativism has no truth-value (or no clear truth-value). To take account of such possibilities, simply replace 'false' with 'not true', so that in perspectives in which relativism has no truth-value it remains the case that relativism is not true.

68. Steven Hales and Rex Welshon, in *Nietzsche's Perspectivism* (Urbana: University of Illinois Press, 2000), pp. 24–25, note that this reading of Nietzsche has been advocated by Alan Schrift, Lawrence Hinman, George Stack, Ken Gemes and E. E. Sleinis.

69. See Hales and Welshon, *Nietzsche's Perspectivism*, pp. 22–23.

70. Meiland, "On the Paradox of Cognitive Relativism," *Metaphilosophy* 11 (1980): 121. Meiland has, in fact, published a string of papers in the 1970s defending the internal coherence of relativism – for references and (an unfortunately poor) critique, see Harvey Siegel, *Relativism Refuted: A Critique of Contemporary Epistemological Relativism* (Dordrecht: D. Reidel, 1987), ch. 1.

71. See R. Lanier Anderson, "Truth and Objectivity in Perspectivism," *Synthese* 115 (1998): 1–32.

72. See Anderson, "Truth and Objectivity in Perspectivism," pp. 23–24.

73. 'Non-realism' understood in this way is consistent with, but not reducible to, the 'hyper-realism' advocated by Caputo in, for example, *The Weakness of God*, pp. 9–12, 121–24, and "For the Love of the Things Themselves: Derrida's Hyper-Realism," *Journal for Cultural and Religious Theory* [www.jcrt.org] 1.3 (August 2000).

   On another point relevant to the above definition of 'non-realism', it might be objected that modern physics no longer countenances 'physical objects', preferring instead to speak of forces, fields, etc. To deal with this objection, we may say that the extension of 'physical objects' should simply be whatever it is that can be examined through the experimental methods typically employed by natural scientists.

74. Parts of the following discussion of D. Z. Phillips's work are drawn from a paper I co-wrote with Graham Oppy, entitled "Religious Language Games,"

published in Andrew Moore and Michael Scott (eds), *Realism and Religion: Philosophical and Theological Perspectives* (Aldershot: Ashgate Publishing, 2007), pp. 103–30. I note that the assessment of Phillips's work in that paper is quite different from the one offered here.

75. See, for example, Phillips, "Religious Beliefs and Language-Games," in his *Faith and Philosophical Enquiry* (London: Routledge & Kegan Paul, 1970), ch. 5.

76. Kai Nielsen, "Wittgensteinian Fideism," *Philosophy* 42 (1967): 191–209.

77. See Phillips, "Religious Beliefs and Language-Games," p. 98 (the distinction between religion and superstition is elaborated further on pp. 101–09). See also Phillips, *Belief, Change and Forms of Life* (Basingstoke: Macmillan, 1986), ch. 1, and *Religion and the Hermeneutics of Contemplation* (Cambridge: Cambridge University Press, 2001), pp. 25–30, where he argues vigorously against the equation of his views with Wittgensteinian fideism.

That Phillips does not think of religious language games as entirely divorced from, or incommensurate with respect to, other language games is often missed by his critics – see, for example, Joseph Runzo, "Realism, Non-Realism and Atheism: Why Believe in an Objectively Real God?" in Runzo (ed.), *Is God Real?* (New York: St. Martin's Press, 1993), pp. 159–60. A critic who has not overlooked this aspect of Phillip's thought is Lance Ashdown, who argues nevertheless that Phillips's position that religious language games are not completely autonomous does not cohere well with his repeated insistence that philosophers ought to stop judging religious beliefs on the basis of criteria borrowed from non-religious forms of discourse (see Ashdown, "D.Z. Phillips and his Audiences," *Sophia* 32 (1993): 1–31). See, however, Phillips, *Religion and Friendly Fire: Examining Assumptions in Contemporary Philosophy of Religion* (Aldershot: Ashgate, 2004), pp. 8–11, where Phillips attempts to meet a similar criticism made by Stephen Mulhall.

78. I borrow this way of characterizing realism from Merold Westphal, "Theological Anti-Realism," in Moore and Scott (eds), *Realism and Religion*, p. 132.

79. Hick, "Believing – And Having True Beliefs," in Runzo (ed.), *Is God Real?* p. 115. Cf. Stephen T. Davis' first two definitions of religious realism in *God, Reason and Theistic Proofs* (Edinburgh: Edinburgh University Press, 1997), pp. 47–48. I should note that Phillips does not think of himself as a non-realist, for in his view both realism and non-realism (including theological versions thereof) are confused, or more precisely, fail to provide a coherent account of what it is to believe something. See Phillips, "On Really Believing," in Runzo (ed.), *Is God Real?* pp. 85–108.

80. A prominent example is Westphal, although this kind of religious non-realism would also comport well with the views of Phillips despite his disavowal of the 'non-realist' label (as indicated in the previous footnote).

81. Phillips, "Philosophy, Theology and the Reality of God," in *Faith and Philosophical Enquiry*, p. 1, emphasis in the original.

82. Ibid.

83. Ibid., pp. 1–2.

84. Phillips, "The Friends of Cleanthes: A Case of Conceptual Poverty," in Phillips, *Recovering Religious Concepts: Closing Epistemic Divides* (Basingstoke: Macmillan, 2000), p. 64. See also Phillips, "In All Probability," *Times Literary Supplement*, 28 May 1982, p. 588, where he reviews Swinburne's *Faith and*

Reason and takes him to task for holding that belief in God is belief in what is merely probable.

85. See Phillips, *Religion Without Explanation* (Oxford: Basil Blackwell, 1976), pp. 174–75, where he draws upon some remarks by Rhees and Wittgenstein.

86. Phillips, *Death and Immortality* (London: Macmillan, 1970), p. 68. A similar point is made in a discussion Phillips had with J. R. Jones on BBC Radio (which was first published in 1970):

> JRJ: What is it that shows that, to take Wittgenstein's example, belief in the Last Judgment has obviously nothing in common with a hypothesis?
> DZP: I think that if we do look at the role this belief plays in at least many believers' lives, we find that it is not a hypothesis, a conjecture, that some dreadful event is going to happen so many thousands years hence. We see this by recognizing that a certain range of reactions is ruled out for the believer. What I mean is this: if it were a conjecture about a future event, he might say, 'I believe it is going to happen' or 'Possibly it might happen' or 'I'm not sure; it may happen', and so on. But that range of reactions plays no part in the believer's belief in the Last Judgment.
> ("Belief and Loss of Belief," in Phillips, *Faith and Philosophical Enquiry*, pp. 112–13.)

> On the 'bedrock' nature of religious belief, see also Phillips, *Religion Without Explanation*, ch. 10, where Phillips notes that the proposition 'God exists' "does not get its unshakeable character from its inherent nature, or from the kind of abstraction which philosophy tries to make of it so often, but from its surroundings, from all the activities that hold it fast. Above all, those activities involving the language of praise and worship" (p. 172).

> I should also point out that, on Phillips's view, the firmness of a religious belief does not mean that it cannot be renounced. For Phillips, however, what erodes religious faith is not evidential considerations (such as evidential arguments from evil), but factors such as the appeal of a rival secular outlook or more pervasive cultural changes. See Phillips, "Belief and Loss of Belief," p. 116, *Death and Immortality*, pp. 73–76, and *Belief, Change and Forms of Life*, pp. 86–93.

87. Phillips, "Philosophy, Theology and the Reality of God," p. 2.

88. Phillips, "Faith, Scepticism, and Religious Understanding," in Phillips, *Faith and Philosophical Enquiry*, pp. 17–18. Phillips makes a similar point in response to Hick's procedure of pointing to religious believers who say that the existence of God is a matter of fact: "I have no doubt, however, that *the same* believers who say that the existence of God is a fact would, if pressed, admit that the discovery of God is not like the discovery of a matter of fact" ("Religious Belief and Philosophical Enquiry," in Phillips, *Faith and Philosophical Enquiry*, p. 71, emphasis in the original).

89. See Phillips, *The Concept of Prayer* (London: Routledge & Kegan Paul, 1965), pp. 21–23.

90. Michael Scott and Andrew Moore, "Can Theological Realism Be Refuted?" *Religious Studies* 33 (1997): 414. As Scott and Moore note (in their fn.18, p. 414), Phillips assumes that the religious realist suffers from the 'philosophical prejudice' that non-physical reality can be understood on analogy with

physical reality. Phillips, to be sure, has further criticisms of this prejudice than those indicated in the main text. He argues, for example, that our criteria of individuation for (empirical) objects are not the same as those we have for God, and that accurate depictions of objects can be constructed, but no such images of God are available. For criticisms of these arguments, see Scott and Moore, "Can Theological Realism Be Refuted?", pp. 414–18. It is also common to find Wittgensteinians arguing that to think of God as an object is to be committed to the view that God is spatially located. Although Wittgensteinians would rely upon logical and linguistic analysis to support this argument, one could also appeal to a principle such as the following: Necessarily, for any (concrete) objects A and B, if A exists independently of B and B is spatially located, then A is spatially located.

91. The quote is taken from Kierkegaard's *Concluding Unscientific Postscript*, trans. David F. Swenson (Princeton: Princeton University Press, 1941), p. 296. Phillips often approvingly quotes this remark – see, for example, "Faith, Scepticism, and Religious Understanding," p. 18; *Faith After Foundationalism* (London: Routledge, 1988), p. 229; and "Philosophers' Clothes" in Charles M. Lewis (ed.), *Relativism and Religion* (New York: St. Martin's Press, 1995), p. 138.

92. Phillips, *Religion Without Explanation*, p. 148. Cf. Phillips, "Religious Beliefs and Language-Games," p. 85. Phillips would not want to deny, however, that 'God' is in some sense a referring expression, but he would add that the sense in which 'God' is taken as a referring expression needs to be made clear (see Phillips, "Philosophers' Clothes," p. 138). As Rush Rhees puts it, "I might say that the language about God certainly does refer to something. But then I should want to say something about what it is to 'talk about God', and how different this is from talking about the moon or talking about our new house or talking about the Queen. How different the 'talking about' is, I mean. That is a difference in grammar" (*Without Answers*, London: Routledge & Kegan Paul, 1969, p. 132).

93. Phillips, "Philosophy, Theology and the Reality of God," p. 2.

94. One may, of course, speak of 'religious facts', but in that case, Phillips notes, "all the grammatical work has still to be done. We have to show how talk of facts in this context differs from talk of facts in other contexts. We would need to be clear about what finding out the facts, discovering the facts, or being mistaken about the facts, would amount to where religious matters are concerned. There would be similarities enough with other contexts, but there would be huge differences. I suspect what is important would lie in these differences" (*Faith After Foundationalism*, p. 230). As pointed out in fn. 92 above, Phillips makes a similar point in regards to calling God an object or 'God' a referring expression.

95. Given that Phillips often extols Wittgenstein's principle of 'leaving everything as it is' as an ideal to which philosophers of religion should aspire (see, for example, Phillips's paper, "Religion in Wittgenstein's Mirror," in *Wittgenstein and Religion*, Basingstoke: Macmillan, 1993, pp. 237–55), it would seem that Phillips is advancing a descriptive rather than a normative claim. Such an approach may be contrasted with the explicitly revisionary non-realism advocated by Don Cupitt in *Taking Leave of God* (London: SCM Press, 1980).

96. A position of this sort has been defended by David Basinger, "Plantinga, Pluralism and Justified Religious Belief," *Faith and Philosophy* 8 (1991): 67–80, and Philip L. Quinn, "The Foundations of Theism Again: A Rejoinder to Plantinga," in Linda Zagzebski (ed.), *Rational Faith: Catholic Responses to Reformed Epistemology* (Notre Dame: University of Notre Dame Press, 1993), pp. 35–45.

97. Some have also appealed to the biblical tradition in support of the (descriptive version of the) anti-evidentialist position. O. K. Bouwsma, for example, discusses biblical accounts of 'exemplars of faith', in particular Abraham, Moses and Paul, to show that notions such as 'belief' and 'faith' are more closely tied with such activities as 'obeying the call of God' rather than 'producing evidence'. Further, the fact that the Bible nowhere attempts to prove the existence of God is taken by Bouwsma as indicating that, in the biblical tradition at least, faith and evidence belong to entirely distinct logical orders, so that it makes no sense to speak of, and search for, evidence in matters of religious faith. See O. K. Bouwsma, *Without Proof or Evidence: Essays of O. K. Bouwsma*, edited by J. L. Craft and Ronald E. Hustwit (Lincoln: University of Nebraska Press, 1984), pp. 1–25.

98. See Phillips, "Sublime Existence" in *Wittgenstein and Religion*, p. 10, and "Return of the Monstrous Illusion" in *Recovering Religious Concepts*, p. 19. See also John Clayton, "The Otherness of Anselm," in Summerell (ed.), *The Otherness of God*, pp. 14–34. Bouwsma, however, mounts a plausible case for thinking that it is Anselm who is misrepresenting Christian discourse – specifically, the biblical language of praise and worship – when offering his ontological argument. See Bouwsma, "Anselm's Argument," in *Without Proof or Evidence: Essays of O. K. Bouwsma*, pp. 40–72.

99. Phillips is no doubt aware of the diversity that exists within the theistic tradition. For example, in response to John Hick's fact-stating account of religious belief, Phillips writes: "One has a vast and various range of persons, all claiming to be religious believers. I do not deny, then, that there are people whose conception of God is similar to that outlined by Hick" ("Religion and Epistemology: Some Contemporary Confusions," in *Faith and Philosophical Enquiry*, p. 127). And later on, he writes: "I do not wish to defend those people whose religious beliefs can be described adequately in Hick's terms. I only wish to stress that there is another kind of belief in God" (p. 129). As Richard Messer points out, the various conceptions of God and the competing views on the nature of religious belief that exist within historical Christianity "overcome the simple charge that Phillips is a revisionist; for there is no single dominant conception of God, even within Christianity, to be revised" (*Does God's Existence Need Proof?* p. 55).

100. Caputo, *On Religion*, p. 93.

101. The evidentialist vis-à-vis religious belief must also contend with the following difficulty, which, I suspect, motivates much of what Phillips has to say on the non-conjectural nature of religious belief: How can religious belief be held tentatively on the basis of (usually flimsy) evidence while at the same time providing the basis for an unconditional and passionate commitment (to God)? For some proposals as to how tentative religious belief can be reconciled with, and even inform and heighten, religious commitment, see

Robert McKim, *Religious Ambiguity and Religious Diversity* (Oxford: Oxford University Press, 2001), pp. 166–70, and C. Stephen Evans, *Philosophy of Religion: Thinking About Faith* (Downers Grove: InterVarsity Press, 1982), pp. 171–76.

102. Critchley, *Continental Philosophy*, p. 34.
103. This is a distinguishing feature of many of the essays collected in C. G. Prado (ed.), *A House Divided: Comparing Analytic and Continental Philosophy*.
104. See, for example, Critchley, *Continental Philosophy*, pp. 41–53.

Chapter 5

1. Edmond Jabès, *Desire for a Beginning, Dread of One Single End*, trans. Rosmarie Waldrop (New York: Granary Books, 2001), p. 9.
2. The novel was entitled in Greek *O ftohúlis tu Theú* (The Little Poor Man of God), and was published in Athens by Difros. Kazantzakis, however, had originally proposed the title, *Pax et Bonum*, this of course being a favourite expression of Francis'. Although the work was first released as a book in 1956, it had already been published in a series of installments by the Athenian newspaper *Eleftheria* from June 1954. The novel was translated into English by Peter Bien and the translation was published in 1962 as *Saint Francis* in the United States (by Simon and Schuster) and as *God's Pauper* in Great Britain (by Cassirer). I prefer the title of 'Poor Man of God', as this is closer to the Greek original. Generally, I follow Peter Bien's translation, and the in-text page references are to the 2005 Loyola Classics edition (published by Loyola Press in Chicago, with an introduction by well-known Catholic troubadour, John Michael Talbot). Occasionally, however, I depart from Bien's rendition, particularly when a more literal translation has seemed preferable. The Greek text I rely upon is that published in Athens by Helen Kazantzakis in 1981.
3. I am relying here on Helen Kazantzakis, *Nikos Kazantzakis: A Biography Based on His Letters*, trans. Amy Mims (New York: Simon and Schuster, 1968), pp. 384–85, where a description of Kazantzakis' working environment in his earlier abode in Aegina is provided.
4. I say 'reignite' as Kazantzakis had already fallen in love with Francis during visits to Assisi in the 1920s, though at that time he tended to view Francis through a political lens as "a great, idealistic communist" who recognized "that the source of every evil is private ownership and forbade . . . his disciples to have any property whatsoever, small or large" (quoted in Peter Bien, *Kazantzakis: Politics of the Spirit*, vol. 1, Princeton: Princeton University Press, 1989, p. 82). Kazantzakis recounts his impressions of Assisi in *Report to Greco*, trans. Peter Bien (New York: Simon and Schuster, 1965), pp. 177–87, 374–82, and in *Journeying: Travels in Italy, Egypt, Sinai, Jerusalem and Cyprus*, trans. Themi Vasils and Theodora Vasils (Boston: Little, Brown and Company, 1975), pp. 9–13 – the latter was written as a newspaper correspondent during a trip to Assisi in 1926 when Italy was under fascist rule. However, Kazantzakis' earliest contact with the Franciscan tradition may have occurred during his brief stay (in 1897–1898) at a school

run by Franciscan friars on the island of Naxos (see *Report to Greco*, pp. 92–103), or even before that, during his upbringing in Crete, where Saint Francis was a popular object of devotion.

5. Helen Kazantzakis, *Nikos Kazantzakis: A Biography Based on His Letters*, p. 513.

6. Quoted in Helen Kazantzakis, *Nikos Kazantzakis: A Biography Based on His Letters*, p. 514. For an excellent account of Kazantzakis' long discipleship to Francis, see Peter Bien, *Kazantzakis: Politics of the Spirit*, vol. 2 (Princeton: Princeton University Press, 2007), pp. 464–79.

7. Quoted in Helen Kazantzakis, *Nikos Kazantzakis: A Biography Based on His Letters*, p. 519. The material that Kazantzakis would have drawn upon in his novel would doubtlessly have included his very own translation, completed in 1943, of the biography of Francis written by the Danish poet and writer, Johannes Jorgensen. (Jorgensen's biography was originally published in 1907, while Kazantzakis' translation was published in 1951.) Kazantzakis describes an encounter with Jorgensen in Assisi in *Report to Greco*, pp. 377–82.

8. Quoted in Helen Kazantzakis, *Nikos Kazantzakis: A Biography Based on His Letters*, p. 550.

9. Norman Malcolm, *Ludwig Wittgenstein: A Memoir*, second edition (Oxford: Clarendon Press, 2001), p. 47, emphases in the original.

10. A. Hecht and A. Memeczek, "Bei Anselm Kiefer im Atelier," *art*, January 1990, pp. 40–41; quoted in Charles W. Haxthausen, "The World, the Book, and Anselm Kiefer," *The Burlington Magazine* 133 (December 1991), p. 851.

11. Kazantzakis, *Journey to the Morea*, trans. F. A. Reed (New York: Simon and Schuster, 1965), pp. 171–72.

12. See Lewis Owens, *Creative Destruction: Nikos Kazantzakis and the Literature of Responsibility* (Macon: Mercer University Press, 2003), where the central theme in Kazantzakis' later fiction is said to be "a dialectic of destruction and creation; a dialectic which, modelled on the process of Bergson's *élan vital*, sees destruction as a necessary prerequisite for renewed creative activity" (pp. 7–8).

13. See Daniel A. Dombrowski, *Kazantzakis and God* (Albany: State University of New York Press, 1997), and Darren J. N. Middleton, *Novel Theology: Nikos Kazantzakis's Encounter with Whiteheadian Process Theism* (Macon: Mercer University Press, 2000).

14. Middleton, *Novel Theology*, p. xix.

15. Middleton, *Novel Theology*, p. 45; see also pp. 98–106, 151–61, 212–17. In resisting such a reduction to metaphysical first principles, Kazantzakis' fiction has much in common with recent work in postmodern and postmetaphysical theology, as Middleton indicates in *Novel Theology*, pp. 38–47, 192–98, and especially in his more recent *Broken Hallelujah: Nikos Kazantzakis and Christian Theology* (Lanham: Lexington Books, 2007), ch. 6, which includes a comparison between Kazantzakis and Caputo.

16. Quoted in Bien, *Kazantzakis: Politics of the Spirit*, vol. 1, p. 36.

17. Bien, *Kazantzakis: Politics of the Spirit*, vol. 1, p. 38.

18. Quoted in Bien, *Kazantzakis: Politics of the Spirit*, vol. 1, p. 248, note 9.

19. Middleton, *Novel Theology*, p. 49.

20. Ibid., p. 216.

21. Ibid., p. 50.

22. *The Sayings of the Desert Fathers: The Alphabetical Collection*, trans. Benedicta Ward (Kalamazoo: Cistercian Publications, 1984), p. 103.

23. This is the title of a recent exhibition of Anselm Kiefer's works at White Cube Gallery in London, 26 January–17 March 2007. For the catalogue to this exhibition, see *Anselm Kiefer: Aperiatur Terra* (London: Jay Jopling/White Cube, 2007).

24. Quoted in Michael Auping, "Introduction" to *Anselm Kiefer: Heaven and Earth* (Fort Worth: Modern Art Museum of Fort Worth, and Munich: Prestel Verlag, 2005), p. 37.

25. Quoted in Karen Wright, "The Ruins of Barjac: Politics, Alchemy, and Learning to Dance in Anselm Kiefer's World," *Modern Painters: The International Art Magazine*, November 2006, p. 71.

26. *The Journals of Søren Kierkegaard*, edited and translated by Alexander Dru (London: Oxford University Press, 1951), p. 528.

27. See, for example, the highly unsympathetic reading of *The Poor Man of God* in Morton P. Levitt, *The Cretan Glance: The World and Art of Nikos Kazantzakis* (Columbus: Ohio State University, 1980), ch. 7, which describes the novel as "the least successful of Kazantzakis' fictions" (p. 142) owing largely to the presumed extreme, life-denying asceticism of its protagonist. A similar criticism is made by Knut Walf, "'My' Francis of Assisi?," trans. David Smith, in Christian Duquoc and Casiano Floristán (eds), *Francis of Assisi Today* (Edinburgh: T & T Clark, 1981), pp. 65–72, esp. pp. 68–69.

28. Tom Doulis, "Kazantzakis and the Meaning of Suffering," *Northwest Review* 6 (1963): 56.

29. Kazantzakis, *Report to Greco*, p. 223.

30. Alfred North Whitehead, *Process and Reality: An Essay in Cosmology*, corrected edition, edited by David Ray Griffin and Donald W. Sherburne (New York: The Free Press, 1978), p. 351.

31. This is not to deny that there are traces of male chauvinism in Francis or in Kazantzakis' other works, but it is to reject as hyperbolic and unjustified Morton Levitt's view that, of all the protagonists in Kazantzakis' major novels, "Francis is probably the worst male chauvinist of them all, the one whose attitudes toward women are most unnatural" (*The Cretan Glance*, p. 146).

32. James Lea concurs in seeing a progression in Kazantzakis' political views from the defence in the 1920s of an amoral and violent approach where the end justifies the means to a position which places spiritual revolution above violent revolution and is expressed best in the novels of the 1940s and 50s. See James F. Lea, *Kazantzakis: The Politics of Salvation* (Tuscaloosa: University of Alabama Press, 1979), pp. 52–54. See also Peter Bien's insightful analysis of Kazantzakis' notorious refusal to condemn Hitler, in "Nikos Kazantzakis' Attitude Toward Hitler in the 1930s," *Modern Greek Studies (Australia and New Zealand)*, vol. 8–9, 2000–2001, pp. 55–70.

33. This is the opening to Kazantzakis' *The Saviors of God: Spiritual Exercises*, trans. Kimon Friar (New York: Simon and Schuster, 1960), p. 43. This was first published in Greek in 1927.

34. Peter Bien emphasizes the dialectical relationship between the Buddhistic or nihilistic and the Bergsonian or life-affirmative elements in Kazantzakis' *Salvatores Dei* and in his oeuvre more generally: see Bien, *Kazantzakis: Politics of the Spirit*, vol. 1, pp. 133–43.

35. Nikos Kazantzakis, "Six Letters of Nikos Kazantzakis to Max Tau" (in Greek, trans. Helen Kontiadis), *Nea Estia* 102 (Christmas 1977), p. 308. This letter was dated 15 September 1951, and was originally written in German.

36. Quoted in Helen Kazantzakis, *Nikos Kazantzakis: A Biography Based on His Letters*, p. 509. The novel Kazantzakis wrote after completing *The Last Temptation* was none other than *The Poor Man of God* (at least according to the chronology given in Peter Bien, *Kazantzakis: Politics of the Spirit*, vol. 1, p. xiv).

37. Quoted in Helen Kazantzakis, *Nikos Kazantzakis: A Biography Based on His Letters*, p. 549. A word of caution: unlike Middleton, I am not calling for a 'rehabilitation' of Kazantzakis as someone whose thought can be placed within "the permissible limits of Christian reflection." Nevertheless, I think Middleton is correct to reject Bien's 'post-Christian' interpretation of *The Poor Man of God* as embodying a purely immanent conception of deity, and to see the novel instead as working out a panentheistic view of God as transcendent-yet-immanent. See Middleton, *Novel Theology*, pp. 113–17, 220–21, and for Bien's most recent statement of his post-Christian interpretation of Francis, see his *Kazantzakis: Politics of the Spirit*, vol. 2, pp. 498–99.

38. Peter Bien takes freedom, and in particular the process by which freedom is obtained, to be the central theme of the novel. See Bien, *Kazantzakis: Politics of the Spirit*, vol. 2, pp. 454–56.

39. Joseph P. Kelly, "Review of Nikos Kazantzakis, *Saint Francis*," *America*, 28 July 1962, p. 549.

40. Epictetus, *The Discourses*, edited by Christopher Gill, translation revised by Robin Hard (London: J. M. Dent, 1995), book 3, ch. 22, p. 194. See further Andrew S. Reece, "Kazantzakis' St. Francis and the Cynics," *Classical and Modern Literature* 18 (1997): 71–77.

41. Jean-Luc Marion, *In Excess: Studies of Saturated Phenomena*, trans. Robyn Horner and Vincent Berraud (New York: Fordham University Press, 2002), p. 61.

42. Candice Dunn and Rebecca Mann, *Kids' View of God* (Sydney: Murdoch Books, 2006).

43. Jacques Derrida, "Sauf le nom (Post-Scriptum)," trans. John P. Leavey, Jr., in *On the Name*, ed. Thomas Dutoit (Stanford: Stanford University Press, 1995), p. 75.

44. Lewis Owens, *Creative Destruction: Nikos Kazantzakis and the Literature of Responsibility*, pp. 94–95.

45. Quoted in "Orthodox Theologian Speaks on Modern Deserts: Interview with John Chryssavgis," published on website of 'Zenit: The World Seen From Rome', 18 July 2006; transcript available at http://www.zenit.org/english/visualizza.phtml?sid=92770 (accessed 19 March 2008).

46. Morton Levitt, *The Cretan Glance*, p. 143.

47. *The Sayings of the Desert Fathers*, p. 6.

48. See Bien, *Kazantzakis: Politics of the Spirit*, vol. 2, p. 459.

49. *The Sayings of the Desert Fathers*, p. 131.

50. Geoffrey Hill, *Tenebrae* (London: André Deutsch, 1978), p. 18.

51. Peter Bien, *Nikos Kazantzakis – Novelist* (Bristol: Bristol Classical Press, 1989), p. 79.

52. Spinoza, *Ethics*, edited and translated by G. H. R. Parkinson (Oxford: Oxford University Press, 2000), Part 4, preface (p. 226) and proposition 4 (p. 231).

53. Michael Leunig, "A Confession," published online at http://www.leunig.com. au/confession/ (accessed 19 March 2008).
54. A transcript of the interview is available from http://www.abc.net.au/tv/ enoughrope/transcripts/s1632918.htm (accessed 19 March 2008).
55. Interview with Rachael Kohn on "The Spirit of Things," ABC Rational National, 2 July 2000; transcript available from http://www.abc.net.au/rn/ relig/spirit/stories/s147548.htm (accessed 19 March 2008).
56. Albert Camus, *American Journals*, trans. Hugh Levick (New York: Paragon House Publishers, 1987), pp. 32, 51.
57. Camus, *American Journals*, p. 52.
58. "A Picture of Dignity and Balance," published in *The Age* (Melbourne), 6 May 2006. Available online at http://www.theage.com.au/articles/2006/05/04/ 1146335867017.html (accessed 19 March 2008).
59. Interview on "Compass," ABC TV, 25 December 1997; transcript available from http://www.abc.net.au/compass/intervs/leunig.htm (accessed 19 March 2008).
60. Edmond Jabès, *Desire for a Beginning, Dread of One Single End*, p. 43.
61. Gerard Manley Hopkins, *Selected Poetry*, ed. Catherine Phillips (Oxford: Oxford University Press, 1996), p. 153.

Chapter 6

1. Kazantzakis, *The Saviors of God: Spiritual Exercises*, p. 128.
2. See Critchley, *Continental Philosophy*, ch. 1.
3. Albert Camus, *The Myth of Sisyphus and Other Essays*, trans. Justin O'Brien (New York: Alfred A. Knopf, 1967), p. 3.
4. W. V. Quine, *Theories and Things* (Cambridge, MA: Harvard University Press, 1981), p. 193. For a spirited critique of the approach to philosophy defended in the above extract by Quine, see Henryk Skolimowski, "Quine, Ajdukiewicz, and the Predicament of 20th Century Philosophy," in Hahn and Schilpp (eds), *The Philosophy of W. V. Quine*, pp. 463–91, esp. pp. 474–77.
5. Scott Soames, *Philosophical Analysis in the Twentieth Century*, vol. 1 (Princeton: Princeton University Press, 2003), p. xiv. Compare, in this context, the following comments on A. J. Ayer made by his biographer, Ben Rogers: "[T]here was an irony in Ayer's fame. For he did as much as anyone to professionalise philosophy, to separate it from the person. He set out quite deliberately to diminish its pretensions, to contain it, to tame it. *No philosopher, or at least no English-language philosopher, did more to insist that philosophy had little to do with life*" (*A. J. Ayer: A Life*, London: Chatto & Windus, 1999, pp. 1–2, emphasis mine).
6. Critchley, *Continental Philosophy*, p. 8.
7. *The Journals of Søren Kierkegaard*, p. 156 (entry made in 1846).
8. The charge that analytic philosophy does not address the questions that truly matter was commonly advanced in the immediate post-WWII period when linguistic analysis was in full swing. For a discussion and partial endorsement of this charge, see H. D. Lewis (ed.), *Clarity Is Not Enough: Essays in Criticism*

of Linguistic Philosophy (London: George Allen & Unwin, 1963), particularly the lead essay by H. H. Price, from whom the title "Clarity Is Not Enough" was borrowed.

9. Robert Solomon, *The Joy of Philosophy: Thinking Thin versus the Passionate Life* (New York: Oxford University Press, 1999), p. 13. Similar sentiments are expressed in Nicholas Capaldi, *The Enlightenment Project in the Analytic Conversation* (Dordrecht: Kluwer Academic Publishers, 1998), and Bruce Wilshire, *Fashionable Nihilism: A Critique of Analytic Philosophy* (Albany: State University of New York Press, 2002), esp. chs 1 and 2.

10. Solomon, *The Joy of Philosophy*, p. 13.

11. Solomon, *The Joy of Philosophy*, p. 13. It should be noted, however, that Solomon does not think that analytic philosophy is inherently doomed: the vices that currently plague it can, in his view, be overcome (see pp. 218–24 of his book). Also, Solomon does not spare the Continental tradition, and at times he is just as critical of Continental philosophy as he is of the analytic tradition (see, for example, his comments on p. 9).

12. Solomon, *The Joy of Philosophy*, p. vi. See also Robert Nozick, *Philosophical Explanations*, pp. 4–8, where the adversarial and coercive character of much analytic philosophy is highlighted.

13. Wilshire, *Fashionable Nihilism: A Critique of Analytic Philosophy*, pp. 5–6, emphases mine.

14. David Tacey, *The Spirituality Revolution: The Emergence of Contemporary Spirituality* (Hove, East Sussex: Brunner-Routledge, 2004), p. 158.

15. Ibid., p. 163.

16. Ibid., p. 164.

17. Ibid., p. 157.

18. Hans Küng, "Rediscovering God," in Hillyer (ed.), *On the Threshold of the Third Millenium*, p. 88.

19. Tacey, *The Spirituality Revolution*, p. 170.

20. Gilles Deleuze, *Difference and Repetition*, trans. Paul Patton (New York: Columbia University Press, 1994), p. xxi.

21. From Walcott's poem "Codicil," in *The Castaway and Other Poems* (London: Jonathan Cape, 1969), p. 61.

22. John Caputo, *Radical Hermeneutics*, p. 234.

23. Ibid., p. 230.

24. Ibid., p. 234.

25. The survey was subsequently published as a monograph, *Higher Education and Human Good* (Bristol: Tockington Press, 2006), edited by Ian McNay, Emeritus professor at Greenwich University, and Jennifer Bone, former pro vice-chancellor of the University of the West of England.

26. Phil Baty, "Academia Has Sold Out, 72% Believe," *The Times Higher Education Supplement*, published online 27 October 2006 [http://www.timeshighereducation.co.uk/story.asp?sectioncode=26&storycode=206308 (accessed 19 March 2008)].

27. Ludwig Wittgenstein, *Culture and Value*, trans. Peter Winch (Chicago: University of Chicago Press, 1984), p. 34e.

28. Kazantzakis, *Report to Greco*, p. 261.

29. Tony Tysome, "Young Guns Ditch Old Values," *The Times Higher Education Supplement*, published online 15 December 2006 [http://www.timeshighereducation.co.uk/story.asp?sectioncode=26&storycode=207146 (accessed 19 March 2008)].

30. Simon Cooper, "Academic Darwinism: The (Logical) End of the Dawkins Era," *Arena Journal* 28 (2007): 114.

31. Quoted in Arnold Davidson's Introduction to Hadot's *Philosophy as a Way of Life: Spiritual Exercises from Socrates to Foucault* (Malden: Blackwell Publishing, 1995), pp. 27, 30.

32. Henry David Thoreau, *Walden*, ed. Stephen Fender (Oxford: Oxford University Press, 1997), p. 15.

33. I owe this analogy between the conferences of learned societies and trade conventions to Theodore Roszak, who in his brilliant essay, "On Academic Delinquency" (in Roszak (ed.), *The Dissenting Academy*, New York: Pantheon Books, 1967, pp. 3–42) discusses many of the problems still beleaguering the academy.

34. Friedrich Nietzsche, *On the Genealogy of Morality: A Polemic*, trans. Maudemarie Clark and Alan J. Swenson (Indianapolis: Hackett Publishing Company, 1998), third treatise, §23, pp. 107–08, emphases in the original.

35. Friedrich Nietzsche, *Untimely Meditations*, trans. R. J. Hollingdale (Cambridge: Cambridge University Press, 1997), p. 36, emphasis in the original.

36. Roszak, "On Academic Delinquency," p. 27.

37. Wilshire, *Fashionable Nihilism: A Critique of Analytic Philosophy*, pp. 41–42. Similar calls have been made by Nicholas Maxwell and the recently established Friends of Wisdom movement, which pushes for a revolution in academia so as to overcome the current dangerous and irrational devotion to the acquisition of factual knowledge and technological know-how dissociated from a more basic concern for wisdom. See the website of Friends of Wisdom: www.knowledgetowisdom.org

38. C. G. Estabrook, "Three Mistakes about Christian Scholarship: Reflections on Remarks by Professor Plantinga," *Common Sense* 7 (1993): 8.

39. Ibid.

40. Ibid.

41. Ibid.

42. This is a quote from Jacques Derrida, "Circumfession," trans. Geoffrey Bennington, in Geoffrey Bennington and Jacques Derrida, *Jacques Derrida* (Chicago: University of Chicago Press, 1993), p. 194.

Bibliography

Adams, Marilyn McCord. *Horrendous Evils and the Goodness of God*. Melbourne: Melbourne University Press, 1999.

Adams, Marilyn McCord, and Robert Adams (eds). *The Problem of Evil*. Oxford: Oxford University Press, 1990.

Adorno, Theodor. *Negative Dialectics*, trans. E. B. Ashton. London: Routledge & Kegan Paul, 1973.

Alston, William. "The Inductive Argument from Evil and the Human Cognitive Condition," *Philosophical Perspectives* 5 (1991): 29–67.

Anderson, R. Lanier. "Truth and Objectivity in Perspectivism," *Synthese* 115 (1998): 1–32.

Ashdown, Lance. "D. Z. Phillips and his Audiences," *Sophia* 32 (1993): 1–31.

Ayer, A. J. *Part of My Life: The Memoirs of a Philosopher*. New York: Harcourt Brace Jovanovich, 1977.

Ayer, A. J. *More of My Life*. London: Collins, 1984.

Ayer, A. J. (ed.). *Logical Positivism*. Glencoe: The Free Press, 1959.

Barthes, Roland. "Science Versus Literature," *The Times Literary Supplement*, 28 September 1967, pp. 897–98.

Basinger, David. "Plantinga, Pluralism and Justified Religious Belief," *Faith and Philosophy* 8 (1991): 67–80.

Bataille, Georges. "Un-knowing and Its Consequences," *October* 36 (1986): 80–85.

Baty, Phil. "Academia Has Sold Out, 72% Believe," *The Times Higher Education Supplement*, published online 27 October 2006. Accessed 19 March 2008. Available from: http://www.timeshighereducation.co.uk/story.asp?sectioncode= 26&storycode=206308

Beaney, Michael. "Analysis," in Edward N. Zalta (ed.), *The Stanford Encyclopedia of Philosophy (Summer 2003 Edition)* URL = http://plato.stanford.edu/ archives/sum2003/entries/analysis/

Bell, David, and Neil Cooper (eds). *The Analytic Tradition: Meaning, Thought and Knowledge*. Oxford: Blackwell, 1990.

Bennington, Geoffrey, and Jacques Derrida, *Jacques Derrida*. Chicago: University of Chicago Press, 1993.

Bernasconi, Robert, and David Wood (eds). *The Provocation of Levinas: Rethinking the Other*. London: Routledge, 1988.

Bien, Peter. *Nikos Kazantzakis – Novelist*. Bristol: Bristol Classical Press, 1989.

Bien, Peter. *Kazantzakis: Politics of the Spirit*, vol. 1. Princeton: Princeton University Press, 1989.

Bien, Peter. "Nikos Kazantzakis' Attitude Toward Hitler in the 1930s," *Modern Greek Studies (Australia and New Zealand)*, vols 8–9, 2000–2001, pp. 55–70.

Bien, Peter. *Kazantzakis: Politics of the Spirit*, vol. 2. Princeton: Princeton University Press, 2007.

Biles, Jeremy. "Review of Slavoj Zizek, *The Puppet and the Dwarf: The Perverse Core of Christianity*," *The Journal of Religion* 86 (2006): 501–03.

Black, Max (ed.). *Philosophy in America*. London: George Allen & Unwin, 1965.

Bone, Jennifer, and Ian McNay. *Higher Education and Human Good*. Bristol: Tockington Press, 2006.

Bouwsma, O. K. *Without Proof or Evidence: Essays of O.K. Bouwsma*, ed. J. L. Craft and Ronald E. Hustwit. Lincoln: University of Nebraska Press, 1984.

Braiterman, Zachary. *(God) After Auschwitz: Tradition and Change in Post-Holocaust Jewish Thought*. Princeton: Princeton University Press, 1998.

Brown, Stuart C. (ed.). *Reason and Religion*. Ithaca: Cornell University Press, 1977.

Burrell, David. *Faith and Freedom: An Interfaith Perspective*. Oxford: Blackwell, 2004.

Butt, John (ed.). *The Poems of Alexander Pope*. London: Methuen & Co., 1963.

Camus, Albert. *The Plague*, trans. Stuart Gilbert. London: Penguin, 1960.

Camus, Albert. *The Myth of Sisyphus and Other Essays*, trans. Justin O'Brien. New York: Alfred A. Knopf, 1967.

Camus, Albert. *The Rebel*, trans. Anthony Bower. Harmondsworth: Penguin, 1971.

Camus, Albert. *American Journals*, trans. Hugh Levick. New York: Paragon House Publishers, 1987.

Capaldi, Nicholas. *The Enlightenment Project in the Analytic Conversation*. Dordrecht: Kluwer Academic Publishers, 1998.

Caputo, John D. *Radical Hermeneutics: Repetition, Deconstruction, and the Hermeneutic Project*. Bloomington: Indiana University Press, 1987.

Caputo, John D. *Demythologizing Heidegger*. Bloomington: Indiana University Press, 1993.

Caputo, John D. *Against Ethics: Contributions to a Poetics of Obligation with Constant Reference to Deconstruction*. Bloomington: Indiana University Press, 1993.

Caputo, John D. *The Prayers and Tears of Jacques Derrida: Religion without Religion*. Bloomington: Indiana University Press, 1997.

Caputo, John D. *Deconstruction in a Nutshell: A Conversation with Jacques Derrida*. New York: Fordham University Press, 1997.

Caputo, John D. "For the Love of the Things Themselves: Derrida's Hyper-Realism," *Journal for Cultural and Religious Theory* [www.jcrt.org] 1.3 (August 2000).

Caputo, John D. *More Radical Hermeneutics: On Not Knowing Who We Are*. Bloomington: Indiana University Press, 2000.

Caputo, John D. *On Religion*. London: Routledge, 2001.

Caputo, John D. "Methodological Postmodernism: On Merold Westphal's *Overcoming Onto-theology*," *Faith and Philosophy* 22 (2005): 284–96.

Caputo, John D. *The Weakness of God: A Theology of the Event*. Bloomington: Indiana University Press, 2006.

Caputo, John D. *Philosophy and Theology*. Nashville: Abingdon Press, 2006.

Cavell, Stanley. *The Claim of Reason: Wittgenstein, Skepticism, Morality, and Tragedy*. Oxford: Clarendon Press, 1979.

Charlton, William. *The Analytic Ambition: An Introduction to Philosophy*. Oxford: Blackwell, 1991.

Cohen, Richard A. *Ethics, Exegesis and Philosophy: Interpretation after Levinas*. Cambridge: Cambridge University Press, 2001.

Cooper, David E. "Analytic and Continental Philosophy," *Proceedings of the Aristotelian Society* 94 (1994): 1–18.

Cooper, Simon. "Academic Darwinism: The (Logical) End of the Dawkins Era," *Arena Journal* 28 (2007): 107–17.

Critchley, Simon. *Continental Philosophy: A Very Short Introduction*. Oxford: Oxford University Press, 2001.

Critchley, Simon, and Robert Bernasconi (eds). *The Cambridge Companion to Levinas*. Cambridge: Cambridge University Press, 2002.

Cupitt, Don. *Taking Leave of God*. London: SCM Press, 1980.

Danto, Arthur C. *Nietzsche as Philosopher*. New York: Macmillan, 1965.

Davies, Brian. "Letter from America," *New Blackfriars* 84 (2003): 371–84.

Davis, Stephen T. *God, Reason and Theistic Proofs*. Edinburgh: Edinburgh University Press, 1997.

Davis, Stephen T. (ed.). *Encountering Evil: Live Options in Theodicy*, first edition: Edinburgh: T & T Clark, 1981; second edition: Louisville: Westminster John Knox Press, 2001.

Deleuze, Gilles. *Difference and Repetition*, trans. Paul Patton. New York: Columbia University Press, 1994.

Deleuze, Gilles, and Félix Guattari. *What Is Philosophy?*, trans. Hugh Tomlinson and Graham Burchell. New York: Columbia University Press, 1994.

DePaul, Michael R., and William Ramsey (eds). *Rethinking Intuition: The Psychology of Intuition and Its Role in Philosophical Inquiry*. Lanham: Rowman & Littlefield, 1998.

Derrida, Jacques. *Limited Inc*. Evanston: Northwestern University Press, 1988.

Derrida, Jacques. *On the Name*, ed. Thomas Dutoit. Stanford: Stanford University Press, 1995.

Derrida, Jacques. *Points . . . Interviews, 1974–1994*, ed. Elisabeth Weber, trans. Peggy Kamuf *et al*. Stanford: Stanford University Press, 1995.

Derrida, Jacques, and Gianni Vattimo (eds). *Religion*. Stanford: Stanford University Press, 1998.

Descombes, Vincent. *Modern French Philosophy*, trans. L. Scott-Fox and J. M. Harding. Cambridge: Cambridge University Press, 1980.

Dombrowski, Daniel A. *Kazantzakis and God*. Albany: State University of New York Press, 1997.

Dostoevsky, Anna. *Dostoevsky: Reminiscences*, trans. and ed. Beatrice Stillman. New York: Liveright Publishing, 1975.

Dostoyevsky, Fyodor. *The Brothers Karamazov*, trans. David McDuff. London: Penguin, 1993 (originally published in Russian in 1880).

Doulis, Tom. "Kazantzakis and the Meaning of Suffering," *Northwest Review* 6 (1963): 33–57.

Dunn, Candice, and Rebecca Mann. *Kids' View of God*. Sydney: Murdoch Books, 2006.

Duquoc, Christian, and Casiano Floristán (eds). *Francis of Assisi Today*. Edinburgh: T & T Clark, 1981.

Edwards, Paul. *Heidegger's Confusions*. Amherst: Prometheus Books, 2004.

Engel, Pascal. "Analytic Philosophy and Cognitive Norms," *The Monist* 82 (1999): 218–34.

Epictetus. *The Discourses*, ed. Christopher Gill, translation revised by Robin Hard. London: J. M. Dent, 1995.

Estabrook, Carl G. "Three Mistakes about Christian Scholarship: Reflections on Remarks by Professor Plantinga," *Common Sense* 7 (April 1993): 1, 8–9.

Evans, C. Stephen. *Philosophy of Religion: Thinking About Faith*. Downers Grove: InterVarsity Press, 1982.

Flew, Antony. "Compatibilism, Free Will and God," *Philosophy* 48 (1973): 231–44.

Gibson, A. Boyce. *The Religion of Dostoevsky*. London: SCM Press, 1973.

Glendinning, Simon (ed.). *Arguing with Derrida*. Oxford: Blackwell, 2001.

Glock, Hans-Johann (ed.). *The Rise of Analytic Philosophy*. Oxford: Blackwell, 1997.

Goodchild, Philip (ed.). *Rethinking Philosophy of Religion: Approaches from Continental Philosophy*. New York: Fordham University Press, 2002.

Griffin, David Ray. *God, Power, and Evil: A Process Theodicy*. Philadelphia: The Westminster Press, 1976.

Hadot, Pierre. *Philosophy as a Way of Life: Spiritual Exercises from Socrates to Foucault*, ed. Arnold I. Davidson, trans. Michael Chase. Malden: Blackwell Publishing, 1995.

Hahn, Lewis Edwin, and Paul Arthur Schilpp (eds). *The Philosophy of W. V. Quine*. La Salle: Open Court Publishing, 1986.

Hales, Steven, and Rex Welshon. *Nietzsche's Perspectivism*. Urbana: University of Illinois Press, 2000.

Hancock, Curtis L., and Brendan Sweetman (eds). *Faith and the Life of the Intellect*. Washington D.C.: The Catholic University of America Press, 2003.

Hasker, William. "The Necessity of Gratuitous Evil," *Faith and Philosophy* 9 (1992): 23–44.

Haxthausen, Charles W. "The World, the Book, and Anselm Kiefer," *The Burlington Magazine* 133 (December 1991): 846–51.

Heidegger, Martin. *Identity and Difference*, trans. Joan Stambaugh. New York: Harper & Row, 1969.

Heidegger, Martin. *Nietzsche*, ed. D. F. Krell, trans. J. Stambaugh, D. F. Krell, and F. A. Capuzzi. San Francisco: Harper, 1991 (originally published 1961).

Hick, John. *Evil and the God of Love*, first edition: London: Macmillan, 1966; revised edition: New York: HarperCollins, 1977.

Hick, John. "God, Evil and Mystery," *Religious Studies* 3 (1968): 539–46.

Hick, John. *Death and Eternal Life*. Glasgow: Collins, 1976.

Hick, John. *Philosophy of Religion*, fourth edition. Englewood Cliffs: Prentice-Hall, 1990.

Hick, John. *An Interpretation of Religion: Human Responses to the Transcendent*, second edition. Basingstoke: Palgrave, 2004.

Hill, Daniel J. *Divinity and Maximal Greatness*. London: Routledge, 2005.

Hill, Geoffrey. *Tenebrae*. London: André Deutsch, 1978.

Hill Jr., Thomas E. "Humanity as an End in Itself," *Ethics* 91 (1980): 84–99.

Hillyer, Philip (ed.). *On the Threshold of the Third Millenium*. London: SCM Press, 1990.

Hoffman, Joshua, and Gary S. Rosenkrantz. *The Divine Attributes*. Oxford: Blackwell, 2002.

Holland, R. F. *Against Empiricism: On Education, Epistemology and Value*. Oxford: Basil Blackwell, 1980.

Honderich, Ted (ed.). *The Oxford Companion to Philosophy*, second edition. Oxford: Oxford University Press, 2005.

Hopkins, Gerard Manley. *Selected Poetry*, ed. Catherine Phillips. Oxford: Oxford University Press, 1996.

Howard-Snyder, Daniel (ed.). *The Evidential Argument from Evil*. Bloomington: Indiana University Press, 1996.

Humphries, Ralph. "Analytic and Continental: The Division in Philosophy," *The Monist* 82 (1999): 253–77.

Jabès, Edmond. *Desire for a Beginning, Dread of One Single End*, trans. Rosmarie Waldrop. New York: Granary Books, 2001.

Kant, Immanuel. *Political Writings*, trans. H. Nisbet. Cambridge: Cambridge University Press, 1991.

Kazantzakis, Helen. *Nikos Kazantzakis: A Biography Based on His Letters*, trans. Amy Mims. New York: Simon and Schuster, 1968.

Kazantzakis, Nikos. *The Saviors of God: Spiritual Exercises*, trans. Kimon Friar. New York: Simon and Schuster, 1960.

Kazantzakis, Nikos. *Journey to the Morea*, trans. F. A. Reed. New York: Simon and Schuster, 1965.

Kazantzakis, Nikos. *Report to Greco*, trans. Peter Bien. New York: Simon and Schuster, 1965.

Kazantzakis, Nikos. *Journeying: Travels in Italy, Egypt, Sinai, Jerusalem and Cyprus*, trans. Themi Vasils and Theodora Vasils. Boston: Little, Brown and Company, 1975.

Kazantzakis, Nikos. "Six Letters of Nikos Kazantzakis to Max Tau" (in Greek, trans. Helen Kontiadis), *Nea Estia* 102 (Christmas 1977): 308–10.

Kazantzakis, Nikos. *O ftohúlis tu Theú*. Athens: Helen Kazantzakis, 1981.

Kazantzakis, Nikos. *Saint Francis*, trans. Peter Bien. Chicago: Loyola Press, 2005.

Kearney, Richard. *The God Who May Be: A Hermeneutics of Religion*. Bloomington: Indiana University Press, 2001.

Kearney, Richard. *Debates in Continental Philosophy: Conversations with Contemporary Thinkers*. New York: Fordham University Press, 2004.

Kelly, Joseph P. "Review of Nikos Kazantzakis, *Saint Francis*," *America*, 28 July 1962, p. 549.

Kiefer, Anselm. *Anselm Kiefer: Heaven and Earth*. Fort Worth: Modern Art Museum of Fort Worth, and Munich: Prestel Verlag, 2005.

Kiefer, Anselm. *Anselm Kiefer: Aperiatur Terra*. London: Jay Jopling/White Cube, 2007.

Kierkegaard, Søren. *Concluding Unscientific Postscript*, trans. David F. Swenson. Princeton: Princeton University Press, 1941.

Kierkegaard, Søren. *The Journals of Søren Kierkegaard*, ed. and trans. Alexander Dru. London: Oxford University Press, 1951.

Lantz, Kenneth. *The Dostoevsky Encyclopedia*. Westport: Greenwood Press, 2004.

Lea, James F. *Kazantzakis: The Politics of Salvation*. Tuscaloosa: University of Alabama Press, 1979.

Leiter, Brian (ed.). *The Future For Philosophy*. Oxford: Clarendon Press, 2004.

Le Poidevin, Robin. *Arguing For Atheism: An Introduction to the Philosophy of Religion*. London: Routledge, 1996.

Leunig, Michael. "A Picture of Dignity and Balance," *The Age* (Melbourne), 6 May 2006. Accessed 19 March 2008. Available from: http://www.theage.com.au/articles/2006/05/04/1146335867017.html

Levine, Michael P. "Contemporary Christian Analytic Philosophy of Religion: Biblical Fundamentalism, Terrible Solutions to A Horrible Problem, and Hearing God," *International Journal for Philosophy of Religion* 48 (2000): 89–119.

Levitt, Morton P. *The Cretan Glance: The World and Art of Nikos Kazantzakis.* Columbus: Ohio State University, 1980.

Levy, Neil. "Analytic and Continental Philosophy: Explaining the Differences," *Metaphilosophy* 34 (2003): 284–304.

Lewis, Charles M. (ed.). *Relativism and Religion.* New York: St. Martin's Press, 1995.

Lewis, H. D. (ed.) *Clarity Is Not Enough: Essays in Criticism of Linguistic Philosophy.* London: George Allen & Unwin, 1963.

Long, Eugene Thomas (ed.). *Prospects for Natural Theology.* Washington, D.C.: The Catholic University of America Press, 1992.

Malcolm, Norman. *Ludwig Wittgenstein: A Memoir,* second edition. Oxford: Clarendon Press, 2001.

Marion, Jean-Luc. *God Without Being: Hors-Texte,* trans. Thomas A. Carlson. Chicago: University of Chicago Press, 1991 (originally published in French in 1982).

Marion, Jean-Luc. *In Excess: Studies of Saturated Phenomena,* trans. Robyn Horner and Vincent Berraud. New York: Fordham University Press, 2002.

Martin, Michael. *Atheism: A Philosophical Justification.* Philadelphia: Temple University Press, 1990.

Martinich, A. P., and David Sosa (eds). *Analytic Philosophy: An Anthology.* Malden: Blackwell, 2001.

McKim, Robert. *Religious Ambiguity and Religious Diversity.* Oxford: Oxford University Press, 2001.

McNaughton, David. "Is God (Almost) a Consequentialist? Swinburne's Moral Theory," *Religious Studies* 38 (2002): 265–81.

Meiland, Jack W. "On the Paradox of Cognitive Relativism," *Metaphilosophy* 11 (1980): 115–26.

Messer, Richard. *Does God's Existence Need Proof?* Oxford: Clarendon Press, 1993.

Middleton, Darren J. N. *Novel Theology: Nikos Kazantzakis's Encounter with Whiteheadian Process Theism.* Macon: Mercer University Press, 2000.

Middleton, Darren J. N. *Broken Hallelujah: Nikos Kazantzakis and Christian Theology.* Lanham: Lexington Books, 2007.

Milton, John. *Paradise Lost,* ed. John Leonard. London: Penguin, 2000 (originally published in 1667).

Montefiore, Alan (ed.). *Philosophy in France Today.* Cambridge: Cambridge University Press, 1983.

Moore, Andrew, and Michael Scott (eds). *Realism and Religion: Philosophical and Theological Perspectives.* Aldershot: Ashgate Publishing, 2007.

Nehamas, Alexander. *Nietzsche: Life as Literature.* Cambridge, MA: Harvard University Press, 1985.

Nielsen, Kai. "Wittgensteinian Fideism," *Philosophy* 42 (1967): 191–209.

Nietzsche, Friedrich. *The Will to Power*, trans. Walter Kaufmann and R. J. Hollingdale, ed. Walter Kaufmann. New York: Vintage, 1967.

Nietzsche, Friedrich. *The Gay Science*, trans. Walter Kaufmann. New York: Vintage Books, 1974.

Nietzsche, Friedrich. *Thus Spoke Zarathustra*, trans. Walter Kaufmann. New York: Penguin, 1978.

Nietzsche, Friedrich. *Untimely Meditations*, trans. R. J. Hollingdale. Cambridge: Cambridge University Press, 1997.

Nietzsche, Friedrich. *On the Genealogy of Morality: A Polemic*, trans. Maudemarie Clark and Alan J. Swenson. Indianapolis: Hackett Publishing Company, 1998.

Nozick, Robert. *Philosophical Explanations*. Cambridge, MA: The Belknap Press, 1981.

O'Connor, David. "In Defense of Theoretical Theodicy," *Modern Theology* 5 (1988): 61–74.

Olthuis, James H. (ed.). *Religion with/out Religion: The Prayers and Tears of John D. Caputo*. London: Routledge, 2002.

Owens, Lewis. *Creative Destruction: Nikos Kazantzakis and the Literature of Responsibility*. Macon: Mercer University Press, 2003.

Passmore, John. "The End of Philosophy?", *Australasian Journal of Philosophy* 74 (1996): 1–19.

Payne, Michael, and John Schad (eds). *life.after.theory*. London: Continuum, 2003.

Penner, Myron B. (ed.). *Christianity and the Postmodern Turn: Six Views*. Grand Rapids: Brazos Press, 2005.

Phillips, D. Z. *The Concept of Prayer*. London: Routledge & Kegan Paul, 1965.

Phillips, D. Z. *Death and Immortality*. London: Macmillan, 1970.

Phillips, D. Z. *Faith and Philosophical Enquiry*. London: Routledge & Kegan Paul, 1970.

Phillips, D. Z. *Religion Without Explanation*. Oxford: Basil Blackwell, 1976.

Phillips, D. Z. "In All Probability (review of Richard Swinburne's *Faith and Reason*)," *The Times Literary Supplement*, 28 May 1982, p. 588.

Phillips, D. Z. *Belief, Change and Forms of Life*. Basingstoke: Macmillan, 1986.

Phillips, D. Z. *Faith After Foundationalism*. London: Routledge, 1988.

Phillips, D. Z. *Wittgenstein and Religion*. Basingstoke: Macmillan, 1993.

Phillips, D. Z. *Recovering Religious Concepts: Closing Epistemic Divides*. Basingstoke: Macmillan, 2000.

Phillips, D. Z. *Religion and the Hermeneutics of Contemplation*. Cambridge: Cambridge University Press, 2001.

Phillips, D. Z. *Religion and Friendly Fire: Examining Assumptions in Contemporary Philosophy of Religion*. Aldershot: Ashgate, 2004.

Phillips, D. Z. *The Problem of Evil and the Problem of God*. London: SCM Press, 2004.

Phillips, D. Z. (ed.). *Religion and Morality*. London: Macmillan, 1996.

Phillips, D. Z., and Timothy Tessin (eds). *Religion without Transcendence?* London: Macmillan, 1997.

Phillips, D. Z., and Timothy Tessin (eds). *Philosophy of Religion in the 21st Century*. Basingstoke: Palgrave, 2001.

Plantinga, Alvin. *The Nature of Necessity*. Oxford: Clarendon Press, 1974.

Plantinga, Alvin. *God, Freedom, and Evil*. Grand Rapids: Eerdmans, 1977.

Plantinga, Alvin. *Warranted Christian Belief*. Oxford: Oxford University Press, 2000.

Pound, Marcus. "Review of *Conversations with Žižek* by Slavoj Žižek and Glyn Daly," *The Heythrop Journal* 47 (2006): 679–80.

Prado, C. G. (ed.). *A House Divided: Comparing Analytic and Continental Philosophy*. New York: Humanity Books, 2003.

Protevi, John (ed.). *A Dictionary of Continental Philosophy*. New Haven: Yale University Press, 2006.

Quine, W. V. *Theories and Things*. Cambridge, MA: Harvard University Press, 1981.

Ramsey, Frank P. *The Foundations of Mathematics and Other Logical Essays*, ed. R. B. Braithwaite. London: Routledge & Kegan Paul, 1931.

Raschke, Carl. "Loosening Philosophy's Tongue: A Conversation with Jack Caputo," *Journal of Cultural and Religious Theory* [www.jcrt.org], vol. 3, no. 2, April 2002.

Raschke, Carl. "The Difference That Faith Makes," *Church and Postmodern Culture* issue 2.1, January–April 2007.

Reece, Andrew S. "Kazantzakis' St. Francis and the Cynics," *Classical and Modern Literature* 18 (1997): 71–77.

Reichenbach, Bruce. "Evil and a Reformed View of God," *International Journal for Philosophy of Religion* 24 (1988): 67–85.

Rhees, Rush. *Without Answers*. London: Routledge & Kegan Paul, 1969.

Rogers, Ben. *A. J. Ayer: A Life*. London: Chatto & Windus, 1999.

Rosenthal, Stephanie. *Black Paintings: Robert Rauschenberg, Ad Reinhardt, Mark Rothko, Frank Stella*. Munich: Hatje Cantz Verlag, 2006.

Roszak, Theodore (ed.). *The Dissenting Academy*. New York: Pantheon Books, 1967.

Roth, John. "Theistic Antitheodicy," *American Journal of Theology and Philosophy* 25 (2004): 276–93.

Roth, John K., and Michael Berenbaum (eds). *Holocaust: Religious and Philosophical Implications*. Minnesota: Paragon House, 1989.

Roth, John K. (ed.). *Genocide and Human Rights: A Philosophical Guide*. Basingstoke: Palgrave Macmillan, 2005.

Rowe, William. "Evil and Theodicy," *Philosophical Topics* 16 (1988): 119–32.

Runzo, Joseph (ed.). *Is God Real?* New York: St. Martin's Press, 1993.

Ryle, Gilbert. "Review of Martin Heidegger's *Sein und Zeit*," *Mind* 38 (1929): 355–70.

Scott, Michael. "The Morality of Theodicies," *Religious Studies* 32 (1996): 1–13.

Scott, Michael, and Andrew Moore, "Can Theological Realism Be Refuted?" *Religious Studies* 33 (1997): 401–18.

Searle, John. "Reiterating the Differences: A Reply to Derrida," *Glyph* 1 (1977): 198–208.

Shand, John (ed.). *Fundamentals of Philosophy*. London: Routledge, 2003.

Sherwood, Yvonne, and Kevin Hart (eds). *Derrida and Religion: Other Testaments*. New York: Routledge, 2005.

Siegel, Harvey. *Relativism Refuted: A Critique of Contemporary Epistemological Relativism*. Dordrecht: D. Reidel, 1987.

Skorupski, John. "The Legacy of Modernism," *Proceedings of the Aristotelian Society* 91 (1991): 1–19.

Sleinis, E. E. *Nietzsche's Revaluation of Values: A Study in Strategies*. Urbana: University of Illinois Press, 1994.

Soames, Scott. *Philosophical Analysis in the Twentieth Century*, vols. 1 & 2. Princeton: Princeton University Press, 2003.

Sobel, Jordan Howard. *Logic and Theism: Arguments For and Against Beliefs in God*. Cambridge: Cambridge University Press, 2004.

Solomon, Robert. *The Joy of Philosophy: Thinking Thin versus the Passionate Life*. New York: Oxford University Press, 1999.

Spinoza, Benedict de. *Ethics*, ed. and trans. G. H. R. Parkinson. Oxford: Oxford University Press, 2000.

Stump, Donald V., James A. Arieti, Lloyd Gerson, and Eleonore Stump (eds). *Hamartia: The Concept of Error in the Western Tradition. Essays in Honor of John M. Crossett*. New York: Edwin Mellen Press, 1983.

Stump, Eleonore. "Suffering and Redemption: A Reply to Smith," *Faith and Philosophy* 2 (1985): 430–35.

Styron, William. *Sophie's Choice*. London: Corgi Books, 1980.

Summerell, Orrin F. (ed.). *The Otherness of God*. Charlottesville: University Press of Virginia, 1998.

Surin, Kenneth. "Theodicy?" *Harvard Theological Review* 76 (1983): 225–47.

Surin, Kenneth. *Theology and the Problem of Evil*. Oxford: Basil Blackwell, 1986.

Sutherland, Stewart R. *Atheism and the Rejection of God: Contemporary Philosophy and 'The Brothers Karamazov'*. Oxford: Basil Blackwell, 1977.

Sutherland, Stewart R. *God, Jesus and Belief: The Legacy of Theism*. Oxford: Basil Blackwell, 1984.

Sutherland, Stewart R. "Horrendous Evils and the Goodness of God," *The Aristotelian Society Supplementary Volume* 63 (1989): 311–23.

Swinburne, Richard. *The Coherence of Theism*. Oxford: Clarendon Press, 1977.

Swinburne, Richard. *The Existence of God*. Oxford: Clarendon Press, 1979.

Swinburne, Richard. *Providence and the Problem of Evil*. Oxford: Clarendon Press, 1998.

Swinburne, Richard. "Reply to Richard Gale," *Religious Studies* 36 (2000): 221–25.

Swinburne, Richard. "Response to My Commentators," *Religious Studies* 38 (2002): 301–15.

Tacey, David. *The Spirituality Revolution: The Emergence of Contemporary Spirituality*. Hove, East Sussex: Brunner-Routledge, 2004.

Terras, Victor. *A Karamazov Companion: Commentary on the Genesis, Language, and Style of Dostoevsky's Novel*. Madison: University of Wisconsin Press, 1981.

The Sayings of the Desert Fathers: The Alphabetical Collection, trans. Benedicta Ward. Kalamazoo: Cistercian Publications, 1984.

Thoreau, Henry David. *Walden*, ed. Stephen Fender. Oxford: Oxford University Press, 1997.

Tilley, Terrence W. *The Evils of Theodicy*. Washington, D.C.: Georgetown University Press, 1991.

Tooley, Michael. "The Argument from Evil," *Philosophical Perspectives* 5 (1991): 89–134.

Trakakis, Nick. "On the Alleged Failure of Free Will Theodicies: A Reply to Tierno," *Sophia* 42 (2003): 99–106.

Trakakis, Nick. "Evil and the Complexity of History: A Response to Durston," *Religious Studies* 39 (2003): 451–58.

Trakakis, Nick. "God, Gratuitous Evil, and van Inwagen's Attempt to Reconcile the Two," *Ars Disputandi: The Online Journal for Philosophy of Religion* [www.ArsDisputandi.org], vol. 3, 2003.

Trakakis, Nick. "What No Eye Has Seen: The Skeptical Theist Response to Rowe's Evidential Argument from Evil," *Philo* 6 (2003): 263–79.

Trakakis, Nick. "Second Thoughts on the Alleged Failure of Free Will Theodicies," *Sophia* 43 (2004): 83–89.

Trakakis, Nick. "Is Theism Capable of Accounting For Any Natural Evil At All?" *International Journal for Philosophy of Religion* 57 (2005): 35–66.

Trakakis, Nick. "Does Hard Determinism Render the Problem of Evil even Harder?", *Ars Disputandi: The Online Journal for Philosophy of Religion* [www.ArsDisputandi.org], vol. 6, 2006.

Trakakis, Nick. "Nietzsche's Perspectivism and Problems of Self-Refutation," *International Philosophical Quarterly* 46 (2006): 91–110.

Trakakis, Nick. "Becoming Children: The Hidden Meaning of the Incarnation," *Theandros: An Online Journal of Orthodox Christian Theology and Philosophy* [www.theandros.com], vol. 3, no. 3, Spring/Summer 2006.

Trakakis, Nick. *The God Beyond Belief: In Defence of William Rowe's Evidential Argument from Evil*. Dordrecht: Springer Publishing, 2007.

Tysome, Tony. "Young Guns Ditch Old Values," *The Times Higher Education Supplement*, published online 15 December 2006. Accessed 19 March 2008. Available from: http://www.timeshighereducation.co.uk/story.asp?sectioncode =26&storycode=207146

Van Inwagen, Peter. "The Argument from Particular Horrendous Evils," *Proceedings of the American Catholic Philosophical Association* 74 (2000): 65–80.

Van Inwagen, Peter (ed.). *Christian Faith and the Problem of Evil*. Grand Rapids: William B. Eerdmans Publishing Company, 2004.

Voltaire, F.- M. Arouet de. *Candide, or Optimism*, trans. John Butt. London: Penguin, 1947.

Wachterhauser, Brice R. "The Problem of Evil and Moral Scepticism," *International Journal for Philosophy of Religion* 17 (1985): 167–74.

Wainwright, William J. (ed.). *God, Philosophy and Academic Culture: A Discussion Between Scholars in the AAR and the APA*. Atlanta: Scholars Press, 1996.

Walcott, Derek. *The Castaway and Other Poems*. London: Jonathan Cape, 1969.

Watson, James R. (ed.), *Portraits of American Continental Philosophers*. Bloomington: Indiana University Press, 1999.

Westphal, Merold. "Prolegomena To Any Future Philosophy of Religion Which Will Be Able To Come Forth As Prophecy," *International Journal for Philosophy of Religion* 4 (1973): 129–50.

Westphal, Merold. *Overcoming Onto-theology: Toward a Postmodern Christian Faith*. New York: Fordham University Press, 2001.

Wetzel, James. "Can Theodicy Be Avoided? The Claim of Unredeemed Evil," *Religious Studies* 25 (1989): 1–13.

Wheeler III, Samuel C. *Deconstruction As Analytic Philosophy*. Stanford: Stanford University Press, 2000.

Whitehead, Alfred North. *Process and Reality: An Essay in Cosmology*, corrected edition, ed. David Ray Griffin and Donald W. Sherburne. New York: The Free Press, 1978.

Wierenga, Edward R. *The Nature of God: An Inquiry into Divine Attributes*. Ithaca: Cornell University Press, 1989.

Wilshire, Bruce. *Fashionable Nihilism: A Critique of Analytic Philosophy*. Albany: State University of New York Press, 2002.

Wittgenstein, Ludwig. *Tractatus Logico-Philosophicus*, trans. C. K. Ogden. London: Kegan Paul, Trench, Trubner & Co., 1922.

Wittgenstein, Ludwig. *Culture and Value*, trans. Peter Winch. Chicago: University of Chicago Press, 1984.

Wright, Karen. "The Ruins of Barjac: Politics, Alchemy, and Learning to Dance in Anselm Kiefer's World," *Modern Painters: The International Art Magazine*, November 2006, pp. 68–75.

Zabala, Santiago (ed.). *Weakening Philosophy: Essays in Honour of Gianni Vattimo*. Montreal and Kingston: McGill-Queen's University Press, 2007.

Zagzebski, Linda (ed.). *Rational Faith: Catholic Responses to Reformed Epistemology*. Notre Dame: University of Notre Dame Press, 1993.

INDEX

Leunig, Michael 109–11
Levinas, Emmanuel 29–30
Levine, Michael 129n38
Levy, Neil 50

Marion, Jean-Luc 63–4, 102
McClleland, Richard 134n74
Messer, Richard 60–1
Moore, A. W. 45

natural theology 49, 57, 74, 79–81
Nietzsche, Friedrich 1, 121
  and perspectivism 58–9, 70–4
non-realism (with respect to religious
    discourse) 60, 63–5, 74–9
  objections to 79–82
Nozick, Robert 2

O'Connor, David 27–8

Pascal, Blaise 60, 89, 95
perspectivism 58–9, 70–4
Phillips, D. Z. 6, 11, 12
  and religious discourse 74–9
  and theodicy 12–17, 22
philosophy
  problems with institutionalization
    of 113–24
  as a way of life 120
Plantinga, Alvin 26–7
  as representative of analytic
    philosophy of religion 37–40
Pope, Alexander 132n60
problem of evil
  non-theodical responses to 96–7,
    133–4n66, 135n84
  theoretical and practical problems of
    evil 24–9

Quine, W. V. 43, 113

Reinhardt, Ad 1, 125n2
relativism 71–4
Roszak, Theodore 122
Rowe, William 7, 49

Scott, Michael 27–8, 131n57
Searle, John 32
Solomon, Robert 114–15
Stump, Eleonore 21
Surin, Kenneth 6, 11, 12, 17–18, 20,
    23–4, 25–6, 28–9
Sutherland, Stewart 19, 133n63,
    135n83
Swinburne, Richard 61, 62, 140n41
  on theodicy 15–17, 128n36, 133n65

Tacey, David 116–17
theodicy 6–30
  appeal to heavenly afterlife 10, 22
  free will theodicy 9–10
  as incompatible with the perfect
    goodness of God 12–15
  nature of 6–8
  and the reality of evil 131–2n60
  soul-making theodicy 8–9, 15–18
  and teleology of suffering 15–18,
    129–30n46
  types of 7–10
  see also anti-theodicy
Tilley, Terrence 12, 25

Westphal, Merold 54–8, 68
Williams, Rowan 30, 127n19
Wilshire, Bruce 115–16, 122
Wittgenstein, Ludwig 67–8, 87,
    140n37
Wittgensteinian philosophy of
    religion 61, 63–5, 74–9

Žižek, Slavoj 44–5

CPSIA information can be obtained at www.ICGtesting.com
Printed in the USA
BVOW022143051211

277667BV00002B/14/P

9 781441 149701